Materialist Feminisms

SO-AII-296

Materialist Feminisms

Donna Landry and Gerald MacLean

BLACKWELL
Publishers

Copyright © Donna Landry and Gerald MacLean, 1993

The right of Donna Landry and Gerald MacLean to be identified as authors of this work has been asserted in accordance with the Copyright, Designs, and Patents Act 1988.

First published 1993

Blackwell Publishers
238 Main Street,
Cambridge, Massachusetts 02142
USA

108 Cowley Road
Oxford OX4 1JF
UK

All rights reserved. Except for the quotation of short passages for the purposes of criticism and review, no part of this publication may be reproduced, stored in a retrieval system, or transmitted, in any form or by any means, electronic, mechanical, photocopying, recording or otherwise, without the prior permission of the publisher.

Except in the United States of America, this book is sold subject to the condition that it shall not, by way of trade or otherwise, be lent, resold, hired out, or otherwise circulated without the publisher's prior consent in any form of binding or cover other than that in which it is published and without a similar condition including this condition being imposed on the subsequent purchaser.

Library of Congress Cataloging-in-Publication Data

Landry, Donna.
    Materialist Feminisms / Donna Landry and Gerald MacLean.
        p.   cm.
    Includes bibliographical references and index.
    ISBN 1-55786-184-6 — ISBN 1-55786-185-4 (pbk)
    1. Feminist literary criticism.   2. Marxist criticism.
    I. MacLean, Gerald M., 1952– . II. Title.
    PN98.W64L36   1993
    801'.95'082–dc20   92-45623
                                                                          CIP

British Library Cataloguing in Publication Data

A CIP catalogue record for this book is available from the British Library.

Typeset in 10½ on 12 pt Garamond
by Photo·graphics, Honiton, Devon
Printed in Great Britain by Biddles

This book is printed on acid-free paper

Contents

". . . I joined a Marxist–Feminist study group."

"Why Marxist–Feminist?"

"Well, you know, when I was in the New Left I never made a decision for myself. Either Jerry or Laura told me what to think. But on my own, actually with some other women in the same pitiful predicament, I started getting my politics together."

"So, what did you decide? Come on Vivian, I want the word." She took a deep breath. "Well, feminism is clearly ahistorical and insufficiently materialist but Marxism has an inadequate analysis of gender relations. I even wrote an article for a theoretical journal in which I stated that woman's relationship to the mode of production is determined by her relationship to reproduction."

I scowled. "Vivian."

Sarah Schulman, *The Sophie Horowitz Story*

The Argument

This is a book about feminism and Marxism written when many people are proclaiming the end of socialism and the end of feminism. The difference between these ends is that socialism is said to have failed in its competition with the capitalist marketplace, while feminism is said to have won all its battles. Women, we are told, have already gained the opportunities for social and economic power they were seeking, so there is no longer any need for a feminist movement.

We find these claims to be both premature and misleading. This book outlines the recent history of debates between feminism and Marxism in Britain and the United States. It then traces the consequences of those debates for other social movements, and for literary and cultural theory.

In literary studies today, another end is often proclaimed – the end of deconstruction and other forms of poststructuralist theory. All these declarations of ends – of feminism, of socialism, of deconstruction – serve similar strategic purposes, rhetorically resolving conflicts while those conflicts continue, sometimes in other forms and in other places. The politics of race, nationality, and ethnicity, of decolonization and the break-up of imperical blocs, have led both to new sites of exploitation and to new forms of social critique and resistance. The status of women and the politics of gender and sexuality remain crucial to these developments.

We shall argue that, far from having come to an end, deconstruction offers strategies of critique and resistance useful for the new social movements, and for literary and cultural critics who wish their work to have progressive political effects. Particularly in the light of global ecological questions, alternatives to thinking of the world as a site of ever-expanding production for profits in the marketplace are urgently needed. In this sense, feminism and socialism are names not so much for theoretical dead-ends as for unfinished business.

Preface

Books tell stories. The story of this book concerns events that mostly took place during the last twenty or so years. Stories often claim to be somehow "true." The stories in history books, for instance, claim to be about real people involved in real events. The stories we find in novels and poems, on the other hand, claim that, although the characters and events are all make-believe, the experiences they stand in for and the feelings they evoke are universal and therefore true to life. The stories found in philosophy books make a different sort of claim, that only by asking questions such as "what is the truth?" can we even begin to understand what words like "life," "experience," "universal," "real event," and "real people" might mean and how they might help us to understand the "truth."

The Women's Movement of the last twenty years constitutes a significant moment in a much longer story, the story of Feminism and Capitalism that started more than three hundred years ago, a story which, in turn, can be seen as a chapter in the even longer story of Women's Oppression and Western Civilization, a story that would take us back to Plato and Aristotle, at least. Our particular story offers a brief critical history of those social, political, and institutional moments in the UK and US women's movements that have, over the last thirty years, made our topic both possible and necessary.

In this book we strive to do at least two things: to present a history of the debates between Marxist and feminist social and cultural theorists in the 1960s, 1970s, and early 1980s, primarily in Britain and the United States, and to analyze what has happened to transform those debates in recent years. The new emphases on race, ethnicity, postcolonialism, gay liberation, and the history of sexuality, and the cultural impact of postmodernism and its intellectual correlative, poststructuralism, have helped to shift the terrain of previous debates from a possible synthesis of Marxism and feminism to the construction of a materialist analysis of culture informed by and responsive to the concerns of women, as well as people of color and other marginalized groups. By poststructuralism, we mean to designate the critique of binary thinking and scientific certainty in structural linguistics, anthropology, and orthodox Marxism made primarily by such figures as Jacques Derrida and Michel Foucault. In recent years, a number of postcolonial critics, African-American critics, and gay historians, including feminists, have made theoretical advances in relation to the work of these writers.

The photography critic Abigail Solomon-Godeau argues that, for a discourse to be critical in a political sense, it needs to emphasize and reflect upon its own discursive and institutional functions:

> Insofar as contemporary critical practices operate within a society in which, as Victor Burgin observes, "the market is 'behind' nothing, it is *in* everything," the notion of an "outside" of the commodity system becomes increasingly untenable. This would suggest that the definition or evaluation of a critical practice must be predicated on its ability to sustain critique from within the heart of the system it seeks to put in question. (Solomon-Godeau 1988: 207)

The institutional space from which this book has emerged will be obvious, as in its pages we are seeking to make available for students of women's studies, literary and cultural studies, history, sociology, and critical theory an introduction to something of the history and prospects of a critical reading practice that might be called materialist feminism. We think that in the current historical moment where information technologies wield considerable power, the terrain of culture is as worth contesting as any other, especially in its historical dimension, where so many fights break out over which version of lived cultural history is true.

Such a question of true history presupposes that there could be a simple answer that would satisfy the desire to know authoritatively, and to have a version of the past that could shore up and affirm the answerer's identity. We hope that reading this book may help make the posing of this and related questions seem rather beside the point. Our notion of materialist feminism as it has evolved since the 1970s is one that takes the critical investigation, or reading in the strong sense, of the artifacts of culture and social history, including literary and artistic texts, archival documents, and works of theory, to be a potential site of political contestation through critique, not through the constant reiteration of home-truths.

Given that the market is "behind" nothing but "in" everything, how should we go about dealing with feminism's, including materialist feminism's, commodification? Signs that feminism has become a marketable commodity in at least the university and the publishing industry are many, one of the most obvious being the publication of books like this one. And in news coverage, films, television, and video there is a complex, sometimes trivializing, sometimes deeply misogynist, obsession with representing women's issues, strong women, or feminist characters. The mass media produce for the market their own versions of feminism, usually in hostile ways. Ironically, another sign of feminism's arrival at commodity status is the proclamation heard in many places that feminism as such is dead.

Imperial or indigenous, capitalist or state-socialist, a patriarchal social order does not love a feminism. Proclaiming its end, its supersession by "postfeminism," is the next best thing to having feminism self-destruct and disappear. Living in a postfeminist era would mean that women have already won whatever struggles once made feminism necessary. That this is not the case in Western Europe and North America, except in the most superficial sense of an increased *visibility* of women in the media and in some corporations and institutions, including the university, seems to us abundantly clear. Attempts in the United States to roll back legislation from the 1970s pertaining to Affirmative Action policies on behalf of minorities, and to reproductive rights (the 1973 *Roe* v. *Wade* decision legalizing abortion as a woman's "right to privacy" and popularly translated into "a woman's right to choose"), the legacy of the Civil Rights and women's movements, suggest that a certain amount of official historical forgetting is going on, as if racial and gender-based inequalities were no longer injustices in need of social action. Ominous sounds from Eastern Europe indicate that the movements towards democracy, and in some cases towards free-market economic policies, may not necessarily bode well for women's emancipation – quite the reverse. When an economic adviser to the Czech government and the former Soviet leader Mikhail Gorbachev can both speak of a need for women to "return" to their "natural and primary role" or "their purely womanly mission," we are in the grip of a patriarchal gender ideology untouched by socialist revolution (Henwood 1990b). The feminization of poverty and the intensified exploitation of women across the international division of labor testify to the fact that the moment of feminism is far from over.

There is much talk these days about a worldwide economic recession. The proportion of debt to Gross National Product in the twenty-five most privileged countries seems to have stabilized at a certain limit beyond which credit has become increasingly hard to obtain. The flip-side of this phenomenon is the increasing squeeze being put upon indebted Third World nations to pay up – whatever the cost to their people and resources. Faced with slow economic growth and intractable inflation, "It's getting harder for the deeply indebted to roll over their debt," one financial analyst observes: "Economically, capitalism could use a real depression – something it couldn't afford politically" (Henwood 1990a: 3). The signs of recession are already plentiful, though in the US continued strategies of crisis management seem more likely than a general financial collapse.

Working as we do in an English department at a large urban university in Detroit, a city whose economy and social life have become so dramatically polarized that it serves as the most frequently cited knee-jerk example of post-industrial urban decay, we find John Kenneth Galbraith's pronouncement some time ago that the United States was a nation of private affluence and public squalor all too self-evident. But reducing the economy to finance does not exhaust the pervasive power of the economic when the market is "in" everything and nothing is incapable of being commodified.

The discipline of critical reading that has developed in academic schools of English studies might once have seemed a long way from the political concerns that have, over the last thirty years, brought Marxists and feminists into dialogue. The literary questions involved in reading the social and cultural practices of our own times, however, are of importance for feminist politics. In particular, the reading of complex or ambiguous textual claims to truth or reality needs to be theorized as a profoundly political activity. In this respect we would agree with the French sociologist, Christine Delphy, that under the sign of materialist feminism we recognize both a call to active political struggle in the everyday, a struggle with and within social institutions, and a revolution in knowledge:

> Materialist feminism is therefore an intellectual approach whose coming is crucial both for social movements, the feminist *struggle, and* for knowledge. This approach would not be – could not be, even if desired – limited to a single population, to the sole oppression of women. It will not leave untouched any aspect of reality, any domain of knowledge, any aspect of the world. As the feminist movement aims at revolution in social reality, the theoretical feminist point of

view (and each is indispensable to the other) must also aim at a revolution in knowledge. (Delphy 1981: 75)

To the extent that *Materialist Feminisms* tells the story of an academic movement that has important relations outside the academy, our story is one of frontiers and borders where limits are set, positions taken, and differences forced into the open. The politics of academic movements may seem limited and circumscribed, but that is no reason to minimize the importance of feminist work within the academy, or to diminish the significance for the women's movement generally of the necessary revolution in knowledge production, a revolution that inhabits those borderlands between academic institutions and self-generating women's groups.

We hope to introduce students engaged in various disciplines to the political urgencies of materialist feminist critical thinking. For there must come a time when, as Catharine R. Stimpson has observed, "We might have to conjoin our awareness of the construction of 'history' and ideology with a deed" (Stimpson 1988: 243). More specifically, we think that the proliferation of minority struggles in recent years has had considerable impact on academic institutions and social practices, and that these movements represent an historical direction from which there will be no simple turning back, politically, socially, or intellectually. A commitment to theory can and should represent an engagement with contemporary struggles around the categories and political realities of feminism, new forms of socialism, anti-racist and anti-imperialist struggles, the lesbian and gay liberation movements, and those loosely allied movements for peace and radical ecological change sometimes called the "green" (or Green) revolution. Within this historical moment, the development of a deconstructive materialist feminist perspective seems to us politically compelling.

Acknowledgments

We should like to thank the Society for the Humanities at Cornell University for fellowships during 1988–9, a year devoted to "Feminism in the Humanities," which made it possible for us to begin writing this book together; many thanks to Jonathan Culler and Dominick LaCapra. During the year in Ithaca, we benefited greatly from conversations with Michèle Barrett, Cynthia Chase, Rita Felski, Heather Findlay, Nelly Furman, Mary Jacobus, Katie King, Biddy Martin, Lisa Moore, Paula Treichler, Hortense Spillers, Charlotte Sussman, and Sharon Willis; our thanks to all. Since then we have benefited from conversations with P. Gabrielle Foreman, Peter Kulchyski, and Janet Langlois. We should also like to thank Tim Dant, Julia Emberley, Tania Modleski, Terry Lovell, and Rajani Sudan for criticism of, advice on, and encouragement with an unwieldy manuscript. Our thanks to Philip Carpenter for encouraging the project at its inception, to Simon Prosser for constant enthusiasm during the writing, revising, and production, and to Linden Stafford for exemplary critical copy-editing. Special thanks to Christopher LeBrun for the use of "Garden Hook" for the cover, and to Gülner Aktug and Gürhan Orhan for looking after us while we worked on final revisions.

Since 1984, when we first co-authored a conference presentation on the work of Gayatri Chakravorty Spivak, we have – together and separately – incurred too many intellectual, political, professional, and personal debts to name everyone without whose material assistance this book would not have been written. But a short list must include John Brewer, Jo Dulan, Bridget and Christopher Hill, Elaine Hobby, Rosemary Hooley, Linda Kauffman, Michael McKeon, Felicity Nussbaum, Hilary Schor, Susan Staves, Angela Tawn, John and Alice Wells, Chris White, and the students at Cornell, the University of Southern California, and Wayne State who have listened to us and asked good questions. This book is dedicated to G.

Introduction

Ends

Introducing *Women's Oppression Today* to the reading public for
the third time since its first appearance in 1980, Michèle Barrett
observes that if she had been writing the book in 1988 she would
have had to consider the issues of racism and ethnicity, but, more
importantly, she would have begun this new book with the question
of feminism and postmodernism. Postmodernism calls feminism into
question. Or at least what Jean-François Lyotard has labeled "the
postmodern condition" calls into question both socialism and feminism as grand political projects, rooted in Enlightenment discourses
of progress and liberty, and dependent upon explanatory historical
narratives of class and gender struggle culminating eventually in
liberation from oppression.

In this book we argue that an understanding of postmodernism,
and in particular of certain intellectual developments of the last
twenty-five years usually categorized loosely as poststructuralism,
need not end in a complete paralysis of political criticism and action,
as has sometimes been claimed. The skepticism towards grand political projects, totalizing theories, and great synthetic narratives characteristic of postmodern or poststructuralist thinking may well prove
indispensable for any radical democratic politics. Socialism must be
re-invented from within feminism and other new social movements,
such as those that contest racism and heterosexism. We hope that
by tracing a genealogy of materialist feminism from some of the
early debates about Marxism and feminism, through more recent
discussions of feminism in relation to anti-racism, poststructuralism,
the history of sexuality, critiques of colonial discourse and postcol-

oniality, and the Green ecological movements, we might be contributing something theoretically towards such a politics.

Our aim in Part I of this book is to introduce certain debates which have, over the last three decades, helped to create and then to transform the political goals of feminist cultural criticism. We do not develop a general theory or offer a synthesis that will solve all existing problems and contradictions, but seek instead to investigate some recent theoretical developments in their historical and political contexts. By "materialist feminisms" we do not wish to name a new and comprehensive feminist theory of knowledge, or to invent a unified feminist politics. Our purpose, rather, is to explore some of the problems in attempting to develop a political analysis of literature and literary theory from a feminist perspective.

But, first, some definitions.

Definitions

Feminism refers principally to those ideas and movements which have sought to challenge and transform the roles ascribed to women in traditional societies. While feminism means different things in different national and regional locations (see, for example, Moi 1987, Lovell 1990, Bono and Kemp 1991, Mohanty, Russo, and Torres 1991, Kauffman 1993), we may notice the following terms commonly used to describe specific feminist positions. Liberal feminism describes the view that women's oppression will end once women have achieved legal equality and equal opportunity with men. Radical feminism argues that the key to women's oppression is men's power over women, a power so embedded in all existing social structures that it cannot be overcome without a general transformation of society. Consequently, radical feminists contend that the concept of legal equality, i.e. equal rights, is insufficient and that all existing social and political institutions need to be uprooted and replaced. This desire has led some radical feminists to the position of feminist separatism, with women establishing their own communities and institutions apart from men. Socialist feminists claim that, unless the economic inequalities and class oppressions of capitalist society are specifically addressed, even radical feminist alternatives will end up by repeating them. Socialist feminists draw a distinction between formal, legal notions of equality and substantive, i.e. economic and social, ones (see Phillips 1987).

At issue in some of these disagreements among feminists is the crucial concept of **patriarchy**. Strictly speaking, patriarchy designates "the rule of the father," but much feminist theory has expanded its implications to cover more general forms of male domination. With Mary McIntosh, Michèle Barrett explores some of the subtle differences between describing a society as "a patriarchy" and trying to tease out exactly which aspects of particular social relations in that society might usefully be described as "patriarchal." Barrett and McIntosh's definition of "patriarchal" social relations, which combine "a public dimension of power, exploitation or status with a dimension of personal servility" (Barrett and McIntosh 1985: 39), is indebted to the work of the American historian Eugene Genovese, who has used the term "paternalism" in a similar sense in relation to slavery in the United States. We use patriarchy in its strict sense of the rule of the father, and the adjective patriarchal to describe social relations that, following Barrett and McIntosh, yoke "public and formal power with private and personal servitude" (1985: 39). The operations of patriarchal power through gender, structures of emotion and affect, sexuality, notions of duty and dependency, and the profound bonds and antagonisms typical of relationships of intimate obligation, make this form of power hard to track. In heterosexual relationships, families, households, and workplaces specifically, patriarchal power proves hard to untangle. This complex interweaving of power in its public and most deeply private forms makes patriarchal power especially difficult to resist.

Materialism exists prior to and independently of Marxism, with which it has frequently come to be associated. As we use it in this book, materialism describes two distinct philosophical tendencies: (a) the proposition that the origins of all forms of existence, including human activity, can be explained in terms of physical being and (b) the critique of idealism, the belief that ideas underlie reality. The moralistic usage of **materialistic**, to describe a selfish and excessive dependence upon status symbols, consumer goods, and making money, is a nineteenth-century development that we may associate with the emergence of industrial capitalism. Marx attempted to distinguish between this **mechanical** materialism, which reduces human agency to a passive reflex of self-interest, and **historical** materialism, which retains human activity as a positive force. "The point that matters," as Raymond Williams explains, "is that **historical materialism** offers explanations of the causes of [the other] sense [of] **materialism** – selfish preoccupation with goods and money – and so far from recommending it describes social and historical ways of overcoming it and establishing co-operation and mutuality" (1983: 200). By transforming Marx's sense of historical materialism – as human interaction – into a theory about the inevitable, scientific unfolding of all natural and physical processes according to universal laws, Marx's sometime collaborator Engels produced **dialectical** materialism. This particular position within Marxism has caused more trouble than any other, provoking many critiques.

We could contend that what is commonly referred to as **orthodox** (or, dismissively, "**vulgar**") Marxism suffers from too heavy a dose of dialectical materialism, pretending to a scientific status unjustified by the evidence of historical events, and ignoring the determining importance of human agency. This kind of Marxism involves the theory that the **economic base** of a society **determines** its **superstructure**, i.e. all aspects of its culture, its legal and political institutions, and its forms of social life. One's place in such a society, or one's **class position**, is determined by one's relation to the economic mode of production – as a factory worker, a police officer, a stock broker, an unemployed single mother receiving assistance from the government's welfare funds, etc.

A number of recent critics in the Marxist tradition have explicitly departed from this so-called orthodoxy without wishing to abandon Marx's project of historical materialism altogether. The **structural Marxism** of Louis Althusser, for instance, influenced by developments in linguistics and philosophy associated with the work of Ferdinand de Saussure, counters determination of the superstructure by the economic base by arguing for the **relative autonomy** of culture and institutions from the economy. We find the concept of culture's relative autonomy useful insofar as it insists upon *some* relation between the category of the economic and particular forms of culture and social life. Further, relative autonomy suggests that the relation between culture and the economic is not simple but complex, that it cannot be known in advance, outside the particular structures of a given society. So the question of economic determination in this version of Marxism is not a case of simple determination but signifies a complexly "overdetermined" relation.

Overdetermination describes how things don't have a single or a simple cause. It requires that we see the relation between, say, the economy and cultural products to be a complex one of mutual interaction. The base does not simply determine or explain the superstructure; neither does the superstructure determine the base. Rather, both intersect in complex ways to produce the peculiar combination of economic and cultural practices characteristic of a particular society. Overdetermination is above all a denial of **essentialist** thinking, by which a complex structure can be reduced to a single kernel of truth, a single essence which "explains" the whole (see Althusser 1969: 89–128, 115–16). Class, for example, cannot be reduced simply to a relation to the mode of production defined in strictly economic terms, any more than woman can be defined exclusively in biological terms, as in the phrase "anatomy is destiny."

Drawing, however unsatisfactorily, upon the psychoanalytic theories of Jacques Lacan (see Barrett 1991: 101–9), Althusser also attempts to unite consideration of the psychic with the social through his model of how **ideology** operates. Ideology is a representation of the lived, yet imaginary relation of individuals to their real conditions of existence (see Althusser 1971: 127–86). In other words, people make sense of the world by imagining themselves as selves, and by thinking about and even fantasizing about their material circumstances as they experience them. Ideology thus carries with it a sense of people's imagining things, a sense of mystification, but in Althusser's model there is no simple escape from ideology either. The ideological representation is also a lived relation, a necessary fiction that is more or less mystified about material reality depending on how much critical knowledge one has about one's circumstances – and about the theory of ideology, as well.

Cultural materialism arises as a critique of certain aspects of structural Marxism. Raymond Williams finds Althusser's model still too mechanical in that it fails to make full use of Marx's own sense of the place of human activity and agency in determining the material conditions of life. V. N. Vološinov provided the first sociological critique of Saussurean linguistics (Vološinov 1973: 58–61). Preferring the linguistic theories of Vološinov and L. S. Vygotsky to Saussure's, Williams himself argues for "the indissoluble connections between material production, political and cultural institutions and activity, and consciousness" (1977: 80). Language for Williams is "practical consciousness" (1977: 44), a way of thinking and acting in the world that has material consequences. Consequently, he regards the study of culture to be as important for grappling with material reality as the study of economics or Marxist philosophy. What is needed, according to Williams, is a supplement to Marx's historical materialism that would develop this recognition further, and so the project of cultural materialism is born, "a theory of the specificities of material cultural and literary production within historical materialism" (1977: 5). Williams thus strives to put human subjects as agents of culture back into materialist debate.

Finally, two terms from poststructuralism which we find especially useful. By **articulation** here we mean not a unified speaking out, but a complex movement of distinct terms with, between, and against each other, as when we describe the action of a knee-joint or the gears of a car's transmission as a "differential articulation." As Michael Ryan comments, "a 'critical articulation' neither makes similarities into identities nor rigorously maintains distinctions. It is more akin to the weaving together of heterogeneous threads into a new product than to the scholarly and disinterested comparison of homogeneous masses whose distinction is respected" (Ryan 1982: xii). Michel Foucault provides the definition of **discourse** as we use it throughout this book: "the term discourse can be defined as the group of statements that belong to a single system of formation; thus I shall be able to speak of clinical discourse, economic discourse, the discourse of natural history, psychiatric discourse" (Foucault 1972: 107–8). Thus discourses are produced by particular institutions within a society, and we can see ideologies circulating through those discourses.

With these definitions in mind, let us return to the question of feminism and materialism in the postmodern era.

Histories

If *Women's Oppression Today* may be said to be a key text in the debates about integrating Marxist and feminist social theories, a founding moment for Anglo-American materialist feminism, then the Introduction to the 1988 edition represents another important moment, in which some of the premises of these debates are called into question. According to Barrett, the "recent fundamental shifts in western philosophy represented by the names and influence of Foucault, Derrida, Lacan, Deleuze and Guattari, Lyotard and so on" (1988: xxxvi) constitute the greatest challenge to both the feminism and the Marxism out of which *Women's Oppression Today* was written. And thus the grounds of any new thinking about the theory and politics of feminism, Marxism, socialism, or materialist feminism will need to have been prepared in the light of these intellectual shifts. Barrett concludes, undaunted:

> But post-modernism is not something that you can be for or against: the reiteration of old knowledges will not make it vanish. For it is a cultural climate as well as an intellectual position, a political reality as well as an academic fashion. The arguments of post-modernism

already represent, I think, a key position around which feminist theoretical work in the future is likely to revolve. (1988: xxxvi)

What are some of the specific issues raised by this new political reality called postmodernism? What qualities or intensities of social life might we expect to find within the "postmodern condition?" Most importantly, who are the "we" who can expect to find ourselves living within this cultural climate?

In *The Postmodern Condition*, which was first published in France in 1979 and written for presentation to the Conseil des Universités of the government of Quebec, Lyotard writes, "The object of this study is the condition of knowledge in the most highly developed societies. . . . Simplifying to the extreme, I define *postmodern* as incredulity toward metanarratives" (1984: xxiii–xxiv). By specifying "most highly developed societies" Lyotard locates his analysis in the metropolitan centers of the advanced-capitalist technocracies of Western Europe and North America. Eastern Europe and the countries of the capitalist periphery or Third World presumably do not suffer from this incredulity to the same extent, ostensibly in direct relation to their relative lack of access to the technologies of information production and circulation so crucial to a post-industrial, "post-Fordist," or at least de-industrializing rather than developing society. In many ways parallel to the discussion of a shift from modernism to postmodernism within culture, there is a body of work, following Antonio Gramsci, on a shift within capitalist industry from the mass production model of Henry Ford and the early automotive industry to a post-Fordist model in which information industries come to dominate consumer societies (see Rustin 1989, Harvey 1990).

Thus Lyotard's implied audience consists primarily of citizens of the metropolitan centers of the West, not of the underdeveloped or developing nations. This is an audience with diverse but at the same time clearly defined relations to the international division of labor. Along an East–West or South–North geopolitical axis, the metropole's highly developed information technologies exact the cost of super-exploitation in the capitalist periphery, and in particular in those "offshore" export-processing zones (EPZs) in which much of the high technology of the microchip revolution is produced (Nash and Fernández-Kelly 1983: viii). Citizens of the metropole, however divided amongst themselves by class, race, gender, sexual orientation, nationality, or ethnicity, still share, however unequally, in a certain metropolitan privilege we could call information access. Donna Haraway, US socialist feminist and historian of science, writes: "[W]e are living through a movement from an organic, industrial society to a polymorphous, information system," from a system of older hierarchical forms of domination to new networks of power. Haraway calls these new networks, terrifying in their complexity and possible consequences in the age of nuclear weapons and "Star Wars" technology, an "informatics of domination" (1991: 161).

Those of us who benefit most from such an international division of labor, as members of the most highly developed societies, are those who, according to Lyotard, are increasingly least willing to believe in the validity of "metanarratives," those particular explanatory narratives which claim to ground, legitimate, and account for other narratives within a culture. In his terms, "Most people have lost the nostalgia for the lost narrative" (1984: 41), for those great universalizing stories of the progress of mankind towards civilization and freedom, which have traditionally been used to legitimate scientific and technological advance as well as political struggles for emancipation. Lyotard's metropolitan citizens are particularly without nostalgia for his two examples of Western master narratives, or *grands récits*: in the wake of the French Revolution, the story of the emancipation of "the people"; and, with the founding of the University of Berlin under the influence of German idealist philosophy, the story of learning or "science" gradually bringing to self-consciousness the ideal "speculative spirit" of humanity.

Lyotard's formulation of such an "incredulity toward metanarratives" has sometimes been taken to mean that, if we accept his analysis of the postmodern moment, all narratives have been discredited, all forms of truth have been relativized out of existence, and all ethicopolitical judgements and actions have been rendered theoretically untenable and thus politically impossible. For those with a stake in political and social change, particularly participants in struggles against imperialism and for self-determination across the globe, feminists, and members of anti-racist and gay liberation groups, such statements are likely to sound reactionary, negating all social agency and the hope for radical political transformation.

Ironically, however, the most outraged objections to Lyotard's analysis have tended to come not from Third World intellectuals but from Euroamerican critics (see Connor 1989, Lovibond 1989). More moderate reservations about the consistency of Lyotard's argument, and hence its potential usefulness for feminism, have been expressed by the US writers Nancy Fraser and Linda Nicholson (1988: 86–91). Meanwhile, a number of Third World or, more precisely, postcolonial intellectuals see more than mere chronological coincidence between movements towards decolonization and the new theoretical perspectives needed to address postmodernity. For the Moroccan writer Abdelkebir Khatibi, for example, "decolonization" and "deconstruction" share ideological affinities, and he sees considerable critical potential in developing their association (1983: 47–8 n.; cited in Harlow 1987: xvi–xvii).

Here we must confront the ways in which feminist theorizing, like other forms of Western thinking, has also often followed an imperial logic, pursuing the goals of empirical information retrieval, and of global prescription on behalf of other women. In this context, Lyotard's description of "postmodern knowledge" and his distinction between a politics of consensus and a politics of justice can prove useful: "Postmodern knowledge is not simply a tool of the authorities; it refines our sensitivity to differences and reinforces our ability to tolerate the incommensurable" (1984: xxv). A feminism based on the assumption that there could be a category "Woman" outside philosophy or male fantasy, or a category "women" within the social world, untraversed by differences of, among other specificities, class, sexuality, race, nationality, or ethnicity, will be bound to repeat the imperial gesture whatever its intentions. A logic of difference by which the incommensurable could not only be tolerated but also enabled to speak is clearly called for, and it is here that we would locate one contribution of poststructuralist thinking to the possibility of a postmodern politics indebted to, but not bound by, the orthodoxies of the Marxist and feminist traditions.

Both Marxism and feminism, in their critiques of ideology, can lead us towards a profound suspicion of everything that presents itself as natural. For what appears natural and unchangeable, Marxism would substitute a notion of the historical, while feminism would substitute the constructed or the coded, recoded, and represented. Both Marxism and feminism can thus be understood to be engaged in the de-fetishization of the self-evidently given, including that most difficult of givens to be critical of and objective about, the form of subjectivity which we experience most concretely as "ourselves." The de-fetishization of concrete experience, paradoxicallly, is one of the most powerful tools of Marxist and feminist ideology critique, for through this process social and political impossibilities become thinkable as possibilities. Thus, although both terms of the title of this book in some sense presuppose those grand nineteenth-century political projects with roots in the Enlightenment of the seventeenth and eighteenth centuries, feminism and Marxism, we hope we have not invoked those projects unproblematically.

If Lyotard were writing *The Postmodern Condition* now in the 1990s, he would presumably have to extend an "incredulity toward metanarratives" to Eastern Europe, the Balkans, and the former Soviet Union, at least. In his terms, the collapse of communist ideology and of a controlled economy into a new rhetoric of reform and free-market economics could be attributed to such incredulity. There is plenty of evidence offered in the Western press for the death of communism as a metanarrative. The social and economic problems of existing socialist regimes are undeniable, but should not be confused with the end of all socialist projects or efforts at collective thinking. As Michèle Barrett and Mary McIntosh have argued, in spite of the bad names collectivism and socialism are receiving with the break-up of the Soviet bloc, new forms of long-term collective thinking are ecologically more urgent than ever: "The market is quite obviously incapable of solving London's traffic problems, let alone global warming. In this context, collectivism and a sense of social responsibility have come to be seen as the only alternative to capitulation to the destructive logic of capitalism's drive towards local profit, whatever the longer-term global price" (1991: 162).

A similar skepticism seems necessary regarding the declaration that we have now arrived at an officially "postfeminist" era. Postfeminism sounds compatible with postmodernism, if not also with such signs of the inarguable "postness" of the contemporary moment as post-Marxism, poststructuralism, post-punk, postcoloniality, post-industrialism, and post-ethnicity.

The sound of the "post-" resonates with up-to-dateness, and with the sophistication of having already been somewhere important, and now having left it behind, no doubt loaded with certain credentials, certain souvenirs of the by now, by definition, kitschy previous moment of Marxism, punkdom, colonialism, or industrialization. Commenting on the significance of the "post-" beyond its sound, R. Radhakrishnan argues:

> The constituency of "the ethnic" occupies quite literally a "pre-post"-erous space where it has to actualize, enfranchize, and empower its own "identity" and coextensively engage in the deconstruction of the very logic of "identity" and its binary and exclusionary politics. Failure to achieve this doubleness can only result in the formation of ethnicity as yet another "identical" and hegemonic [i.e. dominant and dominating] structure. (1987: 199)

The difference between postfeminism and a formulation like "post-ethnicity," we would argue, is that dominant ideologies everywhere, including ethnic communities, have been hoping prematurely and unselfcritically that feminism would go away. It hasn't, of course, and Linda Hutcheon, author of *The Politics of Postmodernism*, argues for "the powerful impact of feminist practices on postmodernism – though not for the conflation of the two." Hutcheon continues:

> If, in the postmodern age, we do live in what has been called a recessionary erotic economy brought about by fear of disease and a fetishization of fitness . . . postmodernism's "de-doxifying" work on the construction of the individual bourgeois subject has had to make room for the consideration of the construction of the *gendered* subject. I say this in full awareness that some of the major theorists of the postmodern have not yet noticed this. . . . [W]e have seen that post-modernism is politically ambivalent for it is doubly coded – both complicitous with and contesting of the cultural dominants within which it operates; but on the other side, feminisms have distinct, unambiguous political agendas of resistance. (1989: 141–2)

The project of "de-doxifying" or critiquing the orthodoxies and home-truths of Western liberal individualism within the global market economy is common to many forms of poststructuralist theory and postmodern art today. This tendency is often what gives them their critical, oppositional force. And the political urgencies of feminist practice in many locations within contemporary metropolitan culture require that feminist political agendas be distinct, and distinctly feminist, and unambiguously engaged in resistance to cultural domi-nants, and to new as well as old forms of domination.

But the certainty with which Hutcheon dictates the form as well as the content of feminist resistance seems misplaced. She establishes a new orthodoxy in the very act of commending the de-doxifiers, the wielders of a critical weapon that is "beyond" *doxa*, beyond traditional truths or reverence for the orthodox. What could be more orthodoxly political, and more pre-postmodern, than the formulation of an *unambiguous* political agenda, untouched by historical contin-gency, unaware of its status as a text, that is, as a linguistic production subject to the metaphorical and ideological slippages of signification characteristic of textuality? The many feminisms in circulation today cannot be so easily subsumed within this model of earnest protest and resistance represented as monolithic, unreflective, and outside complicity with institutional structures of power, either global or local. Whatever it might be, contemporary feminism is neither the feminine other nor the political conscience of postmodernism.

The production of the term postfeminism, then, may well signify a certain cultural impatience and unease at the prospect that the moment of feminism is still far from over. The kinds of feminism, or feminisms, that will be needed in this context, however, are those for which such questions as the whole history of Euroamerican imperialism, colonialism, and ecological exploitation, and the construction of race and nationality or ethnicity as well as class and sexuality as categories through which power operates and augments itself, can no longer be set aside – indeed, can no longer be considered as extricable in any way from considerations of feminism or postmodernism.

In this book we shall trace the complex and sometimes tortuous history of the encounters between Anglophone Marxism and feminism on both sides of the Atlantic. This history will take the form of three exemplary moments, leading to our own argument concerning the politics of deconstruction. In later sections of this book, we shall argue that deconstruction can be useful for overcoming many of the methodological limitations and practical problems in feminist theory. For many feminists, working with socialist and Marxist paradigms has posed the problem of "dual-systems" theories; on what grounds can it be decided whether class takes precedence over gender in the determinations of social life, or vice versa? This predicament becomes even more vexed when attempts are made to address any third or subsequent term such as race, religion, nationalism, regionalism, ethnicity, or sexuality.

Although often hostile to or skeptical of deconstruction, many feminist cultural critics arguing from a socialist position have demonstrated that the material conditions of women's oppression, and hence women's political interests, are themselves historically specific and therefore cannot be framed in terms of gender alone. A feminist politics projected exclusively in terms of women's equality cannot recognize, much less challenge, those currently existing socio-political structures and institutional settings which divide women by class, race, sexuality, and ethnicity, and in which a simple concept of women's equality with men may seem rather beside the point.

We will suggest that when feminist goals are specified solely in terms of gender, or even by a dual-systems approach seeking to include class analysis, political problems arise which deconstructive reading practices can help solve. Thus we are proposing instead the articulation of discontinuous movements, materialism and feminism, an articulation that takes the political claims of deconstruction seriously, without abandoning either class struggle or resistance to gender ideology where these obtain in specific historico-political sites, and opening itself as well to other possible categories of identity and resistance.

We are not proposing that every text requires the same reading strategy, nor is every reading strategy we propose strictly deconstructive. As we argue in Part II, chapter 4, the ends to which different texts are put, the uses readers make of them, are more important for a materialist theory of criticism than are a text's formal properties per se. The materialist theory of textuality that we are proposing is thus distinct from formalism, which views the internal, structural qualities of any specific text as sufficient objects of analysis and evaluation. However, readers do use texts in ways crucially determined by formal properties – is the text in question a detective novel, an autobiographical essay, a diary entry, a romance, a piece of philosophy or social theory, a poem that is also a theoretical manifesto? As a result, our typically deconstructive strategies for reading theoretical texts in Parts I and III may seem to differ in method from those we adopt when reading feminist literary texts in Part II.

We are trying to shift the place of deconstruction from its familiar status as a literary-critical strategy, suitable for use on novels, to a tool of political critique. Consequently, in Part II, chapter 5, when reading some recent examples of feminist fiction, we pay little attention to deconstruction and emphasize instead the commodity status, the conditions of production and reception, and the political and ideological content of these detective novels and novels by women of color. By adopting different reading strategies, we hope to reveal some of the less than obvious features of how fictional as well as theoretical texts do their work.

The first moment of our schematic history in Part I coincides with the political encounter between Marxism and feminism taking place, often in the work of individual feminists who also happened to be Marxists, in Britain and the US from the late 1960s until the publication of Michèle Barrett's *Women's Oppression Today: Problems in Marxist Feminist Analysis* in 1980. The achievement of this moment has been the uneven transformation of existing Marxist and socialist thinking by feminist critique.

The second moment we see as emerging initially in the United States during the 1960s from the political alliances and dialogues between women's liberation and Civil Rights and anti-war activists. This was a moment that had so successfully challenged traditional cultural assumptions by 1985 – the year in which Judith Newton and Deborah Rosenfelt first attempted to elaborate a theory of US-style materialist feminist criticism – that the later 1980s and early 1990s provide ample evidence of a New Right backlash in the US directly aimed at these political gains for women and minorities. And in the last several years the New Right backlash has itself been gaining widespread cultural legitimacy in the work of academic patriarchs like Allan Bloom and E. D. Hirsch, Jr. Debates about multiculturalism, the canon, and political correctness in the US all bear the mark of both the limited institutional success of progressive political ideas and people within American universities, and conservative outrage that this should be so.

The third moment, that of deconstructive materialist feminism, could be said to have been announced in 1976, the year in which Gayatri Chakravorty Spivak's translation made Derrida's *Of Grammatology* available outside France and Francophone circles. This moment also has, however, important though discontinuous origins in the various poststructuralist appropriations and critiques of Lacanian psychoanalysis and post-Althusserian theories of ideology, many of them undertaken in the 1970s within film studies and particularly in the British film journal *Screen*, as well as the British theoretical journal *m/f*. A turning point within this moment could be said to have occurred around 1985, the year in which Newton and Rosenfelt published their anthology, which was heavily indebted to this earlier British theoretical work, and the year in which Toril Moi, a Norwegian specialist in French teaching at Oxford, published her devastating critique of the theoretical shortcomings of Anglo-American feminist literary criticism, as revealed when its texts are read alongside those of French feminist theory.

Moi's case against the Anglo-American resistance to theory, and her consequent celebration of the work of Hélène Cixous, Luce Irigaray, and Julia Kristeva, might seem to pose difficulties for our project of investigating Anglo-American materialist feminism rather than French. After all, we frequently cite work by French intellectuals who are not feminists. Why then do we confine ourselves to so few references to Moi's three big names? An answer will be found in chapter 2. The commodification of feminist theory within the academy, especially in US universities, has enshrined these figures as intellectual icons and fetish objects to such an extent that too often discussion of their work comes to stand for the entire field of feminist theory, globally conceived.

We wish to offer here an alternative story, both historically and theoretically speaking. Matters are more complicated than Moi's survey implies, since the monolithic construction "French feminist theory" is largely an Anglo-American fiction, and disagreements about each of the three terms abound in the French scene. There are, of course, any number of contemporary French writers who might be said to work within a feminist discourse, but who are less well known in the US and UK than Cixous, Irigaray, or Kristeva. Christine Delphy, for example, whom we cited in the Preface, has written manifestos for a materialist feminism. We find her description of this project, however, to be ultimately rather disappointing, and we would make some of the same criticisms of it that we make of Zillah Eisenstein's work in chapter 1 (see also Barrett and McIntosh 1979 for a fuller critique of Delphy). The work of Monique Wittig we touch on in chapter 8 because her most important contribution has been a lesbian intervention, exposing the systematically straight mind behind so much feminist thinking, an intervention that owes something to Marxist theory but more to her own practice as a writer of radically experimental fiction.

In this book, therefore, we have concentrated on what we take to be the crucial issues for materialist feminist debates mainly as they have unfolded in Britain and the United States, with some attention to developments in France when they impinge on one another. And so we have not given the French feminist writers the sustained and contextualixed treatment we give to the British and Americans because to do so properly would require another book, and there have been quite a few books on French feminist theory already (see chapter 2).

Part I offers a schematic history of our three moments of materialist feminism, in relation to Marxist feminist debates and Anglo-American literary studies. Part II focuses on the application of feminist theory to literary history and criticism. What can a materialist feminist critical practice tell us about the writing of histories and fictions, including feminist detective fiction and novels by women of color? In Part III we attempt to question the tidiness of our schematic history in Part I, which could be read as a bluffer's guide to our topic. For readers seeking a quick purchase on the subject matter of this book, Part I provides an overview. The very concept of an overview, however, as we argue throughout, should be regarded with suspicion. The quick fix always has its costs. For starters, it usually comes to an end just as things are beginning to get really interesting.

Part I

Beyond the Marxist–Feminist
Encounter

1

Origins UK and US

Calls for a materialist feminism compatible with historical materialism *def* have been around since the late nineteenth century. We will not attempt a history of relations between socialism, Marxism, and feminism since that time. What follows will be, rather, a reading of certain representative texts organized around particular controversies that we think are crucial for the project of a materialist feminism. The best way of approaching a longer historical view, for those who are interested, would be to read works by some of the important figures in these movements, such as the Owenites and other utopian socialists studied by Barbara Taylor, the socialist sex radicals and reformers analyzed by Jeffrey Weeks, and the writings of August Bebel, Eleanor Marx, Rosa Luxemburg, Alexandra Kollontai, Emma Goldman, Clara Zetkin, Stella Browne, and others.[1]

Where shall we begin, then? Katie King, a US feminist theorist, examining the recent history of the women's movement in the United States, points out:

> Origin stories about the women's movement are interested stories: they construct the present moment, and a political position in it, by invoking the history out of which that moment unfolds. . . . There is no "real" story, only different stories, all concretely situated, all interested. (King 1986: abstract)

King is challenging the assumption that there might be such a thing as a history that would be objective, disinterested, and definitive. The more scientifically objective and ideologically unaligned the presentation, the more likely the interests of the text are to be covert and unexamined, but for that reason peculiarly powerful in the shaping of an historical representation. King's insight contributes to

feminist analysis and anti-racist analysis since it offers an irrefutable
demonstration of the ways in which gender and race operate in
unacknowledged ways in supposedly objective, ungendered, non-
racial accounts, which turn out, upon close critical inspection, to be
both sexist and racist. King's position calls not for the abandonment
of the project of writing histories but for political accountability in
their construction (1986: 84), and that requires more than a declaration of interest; it requires challenging the idea of a unitary history
itself.

In a schematic narrative, the history of materialist feminisms might
begin with the debates among socialists and feminists from the late
1960s onwards regarding the relative political claims of gender and
class analysis. This story would also describe attempts to bring a
psychoanalytical understanding of sexuality and subjectivity to bear
upon a politicized theory of gender differences. In the British context,
it would pay special attention to those feminists, like members of
the Marxist–Feminist Literary Collective, who were seeking to engage
literary theory and psychoanalysis with Marxist analysis of class
struggle to help them formulate strategies in the struggle against the
cultural subordination of women (see Kaplan 1986: 61–4). In the
United States, a history of materialist feminisms would notice how
the "second wave" of feminism, the women's movements of the
1960s and 1970s (the "first wave" being the female suffrage movement
of the nineteenth and early twentieth centuries), largely grew in
connection with the Civil Rights and anti-war movements (see Evans
1979). This story would point to the considerable success of feminists
at transforming institutions, like the higher educational system,
according to women's interests, through the introduction of women's
studies courses and women's resource centers. And it would notice
the recent discontent in both Britain and the US with the racial
blindness and heterosexism undermining many of these reformist
achievements.

But such a narrative might be reductive. The very term "materialist
feminisms" proves contentious, since there has been little general
consensus within the women's movement whether women's interests
can, or indeed should, be addressed in terms of traditional socialist
and Marxist formulas. Heidi Hartmann's essay, "The Unhappy Marriage of Marxism and Feminism: Towards a More Progressive
Union," published in the US in 1981, sparked much debate. Her
position might well make some think of Sarah Schulman's character,
Vivian, as she appears in our epigraph:

We will argue here that while marxist analysis provides essential insight into the laws of historical development, and those of capital in particular, the categories of marxism are sex-blind. Only a specifically feminist analysis reveals the systemic character of relations between men and women. Yet feminist analysis by itself is inadequate because it has been blind to history and insufficiently materialist. (Hartmann 1981: 2–3)

What could be parodied as sounding like an academic exercise in 1984 was still being taken seriously within the US movement in 1981.

UK: The Psychic and the Social

In the British context, Juliet Mitchell began by arguing that feminist questions should be answered by developing Marxist terms, but as her work itself has developed she has increasingly emphasized the necessity for both psychoanalytic questions and answers to be articulated with this Marxist feminist analysis. Although critical of this position, Michèle Barrett's highly influential *Women's Oppression Today* (1980) insists that the way forward for feminists will involve not just direct engagement with, but also a necessary transformation of, Marxist ideological and class analysis if we are to understand the psychic within the social, and respond to various intellectual challenges such as that posed by the discourse theory of Michel Foucault. Parveen Adams and Elizabeth Cowie adopt a more extreme position in their editorial to the final issue of the important UK journal *m/f* (1978–86), stating that "As socialist-feminists we were opposed to the much discussed union of Marxism and feminism," and sought instead "to problematise the notion of sexual difference itself" through a fundamental critique of psychoanalytic categories (Adams and Cowie 1986: 3).

These differences should be understood both as intellectual differences and as political differences that represent partisan disputes within the British left. Here "partisan" is the operative word because feminist involvement with the Labour Party, the Communist Party of Great Britain (CPGB), and various Trotskyist groups was widespread. The situation differs in the USA, where, largely working outside the pressures of party politics but constrained by the memory of Senator Joseph McCarthy's anti-communist witch-hunting in the

1950s, feminists as diverse as Zillah Eisenstein, Lise Vogel, and Donna Haraway identify themselves as socialist feminists. In doing so, they distinguish their work from that of radical and liberal feminists who contend that women's oppression will end with the achievement of women's power or women's equality, respectively, within existing class societies.

There have been several reports of the encounters taking place between feminists and the male-dominated left in Britain during the 1960s and 1970s. The best known of these is probably *Beyond the Fragments: Feminism and the Making of Socialism* (1979) by Sheila Rowbotham, Lynne Segal, and Hilary Wainwright, which begins indignantly by regretting the obvious gap between the left activism of the seventies and the (then) recent election of Margaret Thatcher's Conservative government: "After a decade of intense socialist agitation, more working-class people than ever in post-war years voted Tory at the last election" (1979: 1). One of the arguments of *Beyond the Fragments* is that the male left had failed politically because it had yet to take women and the issues raised by feminism seriously.

For Rowbotham, Segal, and Wainwright, looking back to the sixties from 1979, not much seemed to have changed after two decades of intense feminist agitation. It is sobering to recognize the extent to which Julia Swindells and Lisa Jardine's analysis, *What's Left?*, published in 1990, registers much the same disaffection with an unreconstructed male left who read William Morris "to make good Marx" and unthinkingly consign women to supplying "moral realism" through "a moralism which relies on *art* and on the *family* to carry its burden" (1990: 48, 59–60). Back in 1973, Sheila Rowbotham's *Woman's Consciousness, Man's World* described the political problems facing women seeking to raise feminist issues within left organizations dedicated to "'the correct Marxist position'" (1973: 18). In such contexts, feminist strategies took shape within existing critiques of capitalist society, often by focusing exclusively on the sexual division of labor. Important critiques of women's traditional roles as mothers and housewives linked women's unpaid domestic labor with the reproduction of the capitalist economy. Politically, women came to figure only as members of the working class whose conditions of subordination would end once they were paid for their work. While producing important debates about direct payment for domestic and reproductive labor, this kind of analysis did not produce a specifically feminist politics, since, like the system it sought to critique, it tended to reduce and subordinate women's interests to the struggle for economic control. Nevertheless, putting an end to thê specifically economic exploitation of traditional women's labor still remains of crucial concern for any feminist politics (see Hamilton and Barrett 1986).

The political effects of the encounters between Marxism and feminism in Britain did not work in one direction only. In their introduction to *Feminism and Materialism: Women and Modes of Production*, an important collection of essays published in 1978, Annette Kuhn and AnnMarie Wolpe suggested that British feminists seeking to engage politically with Marxism had initiated a transformation not only of feminist thinking but also of traditional Marxist analysis. They observed:

> It is no coincidence that the attempt to construct analyses of the specificity of the subordination of women in capitalism in terms of orthodox approaches to the labour theory of value through an examination of domestic labour encountered such obstacles that attempts of this sort have by now been virtually abandoned: a situation which suggests that . . . "a correct analysis of the subordination of women cannot be provided by Marxists unless Marxism itself is transformed". (1978: 8)

What this transformation of Marxist theory has meant in practice largely involves the attempt to account for the specifically sexual division of labor and this, in turn, has involved another project of the 1960s, the attempt to bring Freudian theory into dialogue with Marxism.

From the late 1960s on, much feminist analysis in Britain has developed in the midst of what we might call the "New Left" political project, the attempt to identify the popular and working-class struggles against Toryism and British neo-colonialism with the production of a critical reading of orthodox Marxism and psychoanalysis. In Britain, Juliet Mitchell's feminist reading of Marx, Freud, and Lacan has been of considerable importance since the 1960s. Initially trained as a literary scholar, Mitchell has focused on questions concerning the family and childrearing by means of a feminist critique of psychoanalytic theories of sexual development largely based upon a literary-critical examination of texts within the Freudian/Lacanian and Marxist canons. Mitchell's project, continued in her influential *Psychoanalysis and Feminism* (1974) and *Women: The Longest Revolution* (1984), which reprints her 1966 essay and contains exemplary studies of literary texts such as *Wuthering Heights* and *Moll Flanders*, has been to inflect feminist politics with insights from Marxism and psychoanalysis. With Jacqueline Rose, she has continued the engagement between the psychoanalytic theories of Jacques Lacan and materialist feminist thinking in Britain (Mitchell and Rose 1982; see also Coward and Ellis 1977).

Mitchell's 1966 essay, "Women: The Longest Revolution," exemplifies a problem that has vexed Marxist and materialist feminism ever since. On the one hand, Mitchell recognizes that one of the difficulties with the Marxist tradition has been the way in which the question of women is so often framed only in terms of the family. Commenting on the later writings of Marx, including *Capital*, she observes: "What is striking is that here the problem of women has been submerged in an analysis of the family" (Mitchell 1984: 22). Yet Mitchell's own analysis ends up doing much the same thing, since of the four fundamental categories she proposes for specifying women's situation within a general social formation – production, reproduction, sexuality, and socialization – three tend to put women back into the family. Mitchell's later work on psychoanalysis and the family "tells us (what we already know), that the domain of psychoanalysis *is* the familial," and that women have been relegated to the family, first by bourgeois society and then again by Marxist theory (Swindells and Jardine 1990: 78).

Ironically, although Mitchell's work began by trying to analyze the psychic and the social, "the *whole* of women's situation" without fetishizing "any dimension of it" (1984: 50), her recent work is firmly on the side of psychoanalysis, leaving all things social as the proper domain of sociologists. For Swindells and Jardine, this separation fetishizes women's psychic dimension at the expense of everything else, a move they attribute very loosely to "deconstruction" (1990: 83) – an argument to which we shall return.

Mitchell's attention to the psychic as well as social dimensions of Marxist, Freudian, and Lacanian discourses has enabled her to address wide-ranging questions of ideology, literary representation, and the unconscious. This theoretical comprehensiveness has made her work important for subsequent feminist literary studies on both sides of the Atlantic. Of particular interest here are books by Mitchell's British collaborator, Jacqueline Rose (1986), and the American Jane Gallop, who takes Mitchell's *Psychoanalysis and Feminism* as her "point of departure" (Gallop 1982: xiii).

The distinct difference between Rose's and Gallop's work, which Mitchell herself characterizes as Gallop's "trivialising of the subject, of the questions" (Adams and Cowie 1983: 5), exemplifies some of the differences between the British and US intellectual scenes. These differences are important to the development of political strategies that, even when most academic, have continued to resonate with political and social struggles outside universities. In Britain during the 1970s and early 1980s, as we have already mentioned, the development of "cultural materialism" was highly relevant. Meanwhile, the interventionary work of feminists influenced by Althusserian Marxism, and, often through Althusser, by Lacanian theory was starting to prove crucial for the decentering of traditional perspectives in history, psychoanalysis, and the sociology of knowledge both inside and outside the academy. Kuhn and Wolpe (1978: 2) notice how feminist activists had, to a certain extent, already transformed traditional conditions of knowledge production outside traditional educational and academic institutions.

From this theoretically rigorous and politically charged context, Barrett's *Women's Oppression Today* examines encounters between Marxism and feminism by analyzing the paradigmatic problems that had arisen from attempts to bring class and gender analysis together. Despite its race blindness and ethnocentrism, characteristic of the (white) socialist feminism of its moment, Barrett's book established a degree of theoretical coherence and political acumen that renders it in advance of a great deal of feminist theory being constructed today.

Barrett's disciplinary formation as a sociologist is crucial to her achievement, since, especially from a psychoanalytic perspective, "the social" *is* the domain of sociology purely and simply. The great divide between psychic and social formulations of feminism can be emblematized here, in the differences between Mitchell's position and Barrett's. For a sociologist like Barrett, literary questions are contingent rather than central. Yet Barrett's treatment of ideology in *Women's Oppression Today* has been taken up and developed by literary critics. Not surprisingly, then, considering our own disciplinary location, we think that her book, despite its limitations, provides the best analysis of the problems of framing feminist politics within a Marxist perspective, and that her work as a whole is exemplary of both the strengths and the weaknesses of the best white British materialist feminism.

According to Barrett, the political urgencies of women's liberation include the need for a feminist analysis of culture, and it is here that the problematic relationship of Marxism and feminism directly engages questions of literary theory, in particular questions of aesthetics, subjectivity, and ideology. In "Feminism and the Definition of Cultural Politics" (1982), her 1980 lecture to the Communist University of London, Barrett addresses three issues of direct importance to materialist feminist literary theory: (1) the indeterminacy of artistic and literary meaning, (2) the relationship between women's art and feminist art, and (3) the problem of judging aesthetic value and pleasure. This essay is worth considering in some detail here since these questions, and Barrett's treatment of them, characterize the importance of literary theory for materialist feminism.

Barrett asserts that "Feminism has . . . politicized the various forms of artistic and imaginative expression that are more popularly known as culture, reassessing and transforming film, literature, art, the theatre and so on" (1982: 37). Following Raymond Williams, Barrett focuses on the literary problem of " 'signification'," the "systems of signs . . . through which meaning is constructed, represented, consumed and reproduced" (1982: 38). In Barrett's view, artistic and literary meanings are determinable but not fixed, since meaning "may depend on who is reading or receiving . . . and how they do so" (1982: 39). Literary texts and other works of art have no inherent meaning but have specific formal qualities that help to determine the meanings which are given to them in precise socio-historical contexts. A rape scene in a feminist play has different meanings for the feminist viewers from those available to the "men from the rugby club who rushed in from the bar (laughing) when they heard what was going on" (1982: 39). This is not an argument for total indeterminacy, however, since Barrett insists that every work does carry a culturally sanctioned, "dominant, or preferred, reading" (1982: 42) that limits the range of possible meanings: feminist and rugby player can agree that the scene represents rape, where they differ is in their aesthetic response.

For Barrett, literary texts, art objects, and dramatic performances are to be regarded as formally ambiguous and marked by inner contradictions that cannot easily be adjudicated by reference to the artist's life or intentions. She agrees with Rosalind Coward that women's art is not necessarily feminist, since feminism "is an alignment of political interests and not a shared female experience" (1982: 42), though she is reluctant to follow Coward (1980) and abandon female experience entirely as a category within the project of a feminist cultural analysis: "Put another way, feminist art could be seen as a category *within* a tradition of women's art but I fail to see how it could be generated outside it" (1982: 47). She does, however, argue that feminist political interests are not necessarily served by the recovery of women's past artistic achievements, or even by self-proclaimed feminist art works like Judy Chicago's *The Dinner Party*.

Barrett approaches the question how we might distinguish cultural

production in general from "art" within the framework of an historical materialist critique of ideology: "our ideas about art are profoundly influenced by, and entangled with, a particular historical
conception of art which affects feminist as well as other types of
thinking" (1982: 47). Here she is criticizing an influential tendency
within feminist literary criticism that separates reading from writing,
a view that she considers dangerous for feminist politics since it
replicates a division of labor that elevates "art" above "work." "It is
only the degradation of work under capitalist relations of production,
including the degree to which workers have been stripped of mental
control over their labour, that makes us perceive such a huge gulf
between work and what we call 'creative' work" (1982: 48–9). The
ideological formulation of this socio-economic division is the dual
question of aesthetic value and pleasure which, she argues, feminists
ignore to their peril. How can some works of art be judged better
than others? Barrett finds traditional assumptions that value judgements can and should be made highly suspicious for feminist politics,
since they invariably tend to make the values of the dominant classes
appear to be natural and universal.

Barrett's materialist aesthetics seeks to democratize the relation
between the producer and the consumer of art. In order to arrive at
an objective ground on which to base aesthetic judgements that will
prevent the reinscription of dominant and oppressive values, Barrett
suggests that we "consider afresh" (1982: 51) questions of skill and
imagination that have been largely ignored by feminist and other
radical theories of art. "For if we can identify levels of aesthetic skill
in the construction of works of art, and the expression of critical
and fictional representation of the world, it becomes clear that the
reading of the work will inevitably depend upon the corresponding
consciousness and knowledge of the audience" (1982: 52). Skills,
though socially defined, are not innate but acquired and therefore
improvable, while the imaginative rendering of social life in works
of art and literature is typically foreclosed in much feminist criticism
by an undue emphasis upon the work's content as unmediated representation. "We need to work towards the creation of a cultural
milieu in which feminist vision is creatively consumed as well as
imaginatively produced" (1982: 53).

In theorizing this aim, Barrett emphasizes the active role of the
viewer/reader. She suggests that there is no intrinsic merit in avant-
garde forms per se. And she argues that the pleasures to be obtained
from politically regressive art forms (TV soaps, romances) should
not be rejected out of hand by feminist critics. The feminist desire

to reject the sexism of dominant cultural productions and to establish feminist alternatives, she contends, "suffers from the limitations of all lifestyle politics" (1982: 56); not only can it prevent us understanding our desires, but the energy which gets directed at developing alternatives might be used developing "strategies directed at more fundamental changes" (1982: 56). For Barrett, literature and art help constitute social life but do not determine it: "Cultural politics, and feminist art, are important precisely because we are not the helpless victims of oppressive ideology. We take some responsibility for the cultural meaning of gender and it is up to us all to change it" (1982: 58).[2]

The contribution of Barrett's book *Women's Oppression Today*, however, goes beyond strictly literary and aesthetic issues and enters the wider terrain of ideology and culture. Barrett sets out to answer the question why women are oppressed, what constitutes the reasons for their oppression, focusing on contemporary British society in various sites – Marxist and feminist theory; concepts of masculinity, femininity, and sexual practice; ideology and the cultural production of gender; the educational system; the division of labor; the family; the state; and capitalism and women's liberation. Oppression takes many forms: why are women subordinate to men across the whole social structure, why are they economically less powerful than men if not directly dependent upon them, why are they constantly on the short end of the division of labor, and in terms of both gender politics and sexuality, in asymmetrical and unequal relationships with men, shot through with power relations, whether in the workplace or in the family? And why do the state and social policy frequently collude in perpetuating these relations? In addressing the question of women's oppression, then, Barrett is criticizing much previous sociological work on British institutions – the state, the family, the educational system, industrial relations – as well as specifically Marxist feminist debates.

Barrett's answer to the why and how of women's oppression is ironical for a sociologist. She doesn't think the conceptual difficulties of working Marxist and feminist analyses together can be resolved at the level of theory any more than the relation between gender inequality and the industrial (or post-industrial) capitalist social relations we live within can be understood purely theoretically. The answer lies in historical investigation, in establishing the history of gender ideology in relation to the development of capitalist social relations. Barrett writes, "The questions that concern me are the how and why of women's oppression today, but I am sure that the answers to these questions cannot be deduced in strictly theoretical terms. Accordingly, I argue for an historical approach to these questions, drawing on the work of feminist historians, without claiming to provide a systematic historical account" (1980: 5–6).

Contemptuous of those who would assume a purely theoretical stance, "some 'correct' formulation that encapsulates the problem and specifies its answer by juggling with the terms 'capitalism', 'patriarchy' and 'articulation'" (1980: 5), Barrett provides a lucid and sharp critique of the most compelling previous discussions of the issues listed above. Her way around "juggling" with concepts like "articulation" is to argue for the crucial importance of ideology in the construction of gendered subjects and gendered social practices and policies. Ideology, for Barrett, is the theoretical domain in which her own contribution could be said chiefly to lie.

The concept of ideology is also the means by which history enters her discussion. When present-day gender "iniquities" (Barrett 1980: 259) and the needs of capitalist production are examined together, history, and in particular the history of gender ideology, provides the necessary link:

> It has yet to be proved that capitalism could not survive without the present form of domestic labour. On the other hand it is equally difficult to regard the development of the family as unrelated to the changing needs of capitalist production. The available historical evidence suggests that neither generalization is adequate. It might be more useful instead to consider the ways in which pre-capitalist gender divisions have been incorporated, possibly entrenched and exaggerated, into the structure of capitalist relations of production. (1980: 180–1)

The next step might seem to be attributing women's oppression solely to the workings of ideology, but this is a step Barrett refuses to take. She rejects being bound by either of the following alternatives:

> Either you need to hold that ideology is absolutely autonomous of the economic relations of capitalism, in which case it is plausible that a completely dissociated ideology of gender could exist independently of those relations; or you need to hold that ideology is always grounded in material relations but that gender ideology is grounded in economic relations between men and women that exist independently of capitalism. The first view is idealist, divorcing ideology entirely from material conditions; the second view is materialist but poses a different set of material determinants from those specified by Marxism. (1980: 252)

How to resolve this problem? Barrett proceeds with customary caution, so it is worth quoting her conclusions at some length:

> It is, perhaps, possible to resolve this problem without recourse to
> the analytically paralysing thesis of "absolute autonomy," or to a form
> of materialism that displaces the labour/capital contradiction from its
> centrality in the analysis of capitalist society. First, we can note that
> the ideology of gender – the meaning of masculinity and femininity
> – has varied historically and should not be treated as static or unified,
> but should be examined in the different historical and class contexts
> in which it occurs. Second, we can note that the meaning of gender
> in capitalism today is tied to a household structure and division of
> labour that occupy a particular place in the relations of production,
> and that, therefore, this ideology does, concretely and historically,
> have some material basis. Third, we can recognize the difficulty of
> posing economic and ideological categories as exclusive and distinct.
> The relations of production and reproduction of contemporary capi-
> talism may operate in general according to exploitative capital accumu-
> lation processes that are technically "sex-blind," but they take the
> form of a division of labour in which ideology is deeply embedded.
> (1980: 252)

Once again the answer lies in an historical as opposed to a theoretical
understanding of the questions. Anything deeply embedded is difficult to uproot, anything we go to bed with is likely still to be there
in the morning.

Barrett's patient locating of the materiality of ideology – in its
basis and its effects, not in any "materiality" of ideology itself –
distinguishes her work from other theorists who take the construction
of subjects in ideology and representation seriously. Not letting go
of economic relations – we would argue, holding to an Althusserian
concept of relative autonomy, rather than substituting the complete
autonomy of the ideological – Barrett distinguishes her position
"from the feminist appropriation of post-Althusserian theories that
seek to locate all aspects of women's oppression in terms of a theory
of discourse" (1980: 253).

Enter Parveen Adams and Elizabeth Cowie, and the journal *m/f*
as opposed to *Feminist Review*, the feminist journal with which
Barrett was for some years associated. We could oppose Barrett's
continuing interest in Althusserian theories of ideology to Adams's
and Cowie's post-Althusserian interest in psychoanalysis and the
discourse theory of Foucault. For Barrett, this swerve from ideology
to discourse per se not only is idealist but represents a tendency
towards what she calls "discursive imperialism" (1980: 88) or "an

unacceptably expansionist definition of the scope of 'ideology'"
(1980: 253): "The crucial questions concerning the relationship of
ideological processes to historical conditions of the production and
reproduction of material life are left unexamined in this attempt to
colonize the world for a newly privileged concept of ideology in
which everything is material. Yet in drawing the net of ideology so
wide we are left with no means, no tools, for distinguishing anything"
(1980: 90). "Discursive imperialism" and the notion of "colonizing
the world" for a newly privileged notion of ideology: Barrett detects
in these theoretical moves a backing away from those "more fundamental changes" in economic and material practices that marked the
limit of her critique of feminist aesthetics.

For Barrett, there is a real danger in confusing anti-essentialist
critiques of "commonsensical," i.e. ideological, categories with the
abandonment of such categories altogether. In particular this van-
guardism of theory concerning commonsensical and oppressive
notions of gender and sexuality might constitute a problem for a
feminist politics if theoretical sophistication were to prevent feminists
from being able to organize in any sense as "women." From Barrett's
point of view, the psychoanalytical edge of the "discourse theory"
position is suspicious as a position from which to intervene. She
fears that this project would lead to interminable analyses, in both
the clinical-psychoanalytical sense and the academic sense. But it
would be very difficult to tie to any form of political struggle within
institutions or social policies.

By avoiding any discussion of ideology and its relative autonomy
with regard to economic structures, the *m/f* position contains all
heterosexist subordination/oppression directly within explicitly sexual and gendering discursive practices. And these discursive practices
end up not even relatively autonomous, but floating entirely free of
any structural or economic determination. The strength of the *m/f*
position owed a great deal to its historical moment, to its intervention
in a very un-poststructuralized discursive field. Before the debates
about essence and identity, one might say, everyone appeared to be
certain that they knew just who and what women and men were.
With clarity and rigor, writers in *m/f*, including Parveen Adams and
Jeff Minson in "The 'Subject' of Feminism" (1978), insisted on
problematizing such assumptions, and their critiques often fell on
deaf ears. Such was the state of play in Britain around 1980.

The next decade would see some important theoretical changes.
When some of *m/f*'s theoretical points began to be taken up, though
often not in the way that the members of the editorial collective had

hoped, the journal's moment seemed to be over. The last issue of
m/f appeared in 1986, with a mock-funereal cover, and with Adams
and Cowie announcing in their editorial that the moment of the
journal's project had passed, that their "initiatives ha[d] begun to be
taken up elsewhere," and that "Like all feminists we continue to feel
the discontents of women and we continue to feel the need for a
feminist discourse which does not lose sight of that discontent. . . .
As feminism articulates itself, the difficulty of its task becomes more
apparent. We remain committed to these difficult concerns" (Adams
and Cowie 1986: 3). In 1988 a new edition of *Women's Oppression
Today* was published with a new introduction and a new subtitle:
Problems in Marxist Feminist Analysis had become *The Marxist Feminist Encounter*. As Barrett writes in her new introduction, "In some
ways, the intellectual project of reconciling a feminist and a Marxist
understanding of the social world could be said to have been shelved
– it was abandoned rather than resolved" (Barrett 1988: xxiv). Of
her original title, she comments, "perhaps only the word 'problems'
can now be used without some reservation" (1988: vii). By 1991, in
The Politics of Truth, she goes so far as to suggest that Foucault's
theory of discourse offers a way out of the impasse of trying to
adapt Althusser's theory of ideology for feminism.

US: Some Versions of Socialist Feminism

What problems were occupying left-leaning US feminists around
this time? The rather contested notion of socialist feminism in the
United States deserves some scrutiny, since the term means different
things to different people. We alluded earlier to differences between
Zillah Eisenstein's socialist feminism and the socialist feminisms of
Lise Vogel and Donna Haraway. The legacy of McCarthyism and
Red-baiting in the US should not be underestimated, since it accounts
to some extent for the many strategies of disavowal of anything
Marxist we often find in US feminist work. Hence the broader or
more inclusive – but also historically less politically loaded – term
socialist is often employed even where there is a primary, direct
engagement with texts and controversies from the Marxist tradition.
Whether the move to *materialist* constitutes a comparable evasion,
in this case avoiding the insufficiently academic and too political-sounding "socialist," or the too academic and insufficiently
political-sounding "socialist," or a just plain unfashionably old-
fashioned-sounding "socialist" remains to be seen.

Distinguishing between Marxist and socialist feminism, Eisenstein writes, "I choose socialist because it is a more open term, and the unknown dimensions of feminism require this" (Eisenstein 1981: 360–1 n. 4). In another context she distinguishes her position from Michèle Barrett's, which she labels "Marxist-feminist," suggesting that Barrett is preoccupied with strict Marxist definitions and incapable of seeing women as forming a "sexual class" (Eisenstein's term and her thesis) because of holding "economic class as primary" (Eisenstein 1984: 147–8). This account of Barrett consigns her to an economic reductivism and a burying of feminism within orthodox Marxist categories that we have seen Barrett herself directly challenging.

Eisenstein's own position is that women form a "sexual class" though they are also divided by economic class and racial differences:

> My use of the term "class" is therefore neither Marxist nor non-Marxist. It instead further specifies the Marxist notion of class. Women are not a class meaning an economic class. They are a sexual class with a particular status that cuts through economic class lines and is differentiated by these lines. . . . These economic class divisions have yet to be carefully defined in terms of women's positioning in family structures and the racist order. Economic class divisions among women do not invalidate the notion of sexual class; they just require that the economic class differentiations within sexual class be recognized. (1984: 149)

Rather than defining class as a specific relation within a mode of production, Eisenstein insists that, like the proletariat, women as a group perform "socially necessary labor" and this constitutes them as a sexual class. Or is it a status that women occupy within economic class divisions? Eisenstein's language slides back and forth between "class," a Marxist term, and "status," a sociological term, to describe women's position. Sometimes she has one kind of class operating within another. And both economic and racial divisions among women "have yet" to be carefully specified.

Eisenstein attempts to break free from Marxist thought on behalf of a coherent "revolutionary" (her term) feminist program. But has she succeeded? Only one page after the above passage, she returns in a footnote to Marx's *Eighteenth Brumaire* and *The Poverty of Philosophy* to strengthen what she means by "sexual class": that women constitute a class in the sense of a class "for itself" by means of their consciousness as women (1984: 150). Once women have become conscious of themselves as women, according to Eisenstein, they automatically form a class in the Marxist sense. Yet Marx specifies that to be revolutionary such class consciousness must be a consciousness on the part of members of a class "for itself," politically directed towards revolutionary change on behalf of the class in question. In that case, wouldn't "feminist" rather than "women's" consciousness be the more appropriate term here? Surely not all women's consciousness of themselves as women is necessarily politically directed in radical or revolutionary ways. What's revolutionary about groups of women going to watch male strippers, for instance?

It is hard to see how Eisenstein's notion of women as forming a "sexual class" advances our theoretical grasp of the relations between capitalism and patriarchy; it merely reinstates the dualism inherent in previous attempts to talk about "capitalist patriarchy" in relatively static and ahistorical ways (see Eisenstein 1979). And the political strategy Eisenstein advocates strikes us as a backing away from some of the more radical implications of Marxist feminism or other forms of socialist feminism. Through her notion of women as a "sexual class" Eisenstein hopes to form alliances with liberal and radical, as opposed to Marxist, feminists: "I think, as a feminist, there is much more to be *politically* gained by a dialogue between liberal, radical, and socialist feminists than by a dialogue between marxists and feminists. . . . *As a socialist feminist* I think . . . [w]e must begin where most women are – and most women are liberal feminist in their consciousness" (Eisenstein 1981: 341–3).

Like many US feminists, even those on the left, Eisenstein is too quick to generalize from the US situation to a global situation. This American-eye view loses sight of national and geopolitical differences and makes it difficult even to imagine the possibility of a truly international perspective. The purchase of Marxism in many Third World countries far exceeds the purchase of liberalism and certainly of liberal feminism. And forgetting Marxism too often means forgetting any systematic way of thinking globally. As Gayatri Spivak puts it in an interview, "What Marxism really has to offer is global systems." Not coincidentally, in the same interview Spivak mentions Eisenstein while advocating that "discontinuous" movements – feminism, Marxism, anti-racism, anti-imperialism – nevertheless be worked together to "bring each other to crisis":

> the idea in feminism that even the most disenfranchised man has more rights within patriarchal society than the most noble woman, this must seriously bring theories of class to crisis. You can't say like

Zillah Eisenstein that "women are a class." No, but you don't give up the idea of class analysis either. That is the productive sense of crisis. Otherwise, living in a state of perpetual crisis is merely confessional. (Spivak 1990: 138, 139)

By contrast with Eisenstein, Lise Vogel sticks much closer to Marxist theory. Although she describes herself as a socialist and a feminist, she distinguishes her position from that of many American socialist feminists. Describing her simultaneous discovery of the women's movement and Marxist theory in the late sixties, Vogel explains that like many other women at this time she recognized how simply extending Marxist theory to address the concerns of women's liberationists was unsatisfactory. As a solution it was "far too mechanical, and left much to be explained" (Vogel 1983: ix). Although "sympathetic" to the idea of a "socialist-feminist" synthesis, Vogel claims she "continued to pursue the original goal of extending Marxist theory," and while her research has deepened her respect for socialist feminism she remains "convinced that the revival of Marxist theory, not the construction of some socialist-feminist synthesis, offers the best chance to provide theoretical guidance in the coming battles for the liberation of women" (1983: ix–x). Vogel thus describes herself as holding the line with Marxism rather than being borne away from it towards a de-socialized feminism, radical feminism, like many other socialist feminists. We should also notice that she shies away from using the term "feminism" almost entirely, preferring "women's liberation," a term more consonant with both the original sixties project with which she began and with a Marxist-Leninist rather than "socialist-feminist" vocabulary. Vogel defines her project thus:

This book constitutes an argument *for* the power of Marxism to analyze the issues that face women today in their struggle for liberation. It strongly rejects, however, the assumption made by many socialists that the classical Marxist tradition bequeaths a more or less complete analysis of the problem of women's oppression. In this sense, it could be called a socialist-feminist work, although it shares neither the current skepticism among socialist feminists as to the usefulness of Marxist theory, nor their high hopes for radical feminist perspectives. Instead, the text argues that the socialist tradition is deeply flawed, that it has never adequately addressed the question of women, but that Marxism can nevertheless be used to develop a theoretical framework in which to situate the problems of women's oppression and women's liberation. (1983: 2)

Now the burden of Vogel's subtitle becomes clear: *Toward a Unitary Theory*, in which Marxism is transformed from within by a commitment to women's liberation. And this liberation will only be possible when the various forms of women's oppression have been thoroughly understood.

Vogel does not pretend to be able to carry this project through to completion on her own. She begins instead by criticizing existing socialist feminism. She then proceeds to examine writings by Marx, Engels, and other nineteenth-century socialists on the woman question and the family, two problematic starting points which she claims help explain the deep flaws in this tradition. She herself wants to base women's oppression in "social reproduction," in the Marxist sense that every social process of production is, at the same time, a process of reproduction; social reproduction entails the total reproduction of the conditions of production in a particular society. In the capitalist West, Vogel locates contradictions in women's relation to social reproduction, not merely women's dual positioning in relation to wage labor and domestic labor but their "particular dual position with respect to domestic labor and equal rights": "For many women, as for most members of other oppressed groups in capitalist society, bourgeois equality now shows itself as sharply distinct from liberation in a just society" (1983: 168). This is the distinction between formal and substantive equality we have discussed earlier. Vogel seeks to move beyond economistic definitions of women's oppression and address instead "the material foundations that underpin the oppression of women" (1983: 8), and those material foundations include the legal and state apparatuses as well as the economy.

But because this project is so vast she limits her contribution to what she, as a sociologist, can analyze with some rigor, women's relation to social reproduction including, but not limited to, the reproduction of labor power: "In particular, the text does not address directly the psychological, interpersonal, and ideological issues that so often form the main subject of writings on the question of women's liberation" (1983: 8). Silently comparing her project with Barrett's, and having just quoted Barrett to help legitimate her project, Vogel insists that hers is a more modest, and perhaps implicitly a more materialist, treatment of women's oppression because of its more "restricted" focus, leaving questions of ideology and culture to one side: "However restricted the approach may seem from the point of view of the desire for a full-blown exposition of women's oppression, it is necessary to establish these material foundations. Once laid, they will form the indispensable basis for further work" (1983: 138).

Vogel implies without ever stating it that Barrett's attempt at a "full-blown exposition of women's oppression" must be lacking, or her own analysis would not be necessary to supplement it. And Vogel's analysis is useful. Yet it is easy to see why Barrett's and not Vogel's form of materialist approach has proved popular with literary and cultural critics – not least because Vogel hedges on the question of "feminism," though she sounds entirely committed to women's liberation, across class, race, national, and imperial/colonial boundaries.

The case of Donna Haraway's socialist feminism differs yet again. In some respects she could be seen as the most sophisticated exponent of a particular strand within US socialist feminism that Katie King has identified as "standpoint theory." This theoretical position includes Nancy Hartsock's "feminist historical materialism" (1983) and Alison Jaggar's taxonomy of feminisms (1983) which is constructed in such a way that "socialist feminism" seems the ultimate expression of everything all previous forms of feminism have sought but failed to achieve (see King 1986: 73; King 1987: chapter 1). Haraway is a biologist and an historian of science best known for her book *Primate Visions* (1989), which analyzes the interconnections of gender and racial ideologies within the history of primatology as a representative twentieth-century science.

Haraway's clearest statement of her connection to the standpoint theorists is her essay "Situated Knowledges," originally published in 1988 in *Feminist Studies*, the US academic feminist journal with the strongest connection to socialist feminism, and reprinted in her book *Simians, Cyborgs, and Women* (1991). Citing among others Hartsock and Chela Sandoval, theorist of the "oppositional consciousness" of women of color, Haraway comments, "Many currents in feminism attempt to theorize grounds for trusting especially the vantage points of the subjugated; there is good reason to believe vision is better from below the brilliant space platforms of the powerful" (1991: 190). But she is suspicious of identity politics and ontological claims – knowledge claims based on essential being – arguing instead for "mobile positioning" and seeing *from* these multiple, subjugated standpoints critically: "The search for such a 'full' and total position is the search for the fetishized perfect subject of oppositional history, sometimes appearing in feminist theory as the essentialized Third World Woman [citing Mohanty 1984]" (1991: 192, 193).

Haraway's argument is, then, for a socially responsible notion of feminist objectivity and feminist science, knowledge practices that can be held accountable for what they know: "Feminist objectivity is about limited location and situated knowledge. . . . In this way we might become answerable for what we learn how to see" (1991: 190). And she claims that she learned these lessons in part walking with her dogs "and wondering how the world looks without a fovea and very few retinal cells for colour vision, but with a huge neural processing and sensory area for smells" (1991: 190).

Human and animal: the boundaries are where the action is. As Haraway argues in another essay, two centuries of biology and evolutionary theory have rendered the distinction between human and animal "leaky": "Movements for animal rights are not irrational denials of human uniqueness; they are a clear-sighted recognition of connection across the discredited breach of nature and culture. . . . Within this framework, teaching modern Christian creationism should be fought as a form of child abuse" (1991: 152). Haraway may be a scientist but she writes like a polemicist and a poet. Her epigrammatic style yields countless new slogans and images for re-energizing a US socialist feminism that by the mid-1980s often seems to have lost its way.

As one might suspect from her language, Haraway operates very much as a post-poststructuralist feminist critic, so unlike Eisenstein and Vogel she doesn't really belong in this section of our schematic history. But in order to illustrate the diversity of US socialist feminism we need to include her here, chronology notwithstanding. If Haraway takes feminist standpoint theory into the nineties in "Situated Knowledges," she provides one of the most original and provocative contributions to socialist feminist thinking in her "Cyborg Manifesto" (originally published in 1985 in the American journal *Socialist Review*), an essay attempting "to build an ironic political myth faithful to feminism, socialism, and materialism. Perhaps more faithful as blasphemy is faithful, than as reverent worship and identification" (1991: 149). Her irreverent counter-myth counter-poses the cyborg, a figure for both the leaky boundary between human and animal and the equally leaky one between "animal-human (organism) and machine" (1991: 152), to a whole radical feminist mythology of women returning to nature and saving the planet through recovering a lost organicism by means of goddess worship and the repudiation of industrial and post-industrial technology.

Charting the recent effects of science and technology on worldwide social relations, Haraway argues for an updated socialist feminism that can analyze a new object, "The Informatics of Domination," a rearrangement of "White Capitalist Patriarchy" (1991: 162) consonant with the shift from an organic, industrial society to post-industrial polymorphism. This new world order is one in which neo-imperial-ism, the global factory, and the electronic cottage replace older industrial forms, which were never natural but may look that way from a vantage point nostalgic for a simpler world, if not exactly former US President George Bush's "kinder, gentler" world.

It seems that Haraway is responding in particular to US socialist feminist self-criticism, some might even say self-hatred, which mani-fested itself in the 1980s in the course of repeated Republican Party triumphs through the Reagan and Bush presidencies, and a whole host of New Right backlashes against advancements towards social power by women and members of minority groups. Under such pressure, many US socialist feminists looked to the peace and ecology movements for an alternative theory and practice, and what they often found there under the name of feminism was a radical feminism invoking goddesses and organic pasts as empowering images.

A good example of this kind of thinking can be found in the 1985 "fifteenth-anniversary issue" of *Socialist Review*, ironically labeled on its cover "For Leftists who have Considered Suicide when the Rainbow is Enuf" (echoing the African-American feminist playwright Ntozake Shange's title *for colored girls who have considered suicide when the rainbow is enuf* [1976]). The issue contains, among other articles, six responses to the 1984 re-election of Reagan, an essay on teaching courses about the 1960s, and "a conversation" with four US socialist feminists entitled "The Impasse of Socialist-Feminism." One problem with this conversation is that the terms established already assume that socialist feminism is "in trouble." Another prob-lem is that "socialist-feminism" is simultaneously presented as a "theory" and as a form of "self-identification," as if the two were synonymous. This is how the *Socialist Review* facilitator, Ilene Philip-son, addresses the participants: "Some people say that socialist-feminism, as a theory, as a form of self-identification, is dead. Is it?" (Philipson 1985: 101). There is a tendency in US politics to turn every form of opposition to the mainstream into a form of identity politics, a tendency which Haraway, clearly, is writing to resist.

With the exception of Deirdre English, executive editor of *Mother Jones* magazine, the participants – all (San Francisco) Bay Area residents – more or less disavow their relation to "socialist-feminism." English argues that a leftist perspective continues to be "desperately" necessary for the US women's movement, which will be seriously "misled by mainstream feminism without it." She insists that "We need a non-sixties politics that still can talk about the realities of class, that has an international view of women's fate, that can take on the really deep questions about the future of humanity" (Philipson 1985: 106, 109). The others seem much keener on the peace and eco-feminist movements as sources of revitalizing theory and practice. They have given up on socialist feminism, particularly on the socialist half of the equation, as a dead issue. Barbara Epstein, herself a professor of history, goes so far as to say "My perspective is that socialist-feminism has become part of academia and has been killed by it"; she wants to see a combination of feminism with other radical social critiques in which "a movement" and not "academia" is at the center (Philipson 1985: 103, 109).

So, according to some US West Coast feminists on the left, something happened to that "socialist-feminist synthesis," that model of capitalism-plus-patriarchy, that proved it to have been a theoretical dead-end. And from one point of view that something has to do with the universities, with the institutionalization of socialist feminism within academic disciplines, including women's studies. Here we can put a finger on a certain historical shift from the founding of the journal *Feminist Studies* as a graduate student enterprise, with a heavy investment in socialist feminism, to its current institutional importance as an arbiter of what counts within US feminism, its gate-keeping function within feminism as an academic practice. From within the pages of *Feminist Studies* today we are more likely to hear about "materialist feminism" than about "socialist feminism." What does that shift signify?[3]

Notes

1 See, for example, Taylor (1983), Weeks (1981), Bebel (1971), Aveling and Aveling (1886), Luxemburg (1986), Kollontai (1984), and also the biographies of Kollontai by Farnsworth (1980) and Clements (1979), and of Browne by Rowbotham (1977).
2 In "Max Raphael and the Question of Aesthetics" Barrett subsequently restates and refines these questions regarding aesthetic pleasure and value by pursuing the distinction between the capacity of the subject to perceive aesthetic pleasure and the aesthetic qualities of the art object being perceived. Is beauty really in the eye of the beholder or in the object viewed? Can "the aesthetic properties of a work . . . be differentiated from its meaning" (1987: 79)? Returning to her concern for skill and imagination, Barrett argues that "no text can be inherently progressive or reactionary – it becomes so in the act of consumption" (1987: 85).
3 "Materialist feminism is distinguished from socialist feminism in part

because it embraces postmodern conceptions of language and subjectivity" (Hennessy 1993: 5). Hennessy's book, *Materialist Feminism and the Politics of Discourse*, appeared while this book was in production, so we have not been able to engage with its arguments.

2

Institutionalizing Feminism

The achievements of the women's movement in the US, characterized by continuing struggles to institutionalize women's studies in universities and feminist thinking within social institutions generally, find their origins in a very different socio-political moment and a different political dialogue from those which brought Marxism and feminism together in Britain during the 1960s. Although there has been a strong tradition of socialist feminism in the US since the late nineteenth century, it was often feminists associating their struggles with those of the Civil Rights and anti-war movements of the 1960s and 1970s who set the political agenda for feminism in the US.

When Juliet Mitchell investigated the state of the women's movement in the United States in the late sixties, she was struck by its distinctive history and the way in which this history had shaped US feminism. In R. D. Laing's phrase, "the politics of experience" was everywhere to be seen and heard, from the hippie and yippie movements to the shift from Civil Rights to Black Power. Mitchell was even optimistic that contradictions within consumer capitalism might be transformed by this new consciousness in radical ways: "The cult of 'being true to your own feelings' becomes dangerous when those feelings are no longer ones that the society would like you to feel. Testing the quality of your world on your own pulse can bring about some pretty strange heart-beats" (Mitchell 1971: 31). Not surprisingly, the first victories of the women's movement in the US were being won in the name of experience rather than theory, and the effects of this aspect of US feminism's history are still being felt today.

Nevertheless, this history is not as even as it might sometimes seem, since experience and theory are not entirely separable. Cellestine Ware's book, *Woman Power* (1970), for example, is a work of considerable theoretical sophistication that arises directly from radical activist experience; in some respects, its achievements are in advance of much subsequent feminist theory. Perhaps this fact accounts for why it has been largely ignored by academic feminists. Ware's analysis seeks to bring an anti-racist critique of US society together with a revolutionary Marxist-inflected critique of capitalism and a radical feminist critique of social institutions, such as marriage. This last aspect of her project entails a general critique of heterosexism compatible with later lesbian analysis (see King 1986). Ware is very clear about the connection between the black movement and the women's movement:

> The sit-ins and freedom rides brought to the surface the racism and intolerance of America. In learning to deal with increasingly violent confrontations, blacks developed their capacity for aggression, self-assertion and the expression of rage. Mao replaced Gandhi at the universities. Blacks and whites realized that white people were irrelevant to the black struggle, which became essentially a demand for self-determination and the right to develop a truly black identity and organization of energy. Stokely Carmichael's message to white radicals was to look to their own oppression. This admonition was one of the inspirations of the new feminist movement as we shall see. Black Is Beautiful is the direct antecedent to Women Are People. (Ware 1970: 11)

This clarity of expression and purpose, as well as the specific critique of both capitalism and of heterosexist institutions, would soon be lost as academic feminism in the US began to flourish, and white middle-class women began to distance themselves once again both from black women and from revolutionary rhetoric.

The Question of Race

By the late 1970s a problem had emerged in articulating anti-racist together with socialist and feminist positions. Nonetheless, black feminists who were also socialists continued to attempt this articulation, as can be seen in the Combahee River Collective's "A Black Feminist Statement" of April 1977. The members of the collective write: "Although we are in essential agreement with Marx's theory as it applied to the very specific economic relationships he analyzed, we know that this analysis must be extended further in order for us to understand our specific economic situation as black women" (in

Eisenstein 1979: 366). They are clearly interested in theorizing and fighting "interlocking" systems of oppression, "actively committed to struggling against racial, sexual, heterosexual, and class oppression" (1979: 362). We should notice the inclusion of a lesbian critique of heterosexism here, so that the systems of oppression which interlock are as multiple and complex as they were for Ware. The inclusion of "A Black Feminist Statement" in one of the most influential US socialist feminist collections of essays, *Capitalist Patriarchy and the Case for Socialist Feminism*, edited by Zillah Eisenstein (1979), is significant; it is included, but it has to cover race, black feminism, and lesbianism, none of which is adequately dealt with in the other essays in the collection. And the continued republication of the Combahee River Collective's "Statement" in at least two subsequent collections (Moraga and Anzaldúa 1981, 1983; Hull, Scott, and Smith 1982) suggests that as a text it represents a crucial but rather fragile moment in black and US socialist feminist theory.

Certain popular rather than academic histories, histories of women's liberation rather than feminism, would continue some of the theoretical connections that Ware and the Combahee River Collective represent by showing the historical relations between and among anti-racist struggles, the New Left generally, and feminism (see Evans 1979). But feminism was already beginning to be institutionalized, in women's studies programs and feminist literary criticism. The price of this institutionalization was, once again, paid by black women and other working-class women and women of color.

Unlike the attempts by feminists to transform Marxist categories for their own purposes in Britain, dialogues between feminists and Civil Rights activists in the US found their strong point of contact in the politics of empowerment based on a liberal theory of democratic equality. Since the Civil Rights, anti-war, and women's movements of the 1960s in the US were in an important sense, though not entirely, student movements frequently brokered by a disaffected middle class, they aimed at transforming the political status of women, the black communities, and members of other ethnic minorities by empowering them *within* existing institutions such as universities, places they sought to transform rather than abandon or reinvent. This institutional setting and the liberal emphasis on the empowerment of the oppressed within existing structures entailed a necessary emphasis on freedom through education, a precise legacy from three centuries of feminist polemic and activity that nevertheless largely ignores the fundamental challenges of the Marxist critique of capitalism.

Feminist Politics and Literary Theory

This part of our story is exemplified by the development of feminist literary theory within the US academy in recent years. Judith Newton and Deborah Rosenfelt's Introduction to *Feminist Criticism and Social Change: Sex, Class and Race in Literature and Culture* (1985) enthusiastically proclaims the emergence of "materialist feminist criticism." This anthology reprints, among others, important studies by Michèle Barrett, Catherine Belsey, Cora Kaplan, Annette Kuhn, and both editors. The book attempts to bridge the Atlantic gap, to construct a joint materialist project in the name of something more radical than academic-institutional business as usual: "social change" – not explicitly socialist but social, and set in opposition to mere liberalism. It also attempts to include questions of race and lesbian sexuality, continuing an assault on those interlocking oppressions identified by the Combahee River Collective in 1977. Indeed the first essay in the volume is by Barbara Smith, one of the members of the Combahee River Collective and one of the authors of "A Black Feminist Statement," here doing equally ground-breaking work in "Toward a Black Feminist Criticism," an essay first published in 1977.

Despite its announced challenge to liberal feminism and critical formalism, however, we find Newton and Rosenfelt's Introduction in many ways an unsatisfactory statement of a materialist feminist position.[1] In the first place the text never defines either materialism or materialist feminism. Second, there seems an unacknowledged uneasiness about the relation between materialist feminism and socialist feminism. Third, there seems an even greater uneasiness about the relation between their project and certain work in contemporary Marxist theory. Fourth, they indulge in a wholesale dismissal of poststructuralism. Fifth, the movement of their argument ends up privileging gender as the primary category of analysis, precisely the criticism of "materialist feminism" made in a recent article by Rosemary Hennessy and Rajeswari Mohan:

> Materialist feminist and/or socialist feminist interventions into literary studies . . . have involved the recuperation of the most radical features of their critiques by maintaining a privileged status for gender, by failing to extend the materialist understanding of history beyond attention to ideological practice and western culture, and by extending the inclusiveness of "materialism" so broadly that its radical intervention is diffused into an acceptable eclecticism. . . . Our critique is a critique

for feminism. Only it is directed as much against new imperialism, white supremacy, homophobia, and class exploitation as it is against patriarchy. (Hennessy and Mohan 1989: 324–5)

Whether any feminism should presume to encompass all these projects within itself, rather than seeing itself in articulation with other social and political movements committed to these issues, seems to us to be a problematic assumption, though we would endorse Hennessy and Mohan's call for a more globally-directed materialist feminism in which class, race, and sexuality are seen to be as crucial as gender. Finally, in channeling materialist feminist theory towards specific applications in literary and film criticism, Newton and Rosenfelt's collection privileges literature over politics, thereby reversing the priorities of some of its contributors. Thus, despite the importance of some of the essays, this last move seals the volume's fate as yet another exercise in academic feminism losing its political edge by looking fearfully over its shoulder in case anyone institutionally powerful might object to what's going on here.

By privileging literature over politics, and thus running counter to the tenor of many of the essays, certainly those in the first part labeled "Theory" – by Barbara Smith, Paul Lauter, Catherine Belsey, Michèle Barrett, and Ann Rosalind Jones – and many in the second part labeled "Applied Criticism," Newton and Rosenfelt do not succeed very well in challenging the increasing institutional influence of liberal feminism during the 1980s. Moreover, of the two articles about questions of race by black women (there is also one by a white man, Paul Lauter), the second, "Shadows Uplifted," is a classically historicist work of recuperation by Barbara Christian, a scholar who elsewhere vehemently rejects any connection between literary-critical practice and political practice. It irritates Christian that so much contemporary literary criticism seems "but an occasion for espousing [the critic's] philosophical point of view – revolutionary black, feminist, or socialist program" (Christian 1985: xi). As Hazel Carby and Hortense Spillers both observe, in Christian's attempt to separate a critical project from its political dimensions, there is clearly ideology at work (see Carby 1987: 14–15). But Christian isn't interested in concepts like ideology, and it's hard to see how she can have approved of the explicitly political desires of Newton and Rosenfelt's Introduction.

Politically as well as theoretically speaking, the problem here is that Christian's example of black feminist criticism, a critique of negative stereotypes and images of black women based on rather naively mimetic assumptions about the relation of literary texts to social-historical "truth," conforms to the very feminist paradigm from which Newton and Rosenfelt have been at such pains to distance their project. This is surely unfortunate for black feminism and, to borrow from Spillers, "will not help at all if rigor is our dream" (Spillers 1987b: 68).

If Newton and Rosenfelt really wished to connect materialist feminist criticism with feminist politics, they should not have limited their terrain to the literary. The struggle among Marxists to legitimate the relative autonomy of culture and thereby put literary studies onto the political agenda, in spite of certain resistances to privileging the study of culture over other forms of political work, has not only transformed traditional materialist thinking but also produced important and sophisticated theoretical problems for feminists, problems that could, apparently, be ignored by Newton and Rosenfelt working in the US context where Marx is so negatively viewed as to be generally unread. For their version of "materialist feminist criticism" in 1985, the primary concern appears to have been with creating an arena within academic discourse where a plurality of forms of oppressed subject position might find a voice.

Capturing the high ground of left-leaning debate for literature: this feminist phenomenon extends well beyond Newton and Rosenfelt's anthology. On one level, it might be difficult to claim that the Marxist tradition of political theory has been greatly transformed by its encounters with feminism in the US. For example, despite putting Michèle Barrett at the top of its list of editorial advisers, the recently founded journal *Rethinking Marxism* has not given much space to feminist concerns, with the exception of Harriet Fraad, Stephen Resnick, and Richard Wolff's attempt to analyze women's household labor as subsumable under the feudal mode of production (1989, 1990).

Academic Effects

On another level, however, what has been the great and probably the most important single achievement in the history of the Marxist tradition since French intellectuals abandoned the Communist Party after the Soviet invasion of Prague in April 1968 is the successful institutionalization of various positions calling themselves "Marxist thought" within various outposts of the academy in the US. Of course the position of universities themselves within social, cultural, and political life in the US is both marginal and central and, as such, destabilizes this very opposition. Demographically, the academy remains marginal: in 1991 only 21.4 percent of the adult population over twenty-five years old had attended college or university for four or more years.[2] Globally, however, it has achieved a position of power and influence in many fields, partly through the global currency of English, but also as a consequence of its resources for funded research and the pressure for productivity quotients inherent in the frantic American "publish or perish" ethos.

Against trends rightwards during the 1980s, many programs within colleges and universities in the US have maintained impressive control over their own development relative to the situation in the UK, where the question is not "should there be a state curriculum?" but "what is to be its content?" This is not to underestimate the importance of recent recessionary crises and cutbacks in educational programs, particularly in the state university systems. It is just to suggest that the US academy continues to be a site of incomparable privilege and possibility, perhaps as a direct index of its intellectual marginality in relation to mainstream culture.

If Barrett's achievement was to describe the problems inherent in any attempt to articulate Marxist analysis with feminist politics, a problematics that directly addressed and transformed traditional questions of aesthetic pleasure and value, then the asymmetrical development across the Atlantic offers the achievement of socialists, feminists of all sorts, and anti-racist activists to give us a "materialist feminist criticism." In the US context, socialism seems typically overwhelmed by a left-liberal tendency different from the European contexts of New Left Marxism which, since 1968, have been preoccupied with questions of alliance, complicity, organization, and the theoretical critiques of such intellectuals as Althusser and Lacan. Despite its various gestures, the left academic tradition in the US often seems to reject theory even in the very act of embracing it. This is the burden of Toril Moi's controversial objections to – some would say trashing of – what she labeled as Anglo-American feminism in *Sexual/Textual Politics* (1985).

Preferring Virginia Woolf's modernist deconstruction of the unitary self and the critique of the subject found in French poststructuralists to the humanist and empiricist assumptions of much US feminist literary criticism, Moi challenged the work of Sandra M. Gilbert and Susan Gubar, Elaine Showalter, Annette Kolodny, and Myra Jehlen. In their anti-sexist focus on female authors and readers, Moi contends, these and other feminist literary critics who share their views adopt a "'non-contradictory perception of the world'" (Moi 1985: 10) that mystifies rather than disables patriarchal assumptions by positing for itself a place outside ideology. Celebrating women writers and readers reinscribes the unitary self and thereby begs the political questions of agency and resistance, "of how it is that some women manage to counter patriarchal strategies despite the odds stacked against them" (1985: 64).

Even in 1985 this description misrepresented much of the work actually being done by US feminists, some of them in French studies like Moi, some of them doing highly theoretical work in comparative literature, African-American studies, the study of colonial discourse, gay and lesbian studies, and even traditional literary-historical periods. Having designed her book as a polemical critique, she kept claiming that "lack of space" prevented her "from doing justice to the suggestive work of women such as Jane Gallop, Shoshana Felman and Gayatri Spivak" (1985: 98) or that many feminist theoretical works should not be classified as "feminist literary criticism and theory": "Though Marxist or socialist feminists like Rosalind Coward, Annette Kuhn, Juliet Mitchell, Terry Lovell, Janet Wolff and Michèle Barrett have all written on literary topics, their most important and challenging work nevertheless falls outside the scope of this book" (1985: 93). Moi sounds distinctly as if she were having to invent a rationale for not dealing with the theoretical work she found most helpful to her own enterprise. It was surely a mistake for her simply to attack positions she found theoretically wanting, rather than to analyze points of intersection between her position and what other feminists influenced by poststructuralism and French feminism, by the Marxist and socialist traditions – other "materialist feminists" – were also already doing.

The critical strategy Moi prefers to Anglo-American empiricism relies on the work of Cixous and Irigaray, but is most heavily indebted to Julia Kristeva, who investigates avant-garde texts, marginal writers, and the figure of woman in an attempt not to construct positive female alternatives to dominant culture, but to advocate various forms of artistic subversion within it. This combination of allegiances marks Kristeva as a materialist in terms of her approach to texts, according to Moi, though she admits that there are limits to Kristeva's usefulness when it comes to politics. Since Kristeva's work tends to glorify avant-garde figures in individualist and subjectivist, rather than collective and materialist, ways, Moi has reservations about recommending her project wholeheartedly (1985: 169–72).

Despite those reservations, the wide-ranging influence of Moi's book for a whole generation of students of feminist theory, especially in North America, has contributed to the dissemination of interest in Kristeva and French feminist theory generally. Regardless of the claims Moi herself makes for a political materialist feminism, the effect of her critique has often been to turn her readers towards those very forms of individualist rather than collective politics which she criticizes in both their American and their French forms. In these respects, Moi's book might be said to be both a critique of the institutionalization of feminist theory and a symptom of it.

Commodity Feminism

This academic institutionalization of feminist theory, we would argue, can be associated with the commodification of feminism generally. How is feminism being bought and sold in the marketplace? We shall argue that it is useless simply to protest against the commodification of feminism, because the commodification of cultural developments is inevitable within capitalist societies. Rather than declaim against consumer society, we see new forms of consumer practices as potentially new sites of political activity. But it is crucial that we understand how commodification works if we are not to be uncritically caught up in its processes. We need to be able to analyze commodification at work in order to use its contradictions to generate new forms of resistance.

What is commodification? We would do well to begin by remembering what Marx described as the effects of commodification generally:

> The necessary physical properties of the particular commodity . . .
> – in so far as they directly follow from the nature of exchange-value
> – are: unlimited divisibility, homogeneity of its parts and uniform quality of all units of the commodity. As the materialisation of universal labour-time it must be homogeneous and capable of expressing only quantitative differences. Another necessary property is durability of its use-value since it must endure through the exchange process. Precious metals possess these qualities in an exceptionally high degree. (Marx 1970: 49)

Commodity fetishism[3] designates a double movement within ideology and everyday practice, the simultaneous reification of social relations, which become things in themselves, and the personification of the products of our labor, which acquire a life of their own. Marx draws attention to the "peculiar social character" of the labor necessary for commodity production as the key to this precise histori-cal development. Only "private individuals who work independently of each other" will produce commodities: "Since the producers do not come into social contact until they exchange the products of their labour, the specific social characteristics of their private labours appear only within this exchange" (Marx 1977: 165). It is in this exchange that value is constituted, and that a certain abstract equality between exchangeable goods is necessarily presupposed.

We should not forget that commodities have a use-value as well as an exchange-value, though, as Marx makes clear, it becomes increasingly difficult to specify the use-value of commodities within capitalist societies apart from their exchange-value. Feminism's use-value for women lies in its emancipatory potential, the way it can help them as a group to think through solutions to everyday problems. Academic feminism's use-value in this sense can be seen in the material changes within social and political institutions that the women's movements of the last thirty years have brought about. That use-value can also be found in the continuing social innovations and countercultural practices which particular groups of women continue to produce around the globe. When we focus on feminism within the academic marketplace, however, as we shall do here, we are concentrating on feminism primarily in the light of its exchange-value. Its use-value remains, but, within the overdeterminations of the market, such use-value in any pure sense is impossible to isolate. The implications of Marx's theory of the commodity for analyzing the construction of subjectivity within modern capitalist societies are multiple,[4] but what price a feminism constructed thus?

Marx goes so far as to put in play a putative subjectivity for commodities themselves, in a passage that has particular resonances for feminism:

> If commodities could speak, they would say this: our use-value may interest men, but it does not belong to us as objects. What does belong to us as objects, however, is our value. Our own intercourse as commodities proves it. We relate to each other merely as exchange-values. (Marx 1977: 176–7)

Between them, the US feminist Gayle Rubin (1975) and the French feminist Luce Irigaray (1985) have said just about everything important there is to say regarding the status of women as commodities, though nothing about feminism in the marketplace. The exchange of women shores up a homosocial as well as patriarchal social and symbolic order. That is to say, men's primary social relations are with other men, as in male-bonding. Women have social value only in so far as they can be exchanged by men, and they can be exchanged only in so far as they are valued comparatively and interchangeably. As commodities, women mirror back to the men who exchange them their place as men in a phallocratic order in which laws are made by those on the side of the phallus (i.e. men); female commodities cannot by definition mirror each other. Replying to Marx's hypothesis, "If commodities could speak," Irigaray retorts: "*So commodities speak. To be sure, mostly dialects and patois, languages hard for 'subjects' to understand.* The important thing is that they be preoccupied with their respective values, that their remarks confirm the exchangers' plans for them" (Irigaray 1985: 178, 179). As we might expect, Irigaray recommends that women rebel by not going on the market, by not complying with the exchangers' plans, and, instead, initiating forms of commerce – social, sexual, linguistic, and economic – amongst themselves.

Feminist movements constitute one form of strategic resistance to the exchange of women, though the exchange of women itself is a reductive model that does not account for differences of race, class, or sexuality among women. Nor does the exchange of women explain away women's agency and complicity in oppression, again along such axes as class, race, or (hetero)sexuality. It is, however, within feminism's emancipatory potential as a social and political movement, working against patriarchal exchange, that the use-value, rather than the exchange-value, of feminism as a commodity is to be found. But to the extent that feminists happen to be or identify themselves as women, as opposed to the advocates of feminism who are gay or straight men, the exchange of feminisms in the academic marketplace is overdetermined by the traffic in women, or capitalist-patriarchal business-as-usual. "Unlimited divisibility," "homogeneity of its parts," "uniform quality," "durability" within the wear-and-tear of exchange, the absence of social contact among the "private individual" producers except at the moment of exchange, indeed the absence of any sense of value except in exchange, as exchange-value: how does feminism conform or fail to conform to these modelings – unlimited divisibility, homogeneity of the parts, durability?

To take the last of these first, feminism has endured long enough within the academy already to be divided generationally as well as politically. In a recent essay Alice Jardine has proposed a four-way generational split among academic feminists in the United States: those who received their Ph.D.s before 1968, those who got them between 1968 and 1978, those with degrees from 1978–88, and the newest generation, Ph.D.s 1988–98 (Jardine 1989: 85, n. 38). Only the last two generations had any chance at all of training under explicitly feminist mentors, many important developments in feminism seem to have happened "around 1981," as Jane Gallop (1992) has observed, and between 1978 and 1988 many English departments changed their minds dramatically regarding whether or not feminism constituted a theory or acceptable critical approach, so that the penultimate generation is greatly divided in its experience. Jardine's model is in some ways too neat, since some feminists have been in graduate programs for a very long time, or in and out of them, their studies interrupted by the other demands – filial, familial, affectional – so often made upon women. But the divisions to which she points hold true for many if not all cases, especially in the US context.

Recent Ph.D. candidates who do feminism are likely to have been introduced to it in a course and to have had little experience of women's groups, activist organizing around women's issues, or the bad old days of massive institutional silence regarding feminism. As a result, they are likely to think about feminism or women's studies as one field among others, one particularly marketable theoretical or scholarly approach. Here the US context presses heavily, since the academic market is so much larger and more active in its trading in America than it is in Britain, where educational cutbacks have meant a chronic scarcity of academic jobs, especially in the humanities and social sciences. In this sense of feminism as marketable academically, even the presence of feminist courses in the university curriculum is a sign of feminism's commodification through institutional containment as well as evidence of its gradual transformation of institutions.

Feminism's durability, its unfolding history as a social and political as well as intellectual movement, assures that there will be historically significant differences between feminists and feminisms. Paradoxically, those differences, the unlimited divisibility of positions within the movement, can become invisible from the perspective of academic institutions. Unlimited divisibiliity and an increasing homogeneity of the parts: while political, racial, sexual, class, ethnic, and national differences proliferate within feminism, a spurious substitutability may well govern the institutional agenda, particularly with regard to hiring, the academic market in its most nakedly political-economic form, when feminists and feminisms may seem inextricable and interchangeable commodities.

Differences within feminism can take on a peculiarly agonistic quality because they contravene the concept of sisterhood. How can "we" be united against "patriarchy" and "capital" if each of these terms is subject to problematization and to respecification in different concrete situations, different material contexts? How can non-synchronous, sometimes intersecting, sometimes contradictory forms of oppression and self-representation be articulated? Hence the language of multiple and mobile subject positions, and of situated discourses or knowledges within a postcolonial and global context.

To take the academic institution as representative of other institutions once again: when academic institutions mediate some of these real, material differences between women, political differences become professional rivalries, and intellectual differences become counters in the competition for academic status and material rewards. Rather than political debate, and the possibility of working through differences collectively, boundaries are established, positions are consolidated and replicated defensively, and gate-keeping and policing are institutionalized. Since policing has its origins in the defense of private property, the policing of feminism frequently takes the form of claims to ownership of the purest feminist praxis.

The unlimited divisibility of feminism, therefore, works in at least two ways. Politically and intellectually, the public working through of differences can be productive if intensely difficult. But, under the hot lights in the arena of professional competition, the staging of differences tends to devolve into the repressive tactics of the purity police, on the one hand, and the embattled defense of turf on the other.

Feminism looks more homogeneous or heterogeneous depending on where one stands. As socialist-feminist standpoint theorists like Nancy Hartsock and Donna Haraway have amply demonstrated, feminism requires the concept of situated knowledges; so much depends upon a standpoint or, rather, upon mobile, shifting points of view (Hartsock 1983; Haraway 1991: 183–201). As with other commodities, only a committed user can fully experience the fiercer forms of brand loyalty that can make other positions, other brands, just disappear. And it is not simply that to a non-feminist male academic one feminism looks very much like another. Sometimes one feminism is very much like another, and their name might well be "French feminist theory," signified by the Holy Trinity – or is it a limited company? – of Hélène Cixous, Luce Irigaray, and Julia Kristeva: the law according to French feminism (FF). On the academic market in the US today, and to a lesser extent in the UK, feminist theory in a job description is very likely to mean French feminism (so-called), though other varieties like psychoanalytical, deconstructive, black or African-American, postcolonial, lesbian, New Historicist, and, dare we say it, materialist feminism do surface from time to time.

The overdeterminations of the marketplace could well be responsible for this particularly concentrated form of commodification. First there is the continuing romance between US intellectuals and French culture, in which French ideas figure prominently. In this sense US feminism might be said to have absorbed rather uncritically some of the hierarchies of the wider, non-feminist academy. Then, too, French feminist theory as a seemingly tidy package has been made more available than any other feminist theory in summary and book form: Elaine Marks and Isabelle de Courtivron's anthology (1980), Moi (1985), Alice Jardine's *Gynesis* (1985), Gallop's *The Daughter's Seduction* (1982), articles by Ann Rosalind Jones (1981 and 1984) and Spivak (1987: 134–53), books by Judith Butler (1990) and Diana Fuss (1989). We've even made the inevitable reference to Irigaray ourselves, though it was balanced by a reference to a US feminist (who is not a naive essentialist and finds no place in Moi's book), Gayle Rubin. And what gets packaged as French feminist theory sells because, being French, it sounds like Theory, another commodity whose future seems remarkably academically secure at the moment. After all, Derrida did get his honorary degree from Cambridge despite influential protests.[5] Thus a particular charge of being (prematurely) commodified can be brought against the position that labels itself French feminism in the academy, especially when only FF Law, Cixous, Irigaray, and Kristeva are called upon to represent it, and other names for French feminist theory, most notably the materialists, including Simone de Beauvoir, Christine Delphy, and Monique Wittig, are ignored.

This is the sense in which a spurious homogeneity or substitutability in the marketplace, feminism's commodification emerging through what Marx calls its "uniform quality," can also signify academic feminists impeccably dressed in business suits, in uniform and looking uniformly as if they're looking to do as much business as possible on the market, rather than preparing for the crash. Now clothes are not trivial, except when men are making invidious comparisons between important things like sports and trivial things like fashion, as Virginia Woolf observed (Woolf 1957: 77). Differences of sartorial style can mark differences in cultural politics. The left academic of either sex sporting a leather jacket or post-punk haircut when colleagues continue to dress in Harris tweed and wear businesslike hair is making an implicit political statement about his or her countercultural alignments. The lesbian critic who wears lipstick and leather is making a different statement about her lesbianism from the lesbian critic who wears no makeup and jeans, or the one who wears tweed suits. If one takes popular culture to include dress as a form of popular-cultural stylistic production, then the cultural critic cannot be innocent of sartorial style. The problem for feminism in particular with making a case through making fashion statements is the way the larger culture expects women to do just that.

In this sense, the number of references currently made to feminist theories as fashion statements might give us pause, since seeing feminism thus unproblematically could be all too easily conformable with the demands of that other market in which women and not feminisms are exchanged. This may be why invocations of differences between feminisms as sartorial differences often fall flat, as is arguably the case in the by now classic exchange between the American critics Nancy K. Miller and Peggy Kamuf in the summer 1982 issue of *Diacritics* devoted to feminist theory. Miller counters Kamuf's high-heeled deconstructive Parisian feminism with a commonsensical return to "sensible shoes" (Miller 1982: 53), a move that perhaps inadvertently suggests a return to the feminism of good old bourgeois American empiricism, the comfortable feeling of knowing who we are because we are women – i.e. white, successful, middle-class professional women. Thus, although Miller wishes to name her position as "female materialism" (1982: 53) and put that name in opposition to Kamuf's "deconstruction," the metaphor of fashion allows her to sidestep, under a spurious homogeneity conjured around common sense and women, those very material differences of class, race, and sexuality a materialist position might be expected to address.

"Contact of the laborers only at the moment of exchange": marketability leads to mobility. Commodified labor in academic life is what takes place thousands of feet above the clouds in airplanes, shuttling between apartments and conference hotels, commuting in order to have a personal life, living on credit. Such a scene of writing lends new meaning to Marx's description of the private labors of individuals who have no sense of their fellow workers except at the point of exchange – airports, conferences, MLA conventions. These are the conditions of possibility for new forms of social identity that Raymond Williams termed "'mobile privatization,'" identities based on unlimited mobility and consumable resources, mobile shells composed of our relationships with lovers, friends, and relations. As

Williams describes it, "this small-unit entity is the only really significant social entity. . . . It is a shell which you can take with you,
which you can fly with to places that previous generations could
never imagine visiting" (Williams 1989: 171). When lovers and friends
are also professional colleagues, the professional and the personal
are conflated; one's professional life *is* one's personal life and vice
versa.

Unalienated labor or total commodification: which is the result?
And in the long run this is far from a sustainable economy in any
ecological sense. As Williams observes, the price of that space of
mobility, choice, and a very high rate of consumption "has been
paid in terms of the deterioration of the very conditions which allow
it" (1989: 171). The conditions of full employment, easy cheap
credit, easy cheap petrol, which Williams describes, are clearly neither
permanent for those who have enjoyed them nor available for the
majority who have not. Yet this is the space in which feminism, like
other new social movements, has emerged.

The effect of all this exchange-value on feminist writing has often
meant, especially in the United States, taking up a discursive position
grounded in community and political commitment, but one that
manifests itself in highly privatized, marketable forms of professional-
ism, from courses taken in graduate school to the job interview,
from the MLA talk and onwards to competition for grants, salary
raises, and time off – in which to raise one's market value through
publication, and preferably publication of a labor-intensive kind.
Why the research and writing of the successful, mobilely privatized
feminist tends to be labor-intensive can be grasped only if we observe
what kinds of feminist work are most easily assimilated by academic
institutions.

How often do we ask of a new critical approach or a new book,
"But is this really new?" How often has this question been answered
affirmatively within literary studies if the new work offered new
historical research, new facts, rather than merely new strategies of
reading? The recent apparent triumph of New Historicism over
deconstruction in US academic circles seems a case in point, especially
when the new historicism looks remarkably like the old, and the
deconstruction is radical and political rather than simply formalism
by another name. To some extent feminist foraging outside the
canon for increasingly obscure, marginalized, and so theoretically or
politically or even antiquarianly interesting figures or contexts is a
response to culturally imperative desires for the new, the fashionably
novel, the previously unexploited. This cultural imperative often

takes the particular name of the clearing of new professional space, but the space of the profession is not free from larger cultural contingencies.

Like every other artifact in consumerist culture, the plebeian aesthetic object, the proletarian text, the forgotten female novelist, the figure of the laboring woman writer, or the woman of color can and will be fetishized. Valerie Smith has argued that, all too frequently in contemporary criticism, when the time comes to materialize or historicize the discourse, a black woman is invoked (1989). Summoned within the context of the material, of intractable historical reality, the black woman functions as a sign of the engaged nature of the discourse through its sensitivity to race, and as a sign of the critic's mastery of the new critical language of historicity. Thus is the black woman both fetishized and theoretically silenced at the very moment of her appropriation by theory. Chandra Mohanty and Gayatri Spivak have made comparable arguments regarding the fetishization of the Third World or subaltern woman within the critique of colonial discourse (Mohanty 1984, Spivak 1989a). And we should recognize that this specific form of commodity fetishism will occur both despite and because of our institutional complicities with the history of the construction of the international division of labor. The microelectronic revolution, for example, upon which so much professional production depends, is inextricable from Third World proletarianization in the export-processing zones (EPZs) of the capitalist periphery (Nash and Fernández-Kelly 1983). As Spivak observes, "even such innocent triumphs as the hiring of more tenured women or adding feminist sessions at a Convention might lead, since most U.S. universities have dubious investments, and most Convention hotels use Third World female labor in a most oppressive way, to the increasing proletarianization of the women of the less developed countries" (Spivak 1987: 291, n. 44).

These are some of the costs of feminism's commodification. They seem to us to constitute new sites of resistance rather than reasons for nostalgia or despair. We should remember that one of the signs of commodification is an ever-increasing "homogeneity of the parts." Such homogenization leads to greater interchangeability. If we wish to examine and resist commodification, we need to resist gestures towards homogenizing feminism: putting forward one school as definitive, letting a commodified version of, say, French feminism or, for that matter, materialist feminism stand for feminism in all its complex historical variety, employing charged categories like race and colonialism without engaging with contemporary debates in those fields, capitulating to institutional pressures to tokenize feminism by rendering it a special interest while male business-as-usual continues to hold sway.

The peculiar energy with which commodities are charged in the process of their circulation is in some sense a libidinal energy. Commodities are cathected as they are fetishized. We invest the commodities we consume with desire. Feminists would do well not to underestimate the power of that libidinal economy, of those desires, as they overdetermine both the exchange of women and the exchange of their theories in the academic marketplace. To know desire is to be in circulation, and to *desire* to be in circulation.

Notes

1 For a more sympathetic account of Newton and Rosenfelt's project, see Wayne (1991: 3–4).

2 Report of the Census Bureau, *Educational Attainment in the United States: March 1991 and 1990*, Current Population Reports, Series P20: 662 (Washington, DC: Government Printing Office, 1992).

3 "It is nothing but the definite social relation between men themselves which assumes here, for them, the fantastic form of a relation between things. In order, therefore, to find an analogy we must take flight into the misty realm of religion. There the products of the human brain appear as autonomous figures endowed with a life of their own, which enter into relations both with each other and with the human race. So it is in the world of commodities with the products of men's hands. I call this the fetishism which attaches itself to the products of labour as soon as they are produced as commodities, and is therefore inseparable from the production of commodities" (Marx 1977: 165).

4 See, for example, Amariglio and Callari, who argue from a "nondeterminist" position that Marx "depicts the social constitution of the individual as much a 'precondition' for commodity trade as an effect of this trade," and that "Commodity fetishism, therefore, allows Marxist discourse to conceptualize the political and cultural, as well as economic, constitution of individuality as a form of social agency" (1989: 34, 49).

5 Like the "MacCabe affair" of 1981, the controversy surrounding the granting of an honorary degree to Derrida rapidly shifted from an internal dispute within the Cambridge faculty to a media event. In both cases the debate thus soon dispensed with the particulars of the work of Colin MacCabe and Derrida, respectively, usually focusing instead on the place of "Theory" within literary studies or philosophy. See Lonsdale (1992a and 1992b), Bunting (1992), and Kermode (1992).

3

Deconstruction and Beyond

Now the construction of a chronological narrative, however schematic and inconsistent it may have been up to now, gets really tricky.
When does the moment of feminism and deconstruction, or feminism
and poststructuralism more generally defined, begin? We've given as
a provisional starting point the 1976 publication of Gayatri Spivak's
English translation of Derrida's 1967 text *De la grammatologie*. And
we have suggested that 1985 marks an important moment in US
feminist criticism because of the dissemination of a materialist feminist
criticism in the pages of Newton and Rosenfelt's anthology; 1985
also happened to be the year in which Moi published her controversial
critique of a number of the most eminent US feminist critics.

What else happened in 1985? Some Bay Area feminists proclaimed
the death of socialist feminism, as we have seen, but also in 1985
Eve Kosofsky Sedgwick published *Between Men: English Literature
and Male Homosocial Desire*, thus helping to initiate gay studies as
a legitimate field within US English departments, and her declared
method was an attempted articulation of Marxist feminism (ideology
and history) and radical feminism (sexuality and structuralism/
psychoanalysis) (Sedgwick 1985: 11–15). By 1985, in both the UK
and the USA, in spite of the theoretical lack Moi claimed to find in
literary studies, what we might now reasonably call materialist feminist critics sympathetic to deconstructive and poststructuralist methods
of analysis were contributing significantly to literary criticism, film
theory, semiotics, and the study of popular culture, though their
work was often developed independently of socialist politics and
outside traditional Marxist analytical categories. The feminist critics
we have in mind here do work that could be called materialist in
a sense more theoretically rigorous than the attention to material
conditions from which cultural artifacts are produced, the sense in

which Newton and Rosenfelt use the word. What might this kind of materialist analysis look like?

By 1985 the feminist theorists in the Marxist tradition we have already investigated had been poring over the texts of Marx and Engels for two decades, hoping to formulate specifically Marxist feminist or socialist feminist methods of historical investigation. But, as we have seen, they often raised more questions than they answered, and only provided a few provisional and local answers at that. Why should materialism be any more compatible than Marxism with feminism? And why should we in the 1990s now be interested in vaguely nineteenth century-sounding materialist solutions to problems of this postmodern moment?

Materialism and Culture

As Raymond Williams observes, defining human activity, and in particular deciding how much value should be placed on specifically economic activity, has proved to be a problem both in the Marxist tradition and in capitalist societies. As we have already suggested, Williams is notable among Marxist critics for the weight he places on the non-economic and subjective aspects of human activity as crucial for understanding the production and reproduction of social life. His practice as a cultural critic represents what has come to be known as "cultural materialism" in the broadest sense, given his emphasis on, say, conceiving language and the production of cultural artifacts not as purely cerebral activities but as forms of "practical consciousness" which are themselves kinds of material, productive activity: as he terms it, forms of "that practical consciousness which is inseparable from all social material activity" (Williams 1977: 38).

One of the most important tenets of a cultural or literary criticism that calls itself materialist these days might well be the recognition that the production of signs, of signifying systems, of ideology, representations, and discourses is itself a material activity with material effects. Instead of arguing that the material or economic base produces certain effects, like culture and ideology, as part of its superstructure, a cultural materialist would argue that ideology and the discourses generated by social institutions are themselves located in material practices which have material effects that affect even the economic structures of the base. This is a far cry from older Marxist arguments that the economic base determines everything in culture and society in specific and locatable ways. From a cultural materialist position, such arguments suffer from economic reductionism.

Economic reductionism has also presented enormous problems for feminists attempting a Marxist feminist synthesis. If women's responsibilities for childbearing, childrearing, housework and other forms of domestic labor, including emotional and affective work in sexual relationships and families, have often been in contradiction with their participation in economic production, then a too narrow focus on the economic leaves little space for analyzing either the complexities of women's oppression or their historical agency.

In this respect, Williams's project of cultural criticism, his desire to acknowledge the materiality of, and to investigate the interconnections between and among, all the complex human activities necessary for the reproduction of social life, including but not reduced to strictly economic production, could be seen as compatible with feminism. When we argue for the political usefulness of a materialist feminism in literary and cultural criticism and in historical investigation, we are invoking, in part, Williams's attention to the materiality of the many signifying practices of specific cultures, and the importance of analyzing historically changing forms of subjectivity alongside them.

Feminism, Postmodernism, and Marx: Gayatri Spivak and Linda Nicholson

Another shift has proved necessary, however, both within feminism and within Marxism, a shift beyond the recognition of the limitations of economic reductionism and the importance of ideology and cultural production. This shift has to do with the critique of metaphysical essences in philosophy and other disciplines, and the eventual extension of this critique to every aspect of social life. In the work of Jacques Derrida and Michel Foucault in particular, as well as in the work of many feminists, this kind of anti-essentialist, or poststructuralist, critique can be found. We shall have to figure out what the place of Derridian deconstruction is in all of this. For if a poststructuralist project may be said to be allied with materialism, or at least with the materialist critique in philosophy, it is Derrida's project. History and materialism are terms crucially allied in the Marxist tradition. And they remain crucial terms for a materialist feminism. One might think that Derrida's project, if it were materialist, would be productive for thinking about history and politics. And yet

Derrida has often been singled out as the poststructuralist thinker whose work has the least to do with history or with politics, the Henry Ford of French theorists, saying "History's bunk!" Certain aspects of this postmodern project could well be described as extending the materialist critique of mechanical materialism after Marx. They also point the way beyond some of the impasses reached in the 1970s and early 1980s debates about synthesizing Marxism and feminism.

The work of Gayatri Chakravorty Spivak, for example, represents quite a different return to the texts of Marx from what took place in the 1970s. Spivak is Derrida's best-known translator and a subtle critic of Michel Foucault as well as a feminist and postcolonial theorist. When she advocates a return to the texts of Marx, she advocates a deconstructive reading of them, not an orthodox or fundamentalist reading. To use the Derridian shorthand for deconstruction which Spivak herself uses, that means a critical reading of Marx's texts as texts, in all their metaphorical as well as conceptual complexity and contradictoriness, a reading in which the critic is, as Derrida puts it, like Marx himself in his critique of the operations of capital, "[o]perating necessarily from the inside, borrowing all the strategic and economic resources of subversion from the old structure, borrowing them structurally, that is to say without being able to isolate their elements and atoms" (Derrida 1976: 24). In this sense, as Derrida says, "the enterprise of deconstruction always in a certain way falls prey to its own work" (1976: 24). Hoping simply "to go beyond Marx" in one's critique becomes a naive hope; rather, one should hope to reread Marx carefully, to reinvent Marxism "from within the pores of feminism" (Spivak 1989c).

For Spivak as a postcolonial and feminist critic, Marx's narrative of modes of production is not a master narrative, the idea of class is not an inflexible idea, and Marx's texts are by no means univocal. These misconceptions have much more to do with the history of Marxism since Marx than with the texts themselves, as Spivak recently observed in an interview:

> If we look at the production of Marx's own text, we see alternatives based on reading Marx's text carefully. . . . So it seems to me that what is required of the people who would like to think that the choice between Marxism and micropolitics is the giving up of the master narrative – I think the real requirement there is to make time again to look at Marx. If one identifies Marxism with a master narrative one is conflating the history of Marxism with the texts of Marx, and the texts of Marx – I'm not a fundamentalist – the texts of Marx are

precisely the place where there is no sure foundation to be found. . . .
Other ways of analysis can be enabled through Marx's incredible
notion of that "slight, contentless thing" – Marx's way of describing
value, a value that is not necessarily trapped in the circuit of the
general equivalent in all possible contents. (Spivak 1990: 162)

The question of value has been a preoccupation of Marxist feminism
for quite some time. During the 1970s it took the form of the
domestic labor debate, in which participants argued about whether
women's unpaid domestic work was productive in a Marxist sense,
whether it contributed directly or indirectly to the production of
surplus value (the chief mechanism of capital accumulation; productive labor is labor which produces surplus value for the capitalist
in addition to what is necessary for its own maintenance – hypotheti-
cally, the wage; productive labor transforms money and commodities
into capital), whether it should be remunerated (the Wages for Housework campaign), and whether it was unpaid (not valued) because
women had been subordinated to men, or whether women's subordination stemmed from their confinement to unpaid, devalued labor
under capitalism.

Spivak's emphasis on value as a pun, a catachresis, in Marx's work,
not only shifts the grounds of debate from a tendency towards
economic reductionism but opens up potentially productive contradictions in Marx's texts. A catachresis is a signifier for which there
is no adequate literal referent. In a sense, of course, all language is
catachrestical; no referent is fully adequate to the excess of signification generated by the play of the signifying chain. Or, as the
character Robyn Penrose in David Lodge's novel *Nice Work* (1988)
might say, there is a perpetual sliding of the signified (the concept
being referred to) under the signifier (the linguistic marker being
used to refer to it). But the catachresis in Spivak's sense is a particularly clear case of this sliding, and such cases frequently mark productive sites for deconstructive investigation.

By reading Marx's concept of value – "that 'slight, contentless
thing'" – as a catachresis or pun rather than an element of scientific
law, Spivak is above all drawing attention to Marx's writing as
textuality. After poststructuralism, and in particular Derridian deconstruction, reading Marx is very much a matter of *reading*. And
reading means the patient and careful teasing out of the ways texts
may work against themselves, their very nature as pieces of writing,
their text-uality, sometimes going against the grain of their ostensible
arguments. Reading becomes a matter of strategy, of keeping the

political stakes of reading in mind at every critical juncture. A more adequately materialist feminist reading of the texts of Marx than has usually been attempted will require reading them *as* texts. And this project will require some knowledge of Spivak's deployment of deconstruction in the service of a feminist and Marxist politics, including her use of the concept of catachresis to open up a text's most powerful contradictions.

That current work being undertaken in the name of feminism, Marxism, and postmodernism does not necessarily proceed in this way can be illustrated by a look at Linda Nicholson's essay, "Feminism and Marx: Integrating Kinship with the Economic" (1987). Nicholson argues that gender can be crucial in transforming Marxism from a form of analysis that does not recognize its own historical and cultural limitations to a form of analysis that is usefully historical and responsive to cross-cultural differences. This transformation will be brought about if we focus on the history of kinship and the family, and how this sphere of social life came to be separated from the sphere of the economy and the state, because "it may be a function of Marxism's failure to pay sufficient attention to the fundamentality of kinship and its changing relation to other social institutions and practices that has caused the theory to become falsely ahistorical itself" (1987: 27).

For Nicholson, the "ambiguities" in Marx's use of terms like production and reproduction are not sites of productive contradictions for further analysis but "serious problems within the theory" (1987: 19). Marx gets labeled as having been unable to see how not dealing with gender and the family systematically and historically, as sites of pre-capitalist production and capitalist reproduction, respectively, made him a prisoner of the categories of his time. It sounds as if feminism is to come to the rescue of Marxism by filling in the ambiguous spaces of Marx's theory with some unambiguous historical work on kinship and the family. Although Nicholson wants to overcome the industrial capitalist and liberal split between the family, on one hand, and the sphere of politics and economics, on the other, it is hard to see how this kind of feminist supplement to Marx's texts won't end up reduplicating this split and representing the kind of "relatively superficial call to incorporate gender" or women's issues (i.e. kinship and the family) that Nicholson wants to go beyond (1987: 30).

Rereading Marxism

In order to see how a deconstructive (Spivakian) reading of Marx turns the text against itself, rather than finding theoretical holes in it (as Nicholson does), let's take a moment in Marx and Engels's *The German Ideology*. One of the crucially materialist moves in that text is the assertion that consciousness and ideas are materially produced through social labor. They do not occupy an independent or transcendent realm detached from, and therefore somehow superior to, other life-processes, though the division between mental and manual labor so important to the capitalist mode of production might make it appear so:

> Consciousness can never be anything else than conscious existence, and the existence of men is their actual life-process. If in all ideology men and their circumstances appear upside-down as in a *camera obscura*, this phenomenon arises just as much from their historical life-process as the inversion of objects on the retina does from their physical life-process. (Tucker 1978: 154)

That sense of an independent consciousness free to think what it likes, uncontaminated by mere material considerations, constitutes ideology:

> The phantoms formed in the human brain are also, necessarily, sublimates of their material life-process, which is empirically verifiable and bound to material premises. Morality, religion, metaphysics, all the rest of ideology and their corresponding forms of consciousness, thus no longer retain the semblance of independence. They have no history, no development; but men, developing their material production and their material intercourse, alter, along with this their real existence, their thinking and the products of their thinking. (1978: 154–5)

Ideology, including metaphysics, does not develop independently of other forms of social production. The practice of ideology critique therefore historicizes and rematerializes ideology by disclosing how it works to conceal the very means of its own production; to show, in other terms, that what ideology offers as natural or given or real has been constructed in particular and interested ways.

One of the chief categories subjected to ideology critique in *The German Ideology* is the *natural*. If we take the cherry-tree, for example, to be a sign of the "'sensuous certainty'" of the natural world as Feuerbach does, if we think that the cherry-tree represents "nature," we have neglected to remember that the cherry-tree has a history that brought it to Europe in the first place. It is not a natural phenomenon in Germany, but a social and historical one: "The cherry-tree, like almost all fruit-trees, was, as is well known, only a few centuries ago transplanted by *commerce* into our zone, and therefore only *by* this action of a definite society in a definite age has it become 'sensuous certainty' for Feuerbach" (Tucker 1978: 170).

Given the rigor of Marx and Engels's critique of what appear to be natural phenomena, phenomena without history, what then are we to make of an assertion like the following? Inexplicably, Marx and Engels seem to be taking for granted the category of "the natural" when it comes to gender relations:

> With the division of labour, in which all these contradictions [between the forces of production, the state of society, and consciousness] are implicit, and which in its turn is based on the natural division of labour in the family and the separation of society into individual families as opposed to one another, is given simultaneously the *distribution*, and indeed the *unequal* distribution, both quantitative and qualitative, of labour and its products, hence property: the nucleus, the first form, of which lies in the family, where wife and children are the slaves of the husband. (Tucker 1978: 159)

This passage is a good example of what Nicholson refers to as "serious problems within the theory" when it comes to matters of gender. But rather than following Nicholson, and simply accusing Marx and Engels of here falling into the trap of nineteenth-century gender ideology, in which relations within the family are represented as natural, universal, and without history, we recommend reading the text deconstructively instead. Here a deconstructive reading might use the force of Marx and Engels's argument about "nature" and "natural" elsewhere in the text to problematize the use of "natural division of labour in the family" here.

Given that so much of *The German Ideology* is devoted to a critique of ideas of the natural, we need not abandon that critique ourselves when we confront the problem of gender relations. We can thus take Marx and Engels's text a bit further in this specific instance than it seems to go itself. And with a feminist as well as a materialist focus we can take it a bit further towards realizing the crucial importance of gender as both a concept and a metaphor in materialist thinking, as well as indicating the need for further historicization of the categories of gender, sexuality, division of labor according to gender, and the family.

Marx and Engels's text gives us plenty of leverage to use to construct a reading against the tendency to forget that gender and sexual and familial relations have a history, indeed multiple histories that differ across cultures. Marx and Engels have themselves argued *against* arguing from some mythical or metaphysical point of origin in the far-distant past. If they seem to have forgotten this premise when thinking about the family, we need not follow them in ahistorical myth-making, tempting though it may be. Instead we can read this passage as productively contradictory, as testifying to the peculiar difficulty of thinking about gender and the family historically. These social practices have histories as surely as the cherry-tree has one, but even Marx and Engels were tempted to write as if that might not be so. What is it about the categories of men, women, and children that causes prehistoric scenarios to arise in the mind?

These are some of the questions and emphases that a deconstructive materialist feminism might raise in the return to Marxism via textual reading. Perhaps surprisingly, these are not the questions and emphases of most Marxist or materialist feminist analyses, even the most recent ones written in the wake of poststructuralism. We think that a deconstructive take can provide a real breakthrough in working simultaneously towards a feminist and a materialist analysis, by recognizing and working away at the discontinuities and contradictions that occur in the process of articulating these forms of critique.

The Derrida Story

When we use the term deconstruction, we are invoking in the first place the work of the French philosopher Jacques Derrida, but we are not trying to posit a legitimate, paternal authorial origin for deconstruction. In fact, one could say we were trying *not* to do so, since one of Derrida's projects is the destabilization and displacement of concepts like legitimacy based on paternal authority and that system of metaphysical and patriarchal assumptions Derrida designates by the term phallocentrism. Neither do we wish to follow the *New York Times Magazine* in its representation of Derrida as an entrepreneurial genius, a Thomas Edison of intellectual electricity, photo-captioned: "JACQUES DERRIDA. . . . HE INVENTED DECONSTRUCTION,"[1] since Derrida has queried the notion of authorial originality and property manifested in the idea of copyright. Each of these concepts could be understood as controlled by a metaphysics of presence, and Derrida, like Marx and Engels in *The German Ideology* and like Nietzsche, is engaged in a critique of metaphysics.

We wish to give the practice of deconstruction, then, not a proper pedigree but rather an historical location and some textual specificity. The impact of Derrida's work in the US, as exemplified by the *New York Times Magazine* article above, has often been equated with its appropriation by professors of literature at specific US universities, especially Yale, Johns Hopkins, Cornell, and more recently the University of California at Irvine. The Yale school of deconstruction, in particular, has often come to stand for deconstruction as a whole in both North America and Britain, and has come under attack from both left and right. From a Marxist or a feminist point of view, there are reasons for resisting this particular brand of deconstruction, which has presented itself as strictly literary, indeed as another brand of literary formalism not unlike the New Criticism of William Wimsatt and Cleanth Brooks, Yale professors of an earlier generation. Yale deconstruction tends to confine itself to readings of literary texts, and does not suggest, as Michael Ryan does, "that how we read or analyze and how we organize political and social institutions are related forms of practice" (Ryan 1982: xv). We would argue that Derrida's own texts are more open to political reading, and to being put to various political uses, than more narrowly literary or formalist kinds of deconstruction. The interest of a politicized rather than an apolitical (or anti-political) deconstruction for materialist feminism is considerable.

In order to critique radically what he describes as a metaphysics of presence in Western thought, Derrida coins a number of critical terms. Three of the terms through which he situates his object of critique are logocentrism, phonocentrism, and phallocentrism. Logocentrism designates the theological gesture of positing the Word, the logos, as a manifestation of divine presence and a sign of an originary oneness or identity: "In the beginning was the Word." Phonocentrism emphasizes the orality of Western and Judaeo-Christian metaphysics that can be traced right through Saussurean linguistics, when Saussure takes his model for language from speech, with its "sound-images": "In the beginning was the Word" – and it was spoken, not written. In speech, or in phonetic writing systems like our alphabetic one, the plenitude of that originary presence is recalled. Writing is seen as secondary, even parasitic upon such divinely inflected speaking. Phallocentrism marks the equation or complicity in philosophy and psychoanalysis between the Word and the resolutely masculine symbol of power and authority, the phallus. As the psychoanalyst Jacques Lacan has insisted, a phallus is not the same thing as a penis, because, while the penis is a genital organ, the phallus is a floating signifier of power which no one ever fully claims as "his own" since subjectivity is constructed upon lack. However, the phallus's similarity to and consequent symbolic resonance with the penis produces an asymmetrical relation for women and men to this crucial cultural signifier. A phallocentric philosophical or political economy will by definition subordinate if not exclude the feminine, the figure of Woman, or women's real historical interests. Western metaphysics is thus gendered as well as capable of engendering our most fundamental, least-questioned assumptions.

A fourth kind of metaphysical centrism, which is broached by Derrida but remains critically less developed in his writing than the first three, is ethnocentrism. Here subsequent work by Spivak and other critics of colonial and postcolonial discourse has *supplemented* Derrida's own texts – another piece of Derridian vocabulary. The supplement contains within itself a certain doubleness that aptly describes the double relations of appropriation and critique, of homage and resistance, manifested in these texts that put deconstruction to use in the service of a critique of imperialism:

> The supplement adds itself, it is a surplus, a plenitude enriching another plenitude, the *fullest measure* of presence. . . . But the supplement supplements. It adds only to replace. It intervenes or insinuates itself *in-the-place-of*. . . . Compensatory [*suppléant*] and vicarious, the supplement is an adjunct, a subaltern instance which *takes-(the)-place* [*tient-lieu*]." (Derrida 1976: 144–5)

In the work of Spivak and of Homi K. Bhabha, the critique of colonial discourse within a poststructuralist framework seems an apppropriately "subaltern instance" of Euro-deconstruction that both supports Derrida's targeting of ethnocentrism within Western metaphysics and signals the lack of a full-blown critique of it in his texts. Bhabha theorizes "hybridity," with its possibilities for subversive mimicry, as *the* distinguishing effect of colonialist power and its representations, because, rather than consisting of an hegemonic command of authority or the silent repression of native tradtions, "the exercise of colonialist authority requires the production of differentiations, individuations, identity-effects through which discriminatory practices can map out subject populations that are tarred with the visible and transparent mark of power" (Bhabha 1985: 96). For Bhabha, theorizing colonial hybridity in British India means posing questions about "the power and presence of the English" that at once depend on certain Derridian concepts and necessitate a "departure" or "a turning away" from Derrida's own attention to "the vicissitudes of interpretation in the mimetic act of reading" in order to focus on "the question of the effects of power, the inscription of strategies of individuation and domination in those 'dividing practices' which construct the colonial space" (1985: 94). The supplement discloses the necessity of its own coming into being as "supplementary" to a previous lack. Bhabha's departure from Derrida is "also a return to those moments in his essay when he acknowledges the problematic of 'presence'" which Bhabha will put to a different, more explicitly political and historically situated use. As Derrida comments in another context, "And if a certain 'break' is always possible, that with which it breaks must necessarily bear the mark of this possibility inscribed in its structure" (Derrida 1988b: 64).

Near the beginning of Derrida's *Of Grammatology*, in Spivak's translation, there is a section between the author's preface and the beginning of the first chapter called "Exergue." After three short quotations from, respectively, a 1963 French colloquium on writing, Rousseau's *Essay on the Origin of Languages*, and Hegel's *Encyclopedia*, we read:

> This triple exergue is intended not only to focus attention on the *ethnocentrism* which, everywhere and always, had controlled the concept of writing. Nor merely to focus attention on what I shall call *logocentrism*: the metaphysics of phonetic writing (for example, of the alphabet) which was fundamentally – for enigmatic yet essential reasons that are inaccessible to a simple historical relativism – nothing but the most original and powerful ethnocentrism, in the process of imposing itself upon the world, controlling in one and the same *order*:
> 1. *the concept of writing* in a world where the phoneticization of writing must dissimulate its own history as it is produced;
> 2. *the history of* (the only) *metaphysics*, which has, in spite of all differences, not only from Plato to Hegel (even including Leibniz) but also, beyond these apparent limits, from the pre-Socratics to Heidegger, always assigned the origin of truth in general to the logos: the history of truth, of the truth of truth, has always been – except for a metaphysical diversion that we shall have to explain – the debasement of writing, and its repression outside "full" speech;
> 3. *the concept of science* or the scientificity of science – what has always been determined as *logic* – a concept that has always been a philosophical concept, even if the practice of science has constantly challenged its imperialism of the logos, by invoking, for example, from the beginning and ever increasingly, nonphonetic writing. . . .

Nonetheless, it is a peculiarity of our epoch that, at the moment when the phoneticization of writing – the historical origin and structural possibility of philosophy as of science, the condition of the *epistémè* – begins to lay hold on world culture, science, in its advancements, can no longer be satisfied with it. (Derrida 1976: 3–4)

An "exergue," according to the *Oxford English Dictionary* (*OED*), is a small space, usually on the reverse of a coin or medal below the principal device, for any minor inscription, such as the date or the engraver's initials. It can also refer to such an inscription itself. The three short quotations form a triple exergue, a triple "minor inscription" within the coinage of an ethnocentric European philosophy. And Derrida's entire meditation in this section called "Exergue" could be read as an inscription on certain crucial texts within the Western philosophical tradition, an inscription on or reinscription of a certain philosophical currency still very much the medium of intellectual exchange in the West today, in spite of the apparent challenges to its assumptions broached by, for example, new technological developments in microelectronics, telecommunications, and cybernetics.

One of Derrida's concerns is the necessary interchange or crossing over that occurs between philosophical concepts and metaphors: each is defined as distinct from the other; one names a truth and the other a fiction, but even philosophical concepts are dependent upon metaphorical substitutions, for the concept stands in the place of something else, the signified to which it, metaphorically, refers. Such is the play of signification within language, in which meaning is constituted by difference, not identity, and is also always inevitably deferred, indefinitely postponed. Derrida's notion of "différance" plays upon this double sense of differing and deferring, in which we may desire to "say what we mean," but in the process of speaking or writing can only signify or distinguish our desire by its difference from other possible desires. Along the signifying chain of differences activated by that desire to mean, we find both our desire and the meaning of what we mean continually postponed. Nor can we really control the possible reception of our desire as thus represented.

Another of Derrida's concerns addressed by the "Exergue" is the interchange between linguistics and economics. As he writes in "White Mythology" (1974), "The inscription on a coin is most often the point of crossover, the scene of interchange between linguistics and economics. The two kinds of signifier serve for each other in the problematic of fetishism, as much in Nietzsche as in Marx"

(Derrida 1974: 14). Language understood as writing is a material practice. Money as a medium of exchange requires inscription. The project of *Of Grammatology* rematerializes writing as inscriptive practice in order to disclose the dissimulation practiced by Western metaphysics with its idealist, logocentric, phonocentric bias. And ethnocentrism underwrites a metaphysics that would privilege the logos as a unitary point of origin for legitimate learning, while it also permits a certain dissimulation regarding its history of imperialist domination through writing, through the cultural as well as political and economic reinscription of indigenous or native locations as colonial terrain. With the advent of the microelectronic revolution in particular, multinational capitalism controls more and more of the globe, so that an authentically native text can increasingly exist only as a metaphor, as the imaginary Other of the forms of contemporary imperial textuality.

What is Derrida's position, given his linkage of writing with money, of philosophical currency with the means of capitalist exchange, in terms of this global, multinational economic and linguistic commerce? The "Exergue" identifies the concepts of writing and science as levers for a critique that would not be a positive science but would rather establish the conditions of possibility for something other than the metaphysics with which we in the West continue to dissimulate our ethnocentrism, and our imperialist exploitation of the Other in neo- and postcolonial terrains. A deconstructive reading seeks such levers in order to pry open a text, to expose its idealist or metaphysical logic in order to rewrite it, to render it graphically, not logocentrically, in quite a different way. This search for deconstructive levers often means investigating the margins, the throwaway examples or metaphors of a text, rather than only concentrating on the argument. As Derrida notes:

> I do not "concentrate," in my reading . . . either exclusively or primarily on those points that appear to be the most "important," "central," "crucial." Rather, I deconcentrate, and it is the secondary, eccentric, lateral, marginal, parasitic, borderline cases which are "important" to me and are a source of many things, such as pleasure, but also insight into the general functioning of a textual system. (1988b: 44)

To unravel a text's logic requires paying scrupulous attention to what seems beside the point as well as to the main points. This kind of reading can be pleasurable as well as rigorous. It involves a patient engagement with the text in order to inhabit it so fully that one can rewrite it by making the dissimulations of its own logic and history speak.

The fundamental procedure for this reinscription of the object of critique consists of identifying the principal metaphysical oppositions that mark a text's logic and subjecting them to a process of reversal-displacement. As Derrida explains in "Signature Event Context" (1977), the binary structure of metaphysical oppositions requires a double gesture: not simply a reversal, as in privileging writing over orality, but a displacement of the opposition itself:

> Very schematically: an opposition of metaphysical concepts (e.g., speech/writing, presence/absence, etc.) is never the confrontation of two terms, but a hierarchy and the order of a subordination. Deconstruction cannot be restricted or immediately pass to a neutralization: it must, through a double gesture, a double science, a double writing – put into practice a *reversal* of the classical opposition *and* a general *displacement* of the system. It is on that condition alone that deconstruction will provide the means of *intervening* in the field of oppositions it criticizes and that is also a field of non-discursive forces. . . . Deconstruction does not consist in moving from one concept to another, but in reversing and displacing a conceptual order as well as the non-conceptual order with which it is articulated. (1988c: 21)

Such an operation of reversal-displacement discloses the interpenetration and complicity between the two terms, as well as the first, dominant term's dependence on its subordinate. The first term's dominance depends on its status as originary and identical with itself, as pure. The second term's philosophical subordination derives precisely from its secondary, derived status. Derrida comments:

> All metaphysicians, from Plato to Rousseau, Descartes to Husserl, have proceeded in this way, conceiving good to be before evil, the positive before the negative, the pure before the impure, the simple before the complex, the essential before the accidental, the imitated before the imitation, etc. And this is not just *one* metaphysical gesture among others, it is *the* metaphysical exigency, that which has been the most constant, most profound and most potent. (1988b: 93)

Thus the initial gesture of deconstructive practice turns the world upside down in its questioning of metaphysics. If we shift from the register of philosophy to the register of politics, we have the beginnings of a questioning of hierarchical thinking with respect to the effects of power. Power relations based upon difference, and the fact of difference itself being appropriated over and over for the foundation of hierarchies, might then come to be regarded with suspicion.

It cannot be said too often, however: in a deconstructive reading not only is the opposition reversed, it is displaced. This requires showing how the first term is marked in advance by its opposite, how it remains unthinkable without it. Then the priority of the first term collapses, and opposition is replaced by the recognition of complicity. The two terms of the so-called opposition instead disclose themselves as mutually constructive. Thinking about concepts as configurations dependent upon mutual construction rather than as object lessons in transhistorical relations of dominance and subordination has its political as well as philosophically critical uses.

It is not hard to see how the terms "masculine" and "feminine" or "male" and "female" have been written as the hierarchical binary oppositions masculine/feminine and male/female within the phallocentric economy of the metaphysics Derrida analyzes. As Milton put it in *Paradise Lost*, "Hee for God only, shee for God in him" (Book IV, line 299). Eve is Adam's helpmate, derived from his rib, subject to his authority as Adam is to God's. Derrida's project has led him to write of woman as the Other of philosophy, always to be associated either with truth or untruth, and, in *Spurs*, to coin critical terms like "hymen" – "a margin where the control over meaning or code is without recourse" which "poses the limit to the relevance of the hermeneutic or systematic question" (Derrida 1979: 99) – according to a symbolic economy that would not be phallocentric. Derrida reads Nietzsche performing this "feminine" operation, suspending "truth between the tenter-hooks of quotation marks": "The question of the woman suspends the decidable opposition of true and non-true and inaugurates the epochal regime of quotation marks which is to be enforced for every concept belonging to the system of philosophical decidability. The hermeneutic project which postulates a true sense of the text is disqualified under this regime" (1979: 57, 107). Reading Nietzsche, Derrida also engages tentatively with a feminist question about his own investment in this feminine writing or process of inscription, and his investment in recuperating Nietzsche, as it were, for feminism: "But in the midst of all these weapons circulating from hand to hand, passing from one opponent to another, the question still remains of what I am about here. Must not these *apparently feminist* propositions be reconciled with the over-whelming *corpus* of Nietzsche's venomous anti-feminism?" (1979: 57). We may well be disappointed in his answer, which is to reduce feminism to what Nietzsche thought feminism was, "nothing but the operation of a woman who aspires to be like a man," on the side of the "truth, science and objectivity" that distinguish the dogmatic philosopher (1979: 65). Derrida himself might argue that his work is least appropriable for feminism when he addresses the question of woman or the "feminine" most directly:

> It is impossible to dissociate the questions of art, style and truth from the question of the woman. Nevertheless the question "what is woman?" is itself suspended by the simple formulation of their common problematic. One can no longer seek her, no more than one could search for woman's femininity or female sexuality. And she is certainly not to be found in any of the familiar modes of concept or knowledge. Yet it is impossible to resist looking for her. (1979: 71)

Such moments in Derrida's texts may strike the feminist reader as among his most conventional, as among those moments most saturated by gender ideology and thus not without their problematically chivalrous intentions (see McDonald 1982).

We do not, however, wish to cast Derrida as feminism's champion, but rather to suggest that some of his "protocols of reading" (Derrida 1982: 63) are invaluable for a feminist practice. Let us take two further brief examples of such a deconstructive operation of reversal-displacement, one from the intersection of literary and historical studies and one from the continuing feminist debates about sexuality.

Text/Context

If two critical terms can still be seen to carry weight in literary and historical studies even after the posing of the poststructuralist problematic, they are "text" and "context." The text/context couple is invoked too often to bear much thinking about, with primacy and purity going to text, of course, reminding us that the coupling of text/context often represents little more than a superficial shift of vocabulary from those old standbys, "the work of art" and its "background." The "feminized" secondary status of context opens itself to disreputable puns in French, with "con" meaning female genitals, "cunt," as well as "around" or "about." Contexts are, by definition, invariably subordinated to the texts they supposedly clarify or situate historically. In the case of speech-act theory, they may even be put to one side for the sake of "the clarity of the demonstration" of the ideal speech act. Of this exclusion of contexts within speech-act theory, Derrida writes:

To treat context as a factor from which one can abstract for the sake of refining one's analysis, is to commit oneself to a description that cannot but miss the very contents and object it claims to isolate, for they are intrinsically determined by context. The method itself, as well as considerations of clarity should have excluded such an abstraction. Context is always, and always has been, at work *within* the place, and not only *around* it. (1988b: 60)

The context and the text itself are seen to construct one another in such a way that the material conditions of a text's production (composition, transcription, publication), its printing history, and its history of readership inhere in the very idea of the text itself. To read a poem, for example, according to this notion of the text, would not be a matter of simply scanning the words on the page as if they were anonymous, according to certain tenets of "old" New Criticism or Practical Criticism, or as if they were a message in a bottle instead of a manuscript poem or a printed poem, but would require that we retrace and reinscribe through our reading of the text the specific histories of the poems's production, reproduction, and reception as best we can. And in any history of the conditions of textual production and reception today such categories as gender, sexuality, race, and class will prove increasingly important.

The Sex Wars

Our second binary opposition comes out of the 1980s debates in the US and UK around what a feminist sexuality might be like. In many reports of these debates, the possible positions are polarized into two antagonistic camps, the "anti-sex" or "anti-pornography and anti-sadomasochism" camp, and the "pro-sex" camp. The division between pro- and anti-sex feminists was most clearly crystallized in open conflict over the notorious conference at Barnard College in New York City, "The Scholar and the Feminist IX: Towards a Politics of Sexuality," in April 1982, and much has been written on both sides since.

Fueling this division between "anti-" and "pro-sex" activists were differing perceptions of the relations between pornography, sadomasochism (s/m), patriarchy, censorship, and sexuality. Women Against Pornography (WAP) and Women Against Violence Against Women were two groups who campaigned against the conference, urging feminists not to participate in an event where "regressive" practices, such as s/m between lesbians, practices that were by definition "complicitous with patriarchy," were being discussed. Other feminists were opposed to sadomasochism, even between lesbians who chose that practice, on other grounds, whether they characterized s/m as a form of bourgeois decadence, as a commodification of sexuality, as an instance of fascism in everyday life, as an internalization of late capitalist disciplinary repression, or as a residue of male misogynist sexual domination. The "pro-sex" constituency, equally varied in their specific politics, did not balk at name-calling either. To condemn sadomasochism was to be branded a puritan, a sexual conservative, an advocate of sexual censorship, and a covert supporter of the New Right's pro-family and anti-sex policies.[2] Both sides questioned the other's claim to a politics of women's liberation, with the "anti-sex" side tending to insist that it represented "feminism" in the purest sense. In 1985 a similar polarization occurred in London over the question whether s/m groups would be allowed to meet at the London Lesbian and Gay Centre (see Ardill and O'Sullivan 1986).

These polarized positions can be read as constituting a binary opposition. The "anti-sex" stance asserts itself as primary and originary as well as pure; WAP or the London group Lesbians Against Sadomasochism (LASM) make claims to authority by casting themselves as the *true* representatives of feminism. The "pro-sex" group tend to take a defensive line in a sense derived oppositionally from the "anti-sex" group's, that sexual practices such as lesbian s/m *are* feminist because liberating and empowering for women. As we can see, both these terms depend to some extent upon a concept of *a* feminist sexuality. Both manifest the desire to police the terrain of what might constitute that "politically correct" sexuality. But the first term, the "anti-sex" stance, strives to negate the very sexuality upon which it is predicated, and which it tries to police by rendering almost all currently recognizable sexual practices, especially those that play out power relations, deeply suspicious – as residually patriarchal and potentially fascist. As Susan Ardill and Sue O'Sullivan put it:

> We know of many individual lesbians who have taken up the LASM position on the centre because it was presented so heavily as the "correct line." . . . Doubts, ambiguities, confusions are shoved under the carpet under this sort of pressure. The mere expression of dissenting ideas has become synonymous with endorsing oppression. There is no room in the LASM view for struggle, for admitting that we all can harbour reactionary ideas at the same time that we hold on to progressive ones. (Ardill and O'Sullivan 1986: 54)

Thus is the "pro-sex" stance made to seem impure, dangerously parasitical upon the corrupt practices of patriarchal culture. But, as Ardill and O'Sullivan point out, the "pro-sex" advocates can also be found claiming some self-righteously political high ground, mirroring the legislative and moral desires of the "anti-sex" group: "The most absurd extension of the SM political position is the implication that if we all played out our SM fantasies in bed, the world would be a better place. The connecting line between this mode of thinking and the LASM one is striking, even if they draw the opposite conclusions" (1986: 53). By reversing and displacing the opposition between the "anti-" and "pro-sex" stances, a deconstructive reading can disclose their complicity, in particular their complicity with regard to that politically problematical desire to legislate and police a "correct" politics of sexuality.

From what position does one undertake this deconstructive maneuver? It will be a position of acknowledged complicity with the object of investigation, not an olympian position of mastery ostensibly removed from and uncontaminated by its object. We are within the metaphysical enclosure even as we open it to deconstructive examination, alter it by our intervention. We cannot *not* have a politics of sexuality even as we attempt to storm the grounds guarded by the sexuality police. As Spivak notes: "We *must* do a thing *and* its opposite, and indeed we desire to do both, and so on indefinitely. . . . No text is ever *fully* deconstructing or deconstructed. Yet the critic provisionally musters the metaphysical resources of criticism and performs what declares itself to be *one* (unitary) act of deconstruction" (in Derrida 1976: lxxviii). The provisionality of deconstructive practice, then, can be used to prevent any dogmatic fixing of principles abstracted from their contexts. Deconstruction can help us remain vigilant against the freezing into orthodoxy of the strategic, self-reflexive politics desirable, and even necessary, for a materialist feminist practice. As Spivak has so often insisted, "Deconstruction cannot found a political program of any kind" (Spivak 1990: 104). Deconstruction is rather a tool to be used within practical politics, a critical movement that prevents the settling and fixing of foundations and totalities. In order to conduct an argument, we rely on certain premises, and these premises "obliterate or finesse certain possibilities" that question the very grounds of these premises, their availability and validity (1990: 104). This might be understood as the necessary theoretical condition and limitation of all practice. Above all, deconstruction teaches us to pay attention to those moments when the limits and the constructedness of our arguments and positions may otherwise seem to disappear. Complicity between the subject of investigation and its object of inquiry is never greater than when it goes unacknowledged.

Notes

1 Campbell (1986: 21); the full caption reads: "JACQUES DERRIDA OF FRANCE'S ECOLE NORMALE SUPERIEURE, WHO CONDUCTS YEARLY SEMINARS AT YALE. HE INVENTED DECONSTRUCTION."

2 The papers from the Barnard conference have been published as *Pleasure and Danger: Exploring Female Sexuality* (1984), ed. Carole S. Vance. For other pro- and anti-sex arguments, see, for example: SAMOIS (1981); Linden et al. (1982); Rubin, English and Hollibaugh (1982); MacKinnon (1982); Snitow, Stansell, and Thompson (1983); France (1984); the pamphlet distributed at the gates of the Barnard conference by the Coalition for a Feminist Sexuality and against Sadomasochism, reprinted in *Feminist Studies* 9:1 (1983): 180–2; the letter from the Steering Committee of Women Against Pornography in *Feminist Studies* 10:2 (1984): 363–7; the "Forum" on "The Feminist Sexuality Debates" in *Signs* 10:1 (1984): 102–35; Rich (1986); and King (1988).

Part II

Feminism and Cultural Critique

4

Feminism and the History of the Novel

Why have literary texts, especially novels, been crucial for feminist debates both inside and outside the academy? Is there some special relation between women writers or women readers and the novel? It is surely no accident that in *Orlando* Virginia Woolf identifies the moment of Orlando's sex change from aristocratic male sonneteer to female author and adventurer with the later seventeenth century. For during the same historical moment women began to publish under their own names and the English novel began to come into being. Arguably, Aphra Behn could be cited as the first English novelist, if not for *Love Letters Between a Nobleman and His Sister* (1684–7), then for *Oroonoko* (1688). Perhaps because the novel was literally novel or new, a new genre constantly being reinvented by its practitioners, female novelists thrived in the early years of the novel's emergence. And women writers continued to command space in the literary marketplace as popular novelists, with huge reading publics and sometimes also with critical acclaim, right into the twentieth century. There is indisputable evidence that women not only participated in the making of the novel as a literary genre, but were absolutely crucial to its making, to the history of particular forms the genre has undergone over the past three centuries. Why, then, should there be such a gap in our historical knowledge that many readers continue to be amazed to learn that there were any female novelists before Jane Austen?

It should by now be clear that whatever events may have happened in the distant past, accessible to us now only through the processed textuality of the archive and its many scholarly interpreters, institutional forces produce particular versions of the past to suit institutional purposes. All stories are interested stories. So it is with the formation of the canon, the syllabus of sacred texts with which all educated people are expected to be familiar. In practice, the canon operates as those books which get repeatedly taught in schools, colleges, and universities, those books which come to represent their historical moments and the cultural values of the so-called heritage of their readers, generation after generation. To put it crudely, just because the canon, so far as British and American novels are concerned, hasn't included many women writers until quite recently is no reason to suppose that they haven't existed. Feminist scholarship and literary criticism have been concerned, if not obsessed, with re-evaluating existing canons in terms of their politics of exclusion on the grounds of gender, race, class, and sexuality. Feminists have also been busy rediscovering women writers, especially female novelists, in order to produce a more representative and less gender-biased, or even perhaps a feminist, canon.

In historical terms, the classification of texts according to their use-value for feminist purposes can be associated with the emergence, during recent decades, of this feminist recovery work, challenging the existing canons of traditional literary history, particularly through the recovery and republication of texts by lost or neglected women writers, and the development of a broad interest in writing critical, historical, and theoretical studies about women's writings. Feminist use-value may also be found circulating through the production and consumption of novels written within the various subcultures that compose the women's movement, internationally speaking. Many of these books package versions of feminist ideas and feminist politics which get marketed for very different audiences. How might materialist feminist reading strategies prove useful in understanding the ideological work done by such texts?

Women's Writing

In order to answer this question, we shall need to examine some of the work already done around the issues of women's literary production and whether it differs significantly from men's, of whether there is a gender to textuality, and of whether a critical practice calling itself feminist should engage primarily with writings by women and, if so, on what grounds. A gender-based approach to textuality has proved particularly powerful for obvious reasons. Historically, it seems to follow directly from the radical emphasis within the women's movement on the recovery and analysis of women's experiences. The second wave of feminist activity has involved a growing demand for books by, for, and about women, thereby supporting the emergence of commercial publishers such as Virago, The Women's Press, Firebrand Books, The Naiad Press, Zed Books, The Feminist Press, and Kitchen Table: Women of Color Press. Strategically, women's studies programs and courses in universities, schools, and colleges have required a distinctive body of primary and secondary literature to establish their disciplinary credentials; in these contexts, courses on women's writing are necessarily a staple.

Developing a theory of textuality through a focus on women's writing provides an attractive solution to many urgent feminist concerns, not the least of which include the pleasures of reading what women have written, and of providing an arena in which to explore what is most distinctive about women's literary representations. It offers a direct challenge to men's authority over language in the form of a reversal bound up with the terms of its own legitimacy as a distinctly feminist approach. If ideology, language, and literature have been instrumental in establishing the potentially hegemonic conditions of women's subordination, then the recovery and construction of alternative women's textualities, of women's language, might prove directly empowering. And if textuality hasn't been instrumental in establishing the contexts of women's subordination, then why bother with it?

This paradigm provides the general logic for a broad range of feminist literary activities, including the appearance of often opposing but nevertheless influential and ground-breaking feminist studies of textuality. In the Anglo-American context, something of that range may be indicated by suggesting that the diverse and often contradictory views found in books as different as Dale Spender's *Man Made Language* (1980), Sandra M. Gilbert and Susan Gubar's *Norton Anthology of Literature by Women: The Tradition in English* (1985), and Jane Spencer's *The Rise of the Woman Novelist* (1986) in some sense share a common purpose with the French feminist project of *l'écriture féminine*, identified most closely with the work of Hélène Cixous (1976): to write women back into our ideas and histories of language and writing. Some of the contradictions involved in this activity may be characterized as a form of gender-essentialism, one that has replayed certain moves within the Marxist debates over instrumentality and aesthetics by substituting gender for class. One consequence has been miscasting the problem of the material agency of textuality by identifying certain textual forms and strategies with gender-exclusive interests.

What emerges is sometimes an insufficiently historical account of textual instrumentality that, by relying on a mimetic theory of representation, ends up framing a conspiracy theory of language; this is explicit in Dale Spender but no less integral to *écriture féminine* and other versions of women's textuality. Such moves can provide neither a general nor a specifically feminist approach to an aesthetics capable of accounting for a diversity of pleasures, including those to be found in so-called non-feminist texts, and can provide no account of the historical and national differences marking the production and reception of literary texts generally.

Novels Do Cultural Work

For many feminists, the history of the novel has held special signifi-cance, since, from the late seventeenth and early eighteenth centuries at least, the novel has been frequently associated with femininity, romance, domesticity, and what is sometimes called the "feminiz-ation" of modern culture. For the last three hundred years, during the emergence of a so-called feminine "private" sphere cut off from men's "public" activities, the largely private practice of reading novels has been a principal literary activity for many women. Consequently, the association of women and the novel displays a peculiarly modern – and therefore politically relevant – sense of how the history and character of a specific literary form have directly contributed to the construction of currently existing gender distinctions.

The novel has also played an important role in the history of modern feminist thought. At least since Mary Wollstonecraft, femin-ist accounts of literary form have identified the novel as peculiarly and intimately linked with the textual construction of ideas about women. In one recent but already highly influential account, *Desire and Domestic Fiction: A Political History of the Novel* (1987), Nancy Armstrong argues that in the eighteenth century the novel so fully captured the ideological function of the courtesy book that it provided middle-class society as a whole with such a clear and powerful representation of what made a woman desirable that the domestic woman idealized by novels has ever since directly determined how real women imagine themselves to be.

According to Armstrong's account, the bourgeois tradition of conduct books initiated a precise focus on the social position of women, thereby opening up a new discourse of female subjectivity which, towards the end of the seventeenth century, was taken over by the emergence of the novel. By centering gender, Armstrong revises Ian Watt's influential theory in *The Rise of the Novel* (1957) that the realist novel, represented primarily by Defoe, Richardson, and Fielding, proved to be a crucial vehicle for disseminating middle-class values. For Watt, the subject of bourgeois ideology is implicitly a male subject, Robinson Crusoe, hero of economic and Puritan individualism. Crusoe's island represents a particularly pure location for the male assertion of economic will and the bourgeois-epic drama of possessive individualism. According to Armstrong, we need to read Crusoe's management of his island rather differently. The island typifies novelistic space by dint of its private rather than its public nature. For Armstrong, because the novel focuses on domestic space, and because domestic space is associated with women and femininity, Robinson Crusoe's island stewardship should be seen not so much as masculine, public economic activity but more as private, feminine domestic management. According to Armstrong's notion of gender-coding in the eighteenth and nineteenth centuries, Robinson Crusoe is more female than male, but it is not until we get to Richardson's heroines Pamela and Clarissa that the novel really comes into its own domain as domestic fiction. Armstrong's revision of Watt thus consists of arguing not that there were important women novelists to which he should have devoted more space, for her selection of novelists is remarkably similar to his, but that the novel as a genre gave rise to the modern female subject of domesticity, and this explains why the majority of eighteenth-century novels were written by women.

The cultural work of the novel in this view has been to center the domestic woman as the origin and end of modern society. What makes this argument especially compelling is its direct insistence that this is what has really happened, that women today are the specific products of an ideology of domesticity announced and elaborated by the novel. Armstrong also suggests that the model for the bourgeois subject, whether male or female, is fundamentally feminine, that the displacement of aristocratic by bourgeois values constituted a feminization of subjectivity. As the crucial achievement of an emerging capitalist society, the novel dominated cultural activity from the early eighteenth century until the early twentieth century. In advance of social change, the novel imagined into being the way women, and to a certain extent the whole literate public, were supposed to be; it instructed men on what qualities to admire in their wives and themselves, and instructed women how to make themselves desirable agents of their own destiny. In this version of the history of the novel, the agency of textuality is direct; the novel took over the

discursive space of the courtesy book and offered instruction that
people actually took, eventually becoming like the characters whose
lives the novel detailed.

But what happens when we argue in this way that certain literary
forms, like novels, can be said to embody or serve identifiably
gender-specific ideologies? And what are the class implications of
these associations between women's interests and feminist interest in
developing theories of the novel? If the novel is, as has so often
been said, the genre of the emergent bourgeois classes, what does
this mean for women? What are the political implications of the
recent studies of gender and genre, of femininity and domesticity,
that this interest in the novel has generated? How have feminist
theories of and approaches to the novel engaged with the problems
of national history and social identity?

The Problem of Agency: One

Recent concerns over theorizing the political agency of the novel
have not been restricted to feminists or even academics. In reviewing
for *Country Life* in 1985 the English translation of *The House
of Spirits* by Isabel Allende, Dame Marghanita Laski voiced many
traditionally important features of the dilemma over literary agency.
What makes Laski's review worth quoting at length here is that,
after distinguishing political effect from aesthetic quality, she is led
to a remarkable declaration of what can best be called class treachery.
"Tolstoy," Laski reminds us,

> in his long essay *What Is Art?* argued that the best art was that which
> awoke the reader to the desire to remedy social injustice, and this led
> him to the conclusion that *Uncle Tom's Cabin* was the best novel yet
> written. Marxism has adopted a similar stance, and in novel-writing
> the result has been a period of would-be moral tracts judged by criteria
> other than those more properly and classically used for judging art
> than Tolstoy's. In fact, there have been singularly few *good* novels
> [that] have effectively awaked the reader to a sense of social injustice,
> and many great novels have not. Moreover, social injustice must be
> dreadfully timeless for it to move other generations than its own to
> more than imaginative involvement. To become aware of a duty to
> remedy the lives of chimneysweeps or the law's delays are not our
> major reasons for judging Dickens as great.
>
> But still, when, to a novel's other qualities, this is added; when, as
> well as right pace and creative imagination and rich storytelling and

stalwart personal morality, a novel is imbued with the ability to arouse pity and fear on a truly tragic and heroic scale, then the reader recognises greatness, and if this pity and fear is predicated upon social injustice on a national scale, then there is some – not complete – rightness in what Tolstoy was trying to say; though in the end, as always, heroic tragedy must rest not on a political situation but on heroic individuals' response to it.

   This is different, of course, from the moral. The moral here [in Allende's novel], and one we cannot but painfully draw out for ourselves, is the realisation that we, the propertied classes, should not fear the loss of our privileges so much as we should fear what we may be prepared to countenance in the hope of retaining them. (Laski 1985: 528)

The argument here aligns political agency with specific aesthetic qualities found in novels, notably those capable of awakening readers to social injustice. What the critic from the property-owning classes observes about the novel rooted in serious circumstances – its deployment of moral weaponry aimed at forcing readers into an understanding that something must be done because the way things are, clearly, is about to become too terrible to be endured – points directly to the impasse of the heroic mode in our times, despite her attempt to endorse it. For any representation of an individual's moral crises, amidst any historical circumstances, moves us to pity and fear *precisely* of a heroic scale only by limiting all other possibilities of communal or social intervention – by, in other words, containing the social within the individual, a characteristic move in the political arenas of Western bourgeois culture.

   The theoretical implications of Laski's eloquent sentiment – how can we not think of South Africa, Detroit, or Los Angeles? – are worth pondering, since seldom do members of her class reach such an understanding, much less polemicize it. But while no one imagines that readers of *Country Life* are likely to give up whatever claims, real and imaginary, they may have to property because of a book review – or even a novel for that matter – we might usefully address Laski's silence on certain issues. She recognizes the political seriousness of mode and genre – we hear of the heroic and the tragic partially, perhaps, in deference to her author's status – but there is nothing here about the erotic or the comic, and hardly anything about style. And, while she so acutely perceives the international scope of immediate class positions and antagonisms, she is entirely silent on the matter – surely an important one in the context of the book she is reviewing – of gender and the differences it might make.

Beyond Gender and Class

We have already discussed how the rudiments of any materialist
feminism, the problem of developing analytical models capable of
addressing both women's oppression in class-specific terms, and the
profoundly gendered quality of class formations, have sometimes
been presented in terms of "dual-systems theory." This is the solution
recently offered by sociologist Terry Lovell in her history of the
English novel, *Consuming Fiction* (1987). Lovell argues that her book

> is trying to do two things. It attempts to shift the focus of discussion
> of the ideological bearings of the English novel from the context of
> capitalist production to that of capitalist consumption. And it has
> paid as much attention to the conditions of literary production and
> consumption as it has to the text itself. But whether the focus is that
> of the literary system of production, or capitalist consumption, it has
> insisted that the question of sex and gender must be placed at the
> centre of analysis alongside that of class. (Lovell 1987: 17)

While endorsing Lovell's description of a dual systems approach
as a necessary corrective to previous kinds of literary history, we
nevertheless think it provides a statement of the problem rather than
a solution. By no means has all feminist literary criticism been
concerned with class, and the need to continue demonstrating the
importance of class differences for understanding the social construction of women's subordination remains urgent. Yet, in important
ways, the difficulties only start once we recognize the need to center
class analysis "alongside" that of sex/gender systems. We would stress
here once again that materialist feminism is principally a political
problematic, one that has emerged from a variety of socialist and
feminist positions over the last twenty years, but which has developed
during the late 1980s into a broad-reaching social critique sensitive to
politics of difference involving questions of race, sexuality, ethnicity,
nationality, postcoloniality, religion, and cultural identity, as well
as class and gender. A feminist theory of textuality based on gender-
exclusive paradigms will prove incapable of theorizing such differentiated representation of gender differences and the agency of such
representations in the determinations of social life.

Most recently, the critique of essentialism has shown how the
feminist project of writing women back into history commonly
entails the ideological construction, and subsequent reification, of
the category "woman." Gender is a necessary category for materialist

analysis. But gender, like class, is only ever historically specific, a product of social and political differences rather than the reason why those differences exist. The critical articulation of gender with class necessarily points to regional and temporal specificities and differences, since gender and class are primary categories of cultural difference and national identity. Politically, where both gender and class analyses confront their own essentializing tendencies is where ideologies of national identity seek to neutralize oppressive practices or naturalize political differences.

Recent feminist histories of women's writing and the novel, such as those by Terry Lovell (1987), Mary Poovey (1984, 1988), Jane P. Tompkins (1985), Jane Spencer (1986), Linda S. Kauffman (1986), Cathy N. Davidson (1986), Nancy Armstrong (1987), and Janet Todd (1989), have attempted to write women back into literary history, and have successfully extended and challenged the canons of national literatures in important ways. But in doing so they have tended to generalize from the specific positions and experiences of women representing one national or linguistic group, and then to slide from that generalization to "women" as a universal category. Any feminist strategies designed to engage with, and assist in, the liberation struggles of oppressed groups – such as women, racial or sexual minorities or exploited classes – immediately encounter historically specific regional differences, and equally specific cultural efforts to construct ideologies of national and regional identity, that resist such universalizing gestures.

The Problem of Agency: Two

The basic question of textual agency can be stated in the form of a falsifiable either/or. Do literary texts reflect an already existing world that remains identical with itself despite the fact of textual representation? Or do literary texts actually change the world in which they appear and, if so, how? In terms often as crude as these, this dilemma has set the agenda for much literary theorizing since the time when Plato so far feared the effects of literary texts changing the world that he imagined banning poets altogether from his ideal republic. But when the modernist poet W. H. Auden declared that "poetry makes nothing happen" he did more than register a later, opposing opinion or express a sense of his own frustrating inability to change the world by writing about it. For Auden wrote at a time when the debate over questions of literary agency had a long and varied history

all its own, at a time, indeed, when the very ability to debate
questions of literary agency, value, and meaning had long been
central to the legitimizing claims of those classes which identified
themselves with the progress of Western civilization.

This is not the place to rehearse the tale of what Raymond Williams
has called the "long revolution," of how in Britain at least the serious
study of English Literature began replacing training in the Greek
and Latin classics two centuries ago, thereby reflecting or enabling
the emergence of a new social system and class structure suited to
imperial expansion. And which has continued along a supposedly
democratizing cultural path ever since (Williams 1961). Politically,
the question is not whether texts reflect or change the world, but
to what uses they are and have been put, and to what ends they are
and can be used.

We would argue that, in and of themselves, the formal properties
of literary texts such as novels and poems neither reflect nor change
anything. In this view, the material agency of a text is formally
indeterminate, since any text may be used at different times for
different purposes by different people. In other words, we shall
advance the principle that textual agency is always instrumental and
historically specific and consequently not an essential or formal property of the text itself, but an effect of the uses to which it can be
put. With regard to attempts to analyze formal features of texts as
immediate bearers of gender ideology, Rita Felski recently com-
mented in *Beyond Feminist Aesthetics*:

> I suggest . . . that it is impossible to speak of "masculine" and "femi-
> nine" in any meaningful sense in the formal analysis of texts; the
> political value of literary texts from the standpoint of feminism can
> be determined only by an investigation of their social functions and
> effects in relation to the interests of women in a particular historical
> context, and not by attempting to deduce an abstract literary theory
> of "masculine" and "feminine," "subversive" and "reactionary" forms
> in isolation from the social conditions of their production and recep-
> tion. (Felski 1989: 2)

By distinguishing between gender analysis and feminist politics, the
inflection here differs from Lovell's insistence "that the question of
sex and gender must be placed at the centre of analysis alongside
that of class," but Felski's position shares with Lovell's a materialist
concern for national and historical specificity. Unlike Felski and
Lovell, feminist literary historians have too often developed strategies
for reading the textual construction of women's identity by proceed-

ing as if formal properties of texts were essentially gendered in ways that cut across national and historical differences.

A theory of textual agency that attributes formal, textual features with gender-specific qualities relies on an essentializing tendency. Felski seeks to displace this tendency by proposing a feminist theory that avoids gender essentialism while retaining a clear sense of women's interests: "any detailed consideration of the relationship between feminism and literature immediately raises a number of questions which cannot be adequately explained in terms of a purely gender-based analysis" (Felski 1989: 18).

To address the question of what a feminist text might look like, Felski examines texts in which the self-identification of women as an oppressed group is made explicit:

> The emergence of a second wave of feminism in the late 1960s justifies the analysis of women's literature as a separate category, not because of automatic and unambiguous differences between the writings of women and men, but because of the recent cultural phenomenon of women's explicit self-identification as an oppressed group, which is in turn articulated in literary texts in the exploration of gender-specific concerns centered around the problem of female identity. (1989: 1)

Although Felski restricts the focus of her argument to what she calls the "feminist literary genres" of recent years which have explicitly explored the conditions of women's oppression, her approach to the material relations linking literary activity with gender proceeds from an important historical recognition that resonates beyond the contemporary moment:

> One of the main achievements of contemporary feminism has been to show that gender relations constitute a separate and relatively autonomous site of oppression, which cannot, for instance, be satisfactorily explained as a mere function of capitalism. But it does not follow that gender relations can be viewed in abstraction from the complex web of historically specific conditions through which they are manifested. (1989: 18)

In arguing that recent feminist writing may be said to constitute what she calls a "feminist counter-public sphere," Felski is consistently sensitive to the ways in which, in addition and often in opposition to gender, national and social differences generate textual features and strategies. Fiction by Canadian feminists, for example, often engages the opposition between nature and culture not only to examine gender differences, but also to explore questions of national identity "in the face of the homogenizing and imperialistic tendencies of an American culture which is identified with the most negative aspects of modernity." The writings of West German feminists, by contrast, often seem opposed to political movements, displaying instead "the clear influence of a tradition of German idealism in its celebration of female subjectivity as a withdrawal into inwardness" (1989: 149), since even radical German organizations have typically ignored women's interests. Contemporary African-American feminist writers, however, often link the celebration of women's spirituality with collective and activist socio-political goals (1989: 150).

Differing, and even opposed, features specific to the writings of contemporary feminists indicate the need for a theory of literary representation and of textual agency that can account for those national and historical differences which give both specificity and urgency to women's interests.

5

How PC Can a White Girl Be When Her Sisters of Color Can Represent Themselves?

There was a sensibility in black American writing that I liked a lot, which was attention to the underdog, attention to a negative history, a history that was not about being on the Mayflower, and it wasn't about being the best and being the brightest and being the richest and winning all the wars. It was really about trying to carve your own identity from a past that has a lot of negative stuff attached to it. . . . [W]hereas America, as a nationalist identity, what is it? It's about money. There isn't anything else.

Jodie Foster, in Gerstel 1991

If feminist theory or women's studies as an academic enterprise can be both commodified and radical, what of the new women's fiction that addresses itself to an audience influenced by feminism? There are many such books to choose from, since publishers in the English-speaking world have targeted a sizeable audience eager for writing by and about women. We shall focus here on examples from two categories of fiction that seem to us to have generated some of the most interesting debates among readers – feminist detective novels and novels by women of color. The examples we have chosen can easily be used to intervene in contemporary debates about the politics of gender and race, and they package those issues in eminently consumable ways. What are some of the political effects of such a combination of textual coordinates? What strategies of reading might a materialist feminist approach to such texts produce?

Watching the Detectives

During the 1980s a cluster of new detective novels by women writers actively engaged in feminist debate appeared, and now the genre gives every indication of expanding into other forms of popular culture, beginning with film. Sara Paretsky's V. I. Warshawski has made an appearance, so to speak, in an eponymous film starring Kathleen Turner. Perhaps Sue Grafton's Kinsey Millhone, Katherine V. Forrest's Kate Delafield, and Sarah Caudwell's Hilary Tamar will eventually follow suit. There might be a problem with the transposition of Hilary Tamar from print to film, however; the gender of this character remains tantalizingly ambiguous throughout Caudwell's novels, a textual strategy with which Hollywood cinema might have trouble dealing. And, despite the relative success of the film *Desert Hearts* in representing lesbian relationships acceptably for a mainstream audience, Hollywood is probably not ready for Kate Delafield's lesbianism. Then, too, Kinsey Millhone, at least until recently, inhabited a garage, perhaps the smallest single-person dwelling unit in Santa Teresa, California, and she lives too abstemiously to be a full member of shopping-mall consumer culture. Hollywood may not be ready for that kind of moralism. V. I.'s tough-talking feminism, complicated by a familiarizing reliance on urban creature comforts and a liking for fast cars, in a sense represents the most populist and reassuringly mainstream stance of the group.

Clearly, however commodified, the feminism of these detective novels is far from homogeneous. Indeed, the kind of feminist you are might well be revealed by whether you prefer Paretsky or Grafton or Forrest. And although the British detective novel could be said to have been dominated by women writers this century – Agatha Christie, Dorothy Sayers, Ruth Rendell, P. D. James – Paretsky, Grafton, and Forrest are all American writers arguably more directly inspired by the *film noir* crime fiction of Raymond Chandler, Dashiell Hammett, and Elmore Leonard than by the British *grandes dames* of detection.

An Unsuitable Job? P. D. James

A possible predecessor for Warshawski, Delafield, and Millhone might, however, be found in P. D. James's Cordelia Gray, female counterweight to her better-known poet-cop Adam Dalgleish. In *An Unsuitable Job for a Woman* (1972) James established a Cordelia who inherited through apprenticeship a small business as a private investigator, rather like inheriting the genre of the crime novel, and had to feminize it, which meant being unsure all the time if she were up to the job, rather like commenting implicitly on the generic innovations necessary for Cordelia to succeed in the business of a dirty male genre. If Cordelia's name echoes *King Lear*'s apparently most disobedient but actually most loyal daughter, her relation to solving crimes and bringing criminals to justice is similarly unconventional, yet conventional. She disobeys the fathers and transgresses rather than upholds the law, but in the name of principles – truth, personal liberty, the rational tolerance of differences – that the law ostensibly endorses. James's narration is rather coy about whether or not gun-toting private investigation *is* a suitable job for a woman; other characters keep harping on the phrase whenever they meet Cordelia. And Cordelia succeeds in solving her murder, toppling a patriarch, and helping another woman right patriarchal wrongs – up to a point. But she does it largely through a combination of intuition, imaginative empathy with her murdered victim, a fondness for him amounting almost to erotically tinged obsession, and the fortuitous usefulness of a leather belt which had belonged to him and which magically transforms Cordelia's femininity into strength, since wearing it helps her extricate herself from otherwise lethal situations.

James's position on early 1970s feminism, on questions of equal job opportunities for women or women living independently of men, like her position on the opportunities for upward social mobility offered the working class by a booming economy and the welfare state (in fact mainly represented in the text by impoverished members of the lower-middle classes like Cordelia), seems ambivalent but optimistic. There is a pastoral tranquility and beauty to the drop-out's simple-life-lived-in-a-borrowed-cottage, on the outskirts of early 1970s, effetely upper-middle-class Cambridge, to which Cordelia, though an outsider by class, gender, and profession, gains exhilarating access.

Yet James's later novels give us less utopian, more directly Thatcherite heroines, like Inspector Kate Miskin in *A Taste for Death* (1986), who has fought her way out of a tower block, out of a poverty-stricken community of immigrants, and into middle-class feminist independence and comfort through joining the police. A feminist who enforces the Father's Law through a repressive state apparatus? Who sees her achievement of upward mobility as an individual matter of intelligence, industry, and merit, a reward well deserved, and not as a political wedge for altering structures of class privilege and chronic economic deprivation? That is the sort of Thatcherite compromise we will not find the US feminist detective writers harboring in the decade of Reagan and Bush.

A Girl's Gotta Make a Living Somehow! Sara Paretsky and Sue Grafton

A superficial description of each could make Sara Paretsky's V. I. Warshawski and Sue Grafton's Kinsey Millhone sound like similar sorts of feminist heroine, but the reception of these writers has sparked controversy in feminist communities in both the US and the UK. How might a different politics be operative in Paretsky and Grafton, when both seem to be writing for an expressly feminist audience, largely white but sympathetic to minorities, lower-class identified and left-leaning, Democratic rather than Republican, empathizing with the underdog and supportive of social services? As women, both Kinsey and V. I. are fiercely independent and vehemently critical of patriarchal privilege, social snobbery, and the brutal effects of laissez-faire Reaganomics, by which unemployment, ecological disaster, and deindustrialization flourish, the rich get richer, and the poor live in hopeless destitution, having fallen through the skimpiest imaginable safety net of social services – homeless, healthcare-less, food-stampless.

It would be hard to judge just how representative these sentiments are of mainstream political causes in the US today, in spite of the recent election of a Democratic president, Bill Clinton. After all, in the 1988 presidential election the triumphant Republican candidate, George Bush, could accuse his Democratic opponent, Michael Dukakis, of being a card-carrying member of the American Civil Liberties Union, as if liberalism were a dangerously subversive left-wing political platform, and be applauded for it. As we prepare this book for the press during the second month of the new administration (February 1993), it remains unclear how successful Clinton and his appointees will be in implementing liberal policies. What is clear is how strong the social and economic constraints on any such program will be. In such a climate, why should Paretsky's and Grafton's books be so commercially successful, and how can they be said to have packaged *different* feminisms when they sound so similar?

Reading publics are diverse; youth cultures and countercultural groups are more into media than into voting. There would seem to be a difference between what people think they can expect from the political choices provided by a presidential election and the ideas they are prepared to entertain in the books they read. The relative success of these novels suggests that the America of the 1990s may not be, after so many years of the Reagan and Bush administrations, as monolithically neo-conservative as we might have been inclined to think. And, although a female presidential candidate in the near future seems unlikely, and reproductive rights continue to be under siege from rightwing groups, and many young women are suspicious of feminism or at least of being labeled feminists, there is something between the covers of Paretsky and Grafton to which many women and men respond enthusiastically, and which might have been palely reflected in the recent shift of partisan sympathies.

The work of commodification, we remember, involves unlimited divisibility, homogeneity of the parts, uniform quality, durability, and the privatized labor of the producers. The detective novel as one in a series, featuring a particular private eye, a distinctive setting, and a familiar cluster of characters, fulfills in terms of the print artifact some of these criteria. It becomes a perpetual source of renewable pleasures, as does the romance, the serial western, the science fiction trilogy, etc. What is distinctive about the detective novel is the way it structures a narrative around an enigma, as arguably all narrative does, but the murder mystery or novel of detection makes that structure directly visible through the detective as the subject of the narration (see Belsey 1980: 109–17).

In the case of successful detection, the pleasure to be derived from the text is that of a comforting restoration of rational control over otherwise intractably hostile forces. So long as the detective is a woman, exercising her independence in the name of justice, whether inside or outside the apparatus of the law, there is a particularly exhilarating payoff for an audience sympathetic to feminism if she succeeds in exercising individual agency in this way. What the detective genre supplies in the packaging of feminism as a homogeneous and palatable commodity is a powerful investment in the female detective's individual agency: control over her own body, her choices in living arrangements, affectional ties, consumer goods – a whole politics of lifestyle – and control over the social enigmas she decodes and the crimes and corruption in which she intervenes.

Both V. I. Warshawski and Kinsey Millhone manifest this individual agency as private investigators. This marks a difference between them and Kate Delafield, Katherine V. Forrest's lesbian cop, a difference to which we shall return. V. I., daughter of a cop, ex-wife of a successful corporate lawyer, was formerly a lawyer in the public defender's office in Chicago; Kinsey was formerly a Santa Teresa cop; both could be described as having what Kinsey refers to in *"D" is for Deadbeat* as "a constitutional inability to work for anyone else" (Grafton 1988: 1). Both do a lot of investigations for insurance companies, and both have complex relations with the local police, a force both have in some sense broken with, though both acknowledge they owe the police, as father figure or certifying agency or potential help in a tight spot, a certain qualified respect. As women and feminists, they have to take the law into their own hands, so to speak; neither is very sanguine about justice being done through official channels.

Why a feminist reader might favor V. I. or Kinsey seems a matter of tone and atmosphere, of relative optimism about change, including changing relations between men and women. Part of the difference is surely Chicago versus Santa Teresa, teeming metropolis of competing ethnicities and long-established political in-fighting versus southern California pastoral, where the climate is kind even to those without money and around the next curve of the beach could be the romance you are waiting for.

Paretsky's Chicago is a scene of post-industrial wastelands, corporate corruption, pretentious moneyed consumption, and thousands of people, forgotten by trickle-down economic thinking, just making do. There is little reason for optimism about any wide-sweeping political or social changes, just strategies for survival and for keeping the most shameless villains at bay. V. I. is an urban populist who takes on political tycoons and corporate magnates like the courtly, Old World, ruthless Gustav Humboldt in *Blood Shot*, published in Britain as *Toxic Shock* (1988). An enigmatic force behind the scenes of corporate capital, Humboldt embodies patriarchal privilege at its most unmediated. A chapter parodically titled "Humboldt's Gift," echoing the title of a novel by Chicago's best-known novelist and upholder of patriarchal privilege, Saul Bellow, could be read as equating V. I.'s interventions in corporate business-as-usual and Paretsky's interventions in novelistic business-as-usual. Both are scenes of compromise, in which there is no room for moral purity and little for piety.

Though V. I. is committed to fighting for justice for women, ethnic minorities, and the working class – she hasn't forgotten her South Side, Chicago roots – she does battle in expensive clothes, depends on restaurants for her survival, drinks pricey Scotch, and allows herself to be mothered by a Viennese doctor, Lotty Herschel. Lotty's charming, Old World, imperial and imperious manner represents everything the South Side lacks in terms of sophistication and comfort and yet serves as the perfect politically progressive foil to a Humboldt's Old World empire-building.

Families may be in disarray, but the idea of the family, or what

Barrett and McIntosh (1991: 21–42) call familial ideology, still seems necessary for survival within this culture of displaced identities. V. I.'s independence is limited by her dependence on a kind of surrogate family, composed of Lotty and a neighbor, Mr Contreras, a retired machinist always ready to defend V. I. with a pipe wrench or nurture her by cooking her a steak or pasta. There is an uneasy comedy surrounding Mr Contreras, a parody of the industrial working-class hero now retired, narratively rendered obsolescent so that V. I. can take center stage. V. I. is thus caught between her populist loyalties to her Polish-Italian background, supported by her left-leaning Democratic principles, and her impatience with so much of American working-class culture in which neither feminism nor other progressive movements, let alone sophisticated aesthetic pleasures, have yet found much place. When business-as-usual in Chicago means routine corruption, even a radical politics is likely to be compromised, as happens with the Hispanic feminist candidate Roz Fuentes in *Burn Marks* (1990).

If the good guys and the bad guys grow to mirror one another in troubling ways politically, V. I.'s relationships with men are equally vexed. She doesn't put too much stock in romance, though she likes sex. Unfortunately, pleasurable sex often leads to unforeseen complications, such as getting into bed unknowingly with the very objects of her investigations, as happens in *Bitter Medicine* (1987) and *Burn Marks*. You can't trust men these days, even the sympathetic ones, any more than you can trust politicians or corporate capitalists. If you want to have any fun in the straight world, you have to give them a chance, but be prepared to feel a fool when they turn out to be treacherous. As Paretsky's series develops, V. I. increasingly enters relationships with men tentatively, skeptically, almost but not quite pessimistically. Her Chicago is a place where love, friendship, and loyalty count for more than romance or heterosexual passion, which are never denigrated but rarely allowed to appear – nice work if you can get them.

Kinsey Millhone's Santa Teresa may be seedy and down-at-heel, except for the rich folks' estates up on the bluffs, but it is still California, land of opportunity where anything can happen. People in these novels often live in beach motels and trailer parks, and Kinsey herself inhabits a garage apartment attached to the house of a benevolent, elderly, vaguely upper-middle-class landlord who bakes extravagant confections. As a product of trailer parks herself, she is attracted by Henry Pitts's classiness and sometimes regrets the age difference between them. She could almost allow herself to fall for him in spite of it. This is a far cry from Mr Contreras's irritating and risible attempts to be father, mother, and romantic champion to V. I. And, instead of admirable but intimidating Lotty, Kinsey has Rosie, a scrappy, shrewd Hungarian who runs a neighborhood bar at which Kinsey eats most of her meals.

There is no familial friction in these relationships, there are no affective ties that bind Kinsey in the old familial ways. She lives very much alone, a woman waiting for the next exciting adventure to materialize. Twice married and divorced to V. I.'s once, since people in California get married and divorced more often than other people, Kinsey appears ready to eroticize any prospective encounter. Unlike V. I., she doesn't seem to have attracted a surrogate family so much as an assortment of potential objects of desire – the children of wealthy families she knew at school, young people looking for excitement and likely to settle for drugs and casual sex, get-rich-quick artistes of various sorts, characters who embody an uneasy fit between the myth of the American melting pot and deeply felt racial and ethnic antagonisms, beautifully groomed women of all ages, and a succession of sexually desirable men who make her heart beat faster, though she may end up shooting them, as in *"A" is for Alibi* (1982).

Kinsey lives very simply and cheaply, narrowing her wants to a fanatical abstemiousness at odds with the Californian consumer culture around her. Unlike V. I., she is hardly ever out of jeans and a T-shirt. Dressing for a Montebello cocktail party might mean resurrecting a tunic and high heels from the back seat of her car. And she stakes her integrity as an investigator on this higher moral ground: "I pay my bills on time, obey most laws, and I feel that other people should do likewise . . . out of courtesy, if nothing else. I'm a purist when it comes to justice, but I'll lie at the drop of a hat" (*"D" is for Deadbeat*: Grafton 1988: 1–2). Her bare bones of necessity-style solitude and moral earnestness make her vulnerable to temptation when new forms of pleasure arise that also promise security. Even a passionate sexual encounter might be represented in terms like these:

> We lay there afterward, laughing and sweaty and out of breath and then he encompassed me in sleep, the weight of his big arms pinning me to the bed. But far from feeling trapped, I felt comforted and safe, as though nothing could ever harm me as long as I stayed in the shadow of this man, this sheltering cave of flesh, where I was tucked away until morning without waking once. (*"A" is for Alibi*: Grafton 1987: 148–9)

This is the language of the mass-market romance offering temporary escape from the responsibility of individual female agency.

This dream of heterosexual ecstasy as safety and security is the dream Kinsey pursues, in spite of all evidence to the contrary, and in spite of her undoubted self-reliance. As she would say, "Inconsistency has never troubled me" (*"D" is for Deadbeat*: Grafton 1988: 2). Having escaped both family and familial ideology, she finds herself vulnerable when it comes to the ideology of romance. Does her name echo the famous Kinsey report on American sexuality? In the course of serial monogamy, there will always be a next time, and things just might work out if you stick to your principles and keep purifying your own personal space. She's a Californian and can't help it.

Where does your feminism tell you the action is these days – in political spaces best represented by post-industrial Midwestern cities or by suburban southern California? Which is more recuperable or more difficult to shift, the ideology of the family or the ideology of heterosexual romance? How optimistic ought we to be about political and social change? There is a luminous pastoral quality to Kinsey's adventures that recalls the P. D. James of *An Unsuitable Job for a Woman*, a later-1980s optimism about change. V. I.'s world is more charged with cynicism. Sometimes her only defense against the unspeakably corrupt is a wisecrack, a witty remark in exchange for a body blow. A wisecracking populism buttressed by a new definition of familial affections, or a celebration of singularity in search of newer, safer forms of romance: these are the alternatives offered by Paretsky and Grafton's fictions.

Perhaps a further turn towards romantic fantasy-fulfillment with a certain rightward twist can be detected in Grafton's *"G" is for Gumshoe* (1990), a national bestseller. After the demise of her garage apartment in the previous novel, Kinsey is rewarded by her landlord Henry Pitts with a yuppie fantasy-space, a new apartment with loft bedroom and skylights, fitted out like a small yacht. She also indulges in some very unreconstructed suburban white-girl thoughts about people who work in Mexican restaurants and has a hot time with a hard-muscled guy who goes off to make films for improving the security of US military bases abroad by staging enemy-commando infiltrations. Are the turn and the twist related to the national commercial success? Only time, and subsequent novels by Grafton, will tell.

Some Versions of Sexual Difference: Katherine V. Forrest and
Sarah Caudwell

When we leave heterosexual feminism behind for the gay world of
love and ritual in Katherine V. Forrest's novels about Kate Delafield,
the political stakes shift once again. Kate is a Los Angeles cop. If
lesbianism signifies sexual outlawry in a heterosexist society, then
perhaps Kate needs to be on the side of the law so as not to challenge
too many forms of authority all at once. After all, some civil rights
legislation does exist in the US to protect homosexuality, in spite of
many states' oppressive sodomy laws. Changing the law and enforcing the protection of gay rights through the state apparatus is an
important survival strategy for minorities in America, including the
gay community.

As if reluctant to take on too much at once and thus risk losing
everything, Kate is less personally flamboyant than either Kinsey or
V. I. She keeps a low profile, lives in a world of diminished expectations, and takes her erotic pleasures when she can, usually with
mixed results. Including at least one passionate lesbian sex scene is
part of Forrest's modus operandi in each of her novels. In this respect
she shifts generic expectations more dramatically than either Paretsky
or Grafton. There is a consciously polemical edge to her fiction that
has contributed to its achieving a certain cult status in the lesbian
communities of the US and UK. No matter how sordid the crime
or how brutal the violence against which Kate must struggle, the
novels create new spaces for lesbian pleasure and for the celebration
of a racially and ethnically diverse gay community which will one
day be able to abandon the closet altogether. Watching the 1985
Gay Pride parade in West Hollywood at the end of *Murder at the
Nightwood Bar* (1987), Kate is overcome by politically celebratory
emotion: "She remained standing and watching, looking down Santa
Monica. As far as her tear-blinded eyes could see there were thousands of gay people. Thousands and thousands" (Forrest 1987: 220).
Thus the novel, after examining some of the seamier sides of life in
Los Angeles – incest and domestic violence – closes on a note of
epiphany achieved through political solidarity.

In terms of a politics in which traditional identities founded on
essentialist notions of gender, class, sexuality, and race or ethnicity
are put in question, Paretsky, Grafton, and Forrest have produced
texts whose liberal progressive effects would be hard to deny. Oddly
enough, though their feminism comes through loud and clear, and

all three address class and racial prejudices as well as gender ideology, Grafton and Paretsky are less bold when it comes to questioning contemporary notions of gender and sexuality than one might expect. Both construct a fundamentally straight world in which the definition of one's identity as a gendered and sexed person as such is not at stake. Forrest represents the gay community as a crucial alternative to heterosexual practice, but her characters have definite sexual identities; they *are* either men or women, and either gay or straight, quite unproblematically.

In this respect, Sarah Caudwell's whimsical fictions about an Oxford don, Hilary Tamar, whose gender is never specified and whose sexuality seems non-existent, might be said to be more thought-provoking. In a Foucauldian sense (see chapter 8), Hilary's identity is not founded on any sexual truth. For the reader saturated in gender ideology, the question arises again and again – is Hilary a man or a woman? But the texts resolutely refuse to answer to this interrogation even as they excite it. In plots which turn on the escapades of young London barristers who share chambers and each other's every move on the romantic as well as professional fronts, Caudwell explores multiple possibilities of relationship along a spectrum of eroticism and sexual involvement in which gender and sexuality seem mobile, volatile; indeed they can even seem detachable from one another.

A group of friends and colleagues can come to seem more indispensable than any lover, the endlessly renewable conversation in the wine bar more charged with affect than any tryst. Much of the textual play with these ideas happens at the level of suggestion and nuance, just as the plots frequently resolve themselves according to textual cruxes, and are frequently presented in specific textual forms such as lengthy letters posted or faxed to London from the scene of the adventure. Nothing is very explicit apart from some heterosexual couplings, some not-quite-lesbian encounters, Julia Larwood's desire to seduce beautiful young men, most central in *Thus Was Adonis Murdered* (1981), and her tendency to end up in compromising situations wearing only "a small quantity of black underwear," as in *The Shortest Way to Hades* (1984) (Caudwell 1986: 102).

What we could call some Foucauldian or anti-essentialist moves with the concepts of gender and sexuality are, however, arguably made possible by the rather self-enclosed legal and professional atmosphere of Caudwell's fiction. Caudwell's characters traverse the spaces of privilege wittily and enthusiastically because they have been reared to do so. Is it perhaps the case that the whiteness and upper-middle-classness of Caudwell's world ensures a certain ground of experimentation in terms of sexuality and gender?

Feminist Detection in the Marketplace: Anca Vlasopolos and Meg O'Brien

In terms of the commodification of feminist ideas, the status of a cult novelist published by a small press is significantly different from the status of bestselling novelists published by mass-market houses. Katherine V. Forrest is published by the Naiad Press of Tallahassee, Florida, a press well-known for its lesbian publications, including the incomparably comic detective spoof by Sarah Schulman, *The Sophie Horowitz Story* (1984). Which is more disruptive in the literary marketplace, the sexual ambiguity of Caudwell's narratives or Forrest's forthright lesbianism?

There is considerable evidence that the inescapable gayness of Kate Delafield's adventures is likely to be more challenging to most readers in this historical moment, despite the reassuring solidity of her characters as subjects and identities. It would be difficult to find a more globally mainstream publisher than Penguin, who publish Caudwell. Class certainties seem capable of legitimating a number of other narrative innovations by seeming to defuse their radical potential. We could argue that, in terms of packaging detective novels as commodities for the market, the small press status of Forrest's books makes her work *de facto* less commodified than the work of the other writers we have been analyzing. We could also argue that, as we move further from mainstream publishing, the effects of commodification seem rather less totalizing, the possibilities for radical social criticism much greater.

Let's take the case of a feminist detective novel that made the rounds of mainstream publishers but was rejected for being too controversial. No problem with the writing, not even much problem with the politics, which includes an interracial friendship and almost-love affair between a white Detroit sex-crimes cop, Sharon Dair, and her black partner, Robert McNeely, who also happens to be married (to a black woman). Even Sharon's countercultural and artistic friends, including a lesbian couple, seem not to have been at issue. The sticking point in Anca Vlasopolos's *Missing Members*, eventually published by the small Corridors Press in Detroit in 1990, was the kind of crime in which the featured serial killer indulges – lethal castration of a series of men in motel rooms around the city, all of whom seem to have been seeking the services of a prostitute and not got quite what they desired. Too bloody, too graphic, too revolting, Vlasopolos was told. And yet the novel's treatment of these scenes of crime is visually restrained, the opposite of "graphic." It seems rather that it was the *idea* of male castration in itself that struck publishers' readers as too bloody and revolting.

Here we are up against some of the oldest prejudices feminism has had to face. Violence against women, including rape and genital mutilation, are standard fare in crime fiction, but castrated men are beyond the pale. In this respect, Vlasopolos's title is doubly irreverent: "missing members" not only puns on genitals murderously removed but suggests that the male victims have gone missing from the men's club, the patriarchal enclave, from which their social power stems. *Missing Members* thus suffers from confirming, at the level of metaphor and symbol, anti-feminist men's worst fears about feminism as a female conspiracy to emasculate and kill off men. The fact that the text also registers a consistently arch awareness of this possibility, playing ironically with such male fears, apparently escaped those publishers' readers who found it offensive.

We could usefully contrast these non-mainstream qualities of Vlasopolos's feminist detective novel with those of a recent series by Meg O'Brien that seems aimed at capitalizing on the Paretsky/Grafton market while simultaneously abandoning feminism for a postfeminist stance. O'Brien's heroine, Jessica (Jesse) James, is an investigative reporter in Rochester, New York, who, far from representing any form of women's movement, just wants to be one of the boys. We might have been able to predict this tendency from her nickname, with its echo of Wild West outlawry and male bonding – Jesse James and the notorious James Gang. Hard-drinking, wisecracking, jeans-wearing, and avidly heterosexual – especially where men's musculature, the worked-out look of flat stomachs and nice, tight buttocks is concerned – Jesse worships men and chafes against gender difference, from the dress code at one of the papers she works for to her small size and inability to drink without becoming a drunk and continually having to go on the wagon. Taking after her drunken father while dealing obsessively with guilt over his death, Jesse is a Daddy's girl *par excellence*. She goes through the world looking not so much for sex or romance, though she remains interested in them, as for male esteem – for confirmation of her identity as a worthy bondee in the drama of male bonding in which she so strongly desires to participate.

Might it be the case that when detective fiction by a woman, featuring a female detective, is designed for a Paretsky- and Grafton-inspired, so-called feminist market these days it emerges fully commodified from its mainstream publisher? Both of O'Brien's novels appeared in 1990 from Bantam, who also publish Grafton – *The Daphne Decisions* in March and *Salmon in the Soup* in September – and both came labeled as already part of a series, each "a Jessica James mystery." Jesse has all the rebellious trademarks of an independent single woman like V. I. and Kinsey, but in O'Brien's narratives the feminism of Paretsky and Grafton has been replaced by what we would describe as a populist, anti-corruption-in-high-places, but postfeminist stance.

In O'Brien's world, it seems as if all the battles of feminism as a social movement have been fought already, and Jesse's struggle with femininity and independence is a result of her own pathology, her own particular psychic and social history. From tomboy and juvenile delinquent – just one of the guys – to rebellious reporter uncovering real estate fraud and kiddie porn rackets, Jesse is torn between twin male poles of justice, one within and one outside the law. As the projected series develops, where will the female outlaw tend, towards straight-arrow cop Grady North or towards the new-style, anti-violence mobster Marcus Andrelli? The choice of men, the choice of outlawry versus the law, the choice of investigative reporting or of working for the mob, these are all choices in which the gender politics has been decided in advance, in spite of all the quasi-feminist wisecracking and irreverence Jesse can muster, as when she calls in "well" to avoid showing up at her newspaper desk, in *Salmon in the Soup* (1990b: 1, 9). Oddly, these books unfold as if the feminist battle had already been both won and abandoned. Jesse can keep aspiring to honorary masculinity and suffering for her sexual difference, and nothing about social relations between men and women looks likely to change much.

If the Jesse James novels can be read in these terms as postfeminist, at once seeming to render feminism so old hat that it might never have happened and confirming patriarchal business-as-usual, the same could be said of their attitude towards race. Jesse is white, as are most of the other characters in the novels, except for the Genesee Three, Rack Jack, Abe Denton, and Percy Green, black teenagers with police records and families to support, who more or less control Jesse's neighborhood. They came to her aid once when she was mugged and have remained loyal since, helping her pull off assorted illegal operations, no questions asked, saying only " 'You're our main lady' " (*The Daphne Decisions* 1990a: 21). What's a white girl to do, except take advantage of such opportunities for hanging out with the most seriously cool crowd in town? So Jesse gets to be one of the guys again, with these guys, and there's never a black woman in sight. She's *their* "main lady," after all, a kind of tournament queen for whose sake they joust with the law. And they appear in the narrative only as Jesse's protection, not as characters with complex lives lived and leading elsewhere.

Unlike, say, V. I.'s, or Kate Delafield's, or Sharon Dair's friends and acquaintances who are people of color, the Genesee Three only appear at Jesse's convenience. They accept her as one of their own, with that little difference chivalry makes in a gender-conscious world. Does this mean that racial differences and racism have disappeared? O'Brien's narratives of female empowerment depend explicitly on this kind of wish-fulfillment, packaged as if it were unquestionably realistic, the ways things are. Her two novels smooth over precisely those social contradictions and political anxieties which her predecessors in the genre of feminist detective fiction have been at such pains to explore.

Once again, we could argue that, in terms of packaging detective novels as commodities for the market, the small press status of Forrest's books or Vlasopolos's book makes their work *de facto* less commodified than the work of the other writers we have been discussing. We could also argue that the deeper into the big business of mass-market paperbacks we get, the more anything like feminist activism or anti-racism as a social movement, rather than simply a matter of individual choice, tends to disappear.

US Women of Color and the Politics of Textuality

Such generalizations are challenged, however, by the phenomenon of highly successful, critically acclaimed, and widely read novels by women of color in the US. As Hortense Spillers has observed, "the community of black women writing in the United States now can be regarded as a vivid new fact of national life" (Spillers 1985: 249). We shall see in chapter 9 how Spillers is able to use Toni Morrison's *Sula* to argue for a radically African-American and feminist break from patriarchal Judaeo-Christian historiography. What happens when we turn to commercially successful novels like Octavia Butler's *Kindred* (1979) and Gloria Naylor's *Mama Day* (1988), in which questions of gender and race are addressed by black women writers, using genres other than the detective novel, though mysteries and enigmas lurk at the heart of each narrative?

More experimental in terms of form than the detective novels we have been examining, Butler's and Naylor's texts seem particularly well suited to a materialist feminist reading. Both are preoccupied by a notion of history, of how to excavate a few layers of the past in order to determine which of that past's effects might be most susceptible of or resistant to change. We could apply Cherríe Moraga's description of a certain kind of materialism, which she located in writings by radical women of color, to the governing strategy of these novels:

> The materialism in this book lives in the flesh of these women's lives. . . .
> Our strategy is how we cope – how we measure and weigh what is to be said and when, what is to be done and how, and to whom and to whom and to whom, daily deciding/risking who it is we can call an ally, call a friend (whatever that person's skin, sex, or sexuality). We are women without a line. (Moraga 1983b: xviii–xix).

The individual agency of the feminist detective offers too narrow a political scope for these writers. As women of color, accustomed to being politically subjected according to their racial and ethnic identities in addition to their gender, they understand all too well the importance of thinking and acting collectively, not individually.

History As the Ties that Bind: Octavia Butler

Other genres make a collective re-imagining of history and future possibility more thinkable than the detective novel. For Octavia Butler in *Kindred* the solution is science-fiction-style fantasy "without the science," combined with historical reconstruction of life under slavery in the antebellum American south. Butler has rejected the label of science fiction for *Kindred* because there is "absolutely no science in it" (Beal 1986: 14). Naylor returns the novel to its origins in epic and national myth by rewriting a few layers of African-American history in the light of feminist questions about power, gender, race, and sex. Both texts tackle head on the notion that the fictions we carry with us help overdetermine our subjectivity and how we will be subjugated as well as subjected, called into being as subjects within a misogynist and racially oppressive culture.

Kindred problematizes the notions of kin, family, and the ideology of race in a particularly spectacular way. Concepts that operate as metaphors in everyday speech become literalized so that their material reality must be confronted. A young black woman in Los Angeles, an aspiring writer, married to a young white man who is also a writer, finds herself catapulted into nineteenth-century Maryland, into a series of episodes from her family history during slavery. Her experience of telekinesis and chronoportation is not at all investigated by the text; Dana simply disappears from 1976 Los Angeles through a swooning nausea and re-emerges in 1810, and later in subsequent years, always when a white man named Rufus Weylin, a slaveowner who turns out to be one of her ancestors, is in danger. Dana tries to educate Rufus in progressive ways; she also learns how easy it is to slip into a slave's mentality within that peculiar institution, the effects of which are still all too apparent in American society.

What the novel's time travel literalizes is how the past never really vanishes; we are always already marked by our histories. On her last visit to Rufus, Dana is nearly raped by him and she escapes only by stabbing him and leaving her left arm behind in his grip when the telekinesis begins again. Thus does the live hand of the past leave its literal mark on the bodies of the living. Thus does slavery leave its mark. Dana learns a new meaning of "kindred," in addition to the feeling of "kindred spirits" she has with Kevin, in spite of his whiteness (Butler 1988: 57), and in addition to the notion of "kin" as genealogy, family history. She learns to live through, to go beyond the "dread" of discovering her own racial past within the history of slavery, to go beyond dreading to discover that hers is a history of complicity as well as rebellion, that her kin were white slaveowners as well as black slaves, and that the nexus of this relation is the body of the female slave.

There is an uneasy tension in the text over Rufus's attempted rape of Dana; it seems almost gratuitous, almost trite. Does Butler end up essentializing the female body, making rape the final ground of battle between men and women, whites and blacks, since Dana's last stand, her final rebellion, is a gesture of self-defense against rape? And, if so, what might this signify? Could it be a case of strategic essentialism rather than a limit to the text's capacity for ideology critique? There is much historical evidence to support the centrality of the body of the female slave in the slaveowning, racist imaginary. If Dana's body as object of Rufus's desire to punish and control seems stereotypical and reductive, that doesn't mean that such stereotypes are not powerfully with us still, or that employing them might not have a critical rather than an essentializing function.

Rather than reading this attempted rape as a falling back upon an essentialized female body the previous text has done so much to question, we might see how some attention to the historical context of interracial rape within slavery could alter this reading. As Valerie Smith has observed, some of the most fruitful ground for critique of assumptions about race and gender occurs in what she, following Mary Poovey, calls "border cases," of which interracial rape is a prime instance: " 'Border cases' are precisely those issues that problematize easy assumptions about racial and/or sexual difference, particularly insofar as they demonstrate the interactions between race and gender" (Smith 1990: 272). Smith argues that interracial rape "can never be read solely as an offense against women's bodies. It is always represented and understood within the context of a variety of public issues, among them race, imperialism, and the law" (1990: 274).

So, rather than seeing Dana's resistance to Rufus's forcing himself on her as a return to an ideology in which simple violence against women is the final ground of feminism, and a woman's body the final ground of her individual integrity – both essentialist assumptions common to liberalism – we might read the scene as a nexus of ideologies about race, imperialism, and the law in which the traditionally most socially powerless victim, the black female slave, succeeds in defending herself, in striking back against the past and the legacy of slavery, though at the expense of her bodily integrity, as it were; she loses an arm. "You give them a hand, they'll take your arm," the adage goes. Dana has rescued Rufus again and again, given him a hand to save his life and to work against the prejudices with which he has been saturated. No resistance is free, the text suggests, neither free of complicity nor of the price of pain.

To this reading we might also add Hortense Spillers's arguments about the construction of African-American subjectivity within slavery, in particular its de-genderedness when viewed alongside nineteenth-century white subjectivity, with its imperial and patriarchal notions of masculinity and its cult of domesticity and true womanhood, all of which were denied slaves by a process of deracination and commodification. For chattel slaves are property. Slave women produce property, produce capital for their owners. Children born into slavery are given their mother's, not their father's name, but their mother has no legal entitlement to them, no "mother right." As property, slaves grow up without any necessary relation to kinship systems or their accompanying affective ties. And the market in slaves remains crucial to the perpetuation of slavery; biological reproduction within slavery is not sufficient to secure its continuance. Spillers argues that, to the extent that the slave market overrides notions both of femininity and of motherhood held to be natural in other social spaces,

> To that extent, the captive female body locates precisely a moment of converging political and social vectors that mark the flesh as a prime commodity of exchange. While this proposition is open to further exploration, suffice it to say now that this open exchange of female bodies in the raw offers a kind of Ur-text to the dynamics of signification and representation that the gendered female would unravel. (Spillers 1987b: 75)

So saturated by ideologies of gender are we, it is difficult to comprehend this Ur-text. Dana herself has difficulty comprehending it. She cannot quite believe that Rufus can see her as property-in-the-flesh, his property, in this way. If we bring to bear upon the novel this history of commodification within slavery, the attempted rape is far from simple, though it may still read as narratively gratuitous. The very awkwardness of the scene and its faintly embarrassing quality themselves testify to its critical function as a border case in which ideologies of gender and race intersect disturbingly, problematically, in the contexts of imperialism and the law.

History as Woman Power: Gloria Naylor

A comparable form of border-casing occurs in Gloria Naylor's novel *Mama Day*. Naylor explores the novel's epic and mythological roots by mixing rhetorical modes and narrative voices while superimposing some speculations on the history of slavery in the southern community of Willow Springs upon a contemporary urban romance between Cocoa, a light-skinned girl born in Willow Springs, and George, a darker-skinned New Yorker. The enigmas to be understood operate on at least three historical levels: (a) What happened in Willow Springs in 1823 between the black slave Sapphira and her white owner Bascombe Wade in such a way that Sapphira's descendants inherited the island? (b) What kind of power/knowledge could a slave woman have that might be inherited by her daughters and granddaughters, including Cocoa's great-aunt Miranda (Mama Day), and possibly Cocoa herself? (c) What kind of feminist relationships are possible today given contemporary intersections of racial and gender ideologies, and how might the past offer some resources of women's power and knowledge difficult for modern feminists to comprehend?

Mama Day is both a brilliant examination of how romantic ideology works its way through contemporary relationships among urban black people in the racist, sexist US context and an attempt to provide an empowering new mythology about what certain slaves made of a history lived within an oppressive institution not of their own making. The contrast between the cultures of New York and Willow Springs is dazzling and instructive at the level of the narration itself, so that the text gives each culture linguistically its distinctive material reality. When Cocoa and George narrate the delicate negotiation of their sexual attraction and eventual marriage, they do so within a context of racial and other social and political issues. When George uses an elaborately romantic ploy for asking her out to dinner, Cocoa thinks, "Now, what kind of fudge stick asked a woman out like this – who's this guy used to dating, Mary Tyler Moore?" (Naylor 1989: 58). As readers we may find ourselves wondering about Cocoa's lexicon of food-names for racial and ethnic differences, only to hear George call her on it directly, "why are people food to you?": "that's what you've been saying most of the evening – fudge sticks, kumquats, bagels, zucchinis. You just called Herman Badillo a taco. Number one, it's ignorant because tacos aren't from Puerto Rico, and number two, your whole litany has turned the people in this city into material for a garbage disposal" (1989: 62). With difficulty, Cocoa answers that she is scared of New York, where there are more people living on her block than on the whole island of Willow Springs, and where, unlike Willow Springs with its pastoral change-lessness, nothing stays the same:

> Because just when you think you've gotten a handle on it, there's a new next-door neighbor or the Laundromat at the corner becomes a hole in the ground and the next year it's a high rise with even more people for you not to know. A whole kaleidoscope of people – nothing's just black and white here like in Willow Springs. Nothing stays put. So I guess the way I talk is my way of coming to terms with never knowing what to expect from anything or anybody. I'm not a bigot, but if I sound like one, I guess its because deep down I'm as frightened of change and difference as they are. (1989: 63)

The question posed by this sort of "New York" narration is "Can this relationship be saved?" when differences of class and regional upbringing and family history as well as tonalities of skin color within a black community in a racially divided society collide with and construct gender differences.

And this question leads to the question posed by the climactic events of the Willow Springs sections of the novel: what is it George is supposed to find in the henhouse and bring back to Mama Day to save Cocoa when she is wasting away because of a voodoo spell put upon her by a jealous woman? The very terms of these questions are so different from one another that the narrative gap between sections of the novel is plain. In the articulation of these different narrative terrains lies much of the critical potential of the text. George can't believe in voodoo spells, yet Cocoa appears to be dying. In desperation, he tries to follow Mama Day's instructions, but he can't quite believe that returning to her with nothing but his empty hands will be good enough. He lashes out, fighting the hens, smashing the henhouse, and has a heart attack. He has done it his way, his death for Cocoa's life. Was there any other option? The novel implies that there might have been, had George been the product of a different, less rationalistic history.

We approach Mama Day's world, her knowledge of healing herbs and powerful rituals, by implication and contrast with the familiar, rational modern world rather than directly. There is no insistence on our accepting that things could be differently organized if Mama Day were officially in charge, that her rural poverty and alternative knowledges might offer a solution to contemporary urban and global conflicts. There is merely the suggestion that things *are* differently organized in particular locations away from the mass media's gaze, and that in spite of male domination and class hierarchy and racism, some women already possess particular powers as yet unthinkable to the modern urban feminist, particular powers that collectively make the world a more mysterious, less oppressive place than it would otherwise be.

In what sense, then, do *Kindred* and *Mama Day* exemplify the commodification of feminism? As we hope to have made clear, the charge of commodification is a complex and potentially productive one. When politically progressive ideas are put in circulation through the marketing of print culture, the possibility of new political spaces and new forms of resistance being created is increased. These two novels by women of color simultaneously package critically powerful strategies for questioning old assumptions about relations between the genders and the races, and they make the voices of African-American women available to be heard – and consumed. Arguably, these two texts, in which forms of black feminist theorizing and thinking about history are represented by black women representing themselves, go further in a critical sense than the politically progressive detective fiction of white writers like Grafton and Paretsky.

Women of Color and Postcolonial Textuality

What happens when we look across the Atlantic to the scene in the UK? No comparably celebratory commodification of novels by women of color can be found. West Indian, African, and subcontinental women writing and publishing in the UK abound, but they tend to be published by small presses and not to garner prestigious literary prizes or even many reviews. Celebrated women writers associated with radical politics and feminism, such as Angela Carter and Jeanette Winterson, tend to be white. Winterson's unabashedly lesbian autobiograpical novel, *Oranges Are Not the Only Fruit* (1985), proved to be a prelude to sexually complicated and experimental fictions, *The Passion* (1987) and *Sexing the Cherry* (1989), which have met with great critical and commercial success.

A similarly serious, though not uncontroversial, critical reception greeted Alan Hollinghurst's *The Swimming-Pool Library* (1988), a novel in which gay male sexuality is celebrated from public-school lavatories, conduits to the corridors of power, through the pool and showers of the more democratic Corinthian athletic club. Our upper-middle-class hero's adventures in the sub-aqua prick-forest of London reveal the paradoxical status of male homosexuality within English culture, its cross-class and cross-race lusts and its fundamental associations with upper-class institutions like the public school and the colonial civil service. Readable as gay male porn, Hollinghurst's novel is also paradoxically a classic realist English novel about social distinctions and anxieties. Its critical success is thus in some ways less surprising than the success of Winterson's formally more experimental and "difficult" fictions.

In order to locate the cultural work being done in Britain on something approaching a mass scale by women writers of color, or at least by writers of color who address feminist concerns, we need to look rather at two movements or moments within UK publishing, the tradition of publishing colonial, particularly African, writers in English, and the recent, not entirely uncritical, splash made by

Hanif Kureishi's *The Buddha of Suburbia* (1990). Publication in the Heinemann African Writers Series, founded by Chinua Achebe, guarantees at least a modicum of critical and commercial recognition. Some richly distinguished novels useful for feminist work on race and gender have appeared in it, including Bessie Head's *A Question of Power* (1974) and Mariama Bâ's *So Long a Letter* (1981), winner of the Noma Award for publishing in Africa. Once again, the more formally experimental and wonderfully radical *Our Sister Killjoy or Reflections from a Black-Eyed Squint* (1979), by Ama Ata Aidoo, published by NOK International of New York, London, and Lagos, has not only been comparatively marginalized by being published with a less well-established press than Heinemann, but it is now out of print. And what does it suggest that one "funny kind of Englishman," a postcolonial Pakistani-Englishman, whose jacket blurb describes him as having been "born and brought up in Kent, England" and as having "read philosophy at King's College, London, where he started to write plays," has been responsible for producing three of the most provocative and commercially successful documents about race, gender, sexuality, and postcoloniality of the 1980s, the screenplays *My Beautiful Laundrette* (1986) and *Sammy and Rosie Get Laid* (1988), and the novel *The Buddha of Surburbia*?

The shift in critical categories we have just made – from "race and gender" to "race, gender, sexuality, and postcoloniality" – is an important one. The critique of race is not identical with, and should not be confused with or substituted for, the critique of imperialism and colonialism. More on this distinction will follow in chapter 9.

Writing Africa: Bessie Head and Mariama Bâ

The question of formal difficulty in contemporary fiction is a vexed one. What is the status of realism, as opposed to more experimental, non-mimetic fictional modes, for our critical and political purposes? Moi argues strongly for what she calls "pioneering modes of textual production" (Moi 1985: 11), for the radical possibilities of the high-modernist tradition as represented by Virginia Woolf. Through its deliberate difficulty and preoccupation with formal experimentation, Moi insists, this tradition destabilizes liberal-humanist notions of masterful and non-contradictory subjectivity. Yet the more commercially successful a book tends to be, here in the last decade of the twentieth century, the less likely it is to play with high-modernist-style, non-mimetic, self-consciously experimental modes of represen-

tation. And, arguably, if a book aims to do its cultural work among
the unconverted, there is something to be said for at least some
attention to the mimetic, to realist conventions, in order to address
possible readers unschooled in the conventions of literary modernism.
Bessie Head's *A Question of Power* tackles this problem directly:

> "In our country culture has become so complex, this complexity is
> reflected in our literature. It takes a certain level of education to
> understand our novelists. The ordinary man cannot understand them
> [sic] . . ." . . .
>   And she reeled off a list of authors, smiling smugly. It never
> occurred to her that those authors had ceased to be of any value
> whatsoever to their society – or was it really true that an extreme
> height of culture and the incomprehensible went hand in hand? (1974:
> 79)

The character who smugly reels off a list of authors famous for being
almost impossible to understand is Camilla, a Danish agricultural
expert working in Botswana, whose method of teaching stands in
stark contrast to the sympathetically rational, methodical explanations
of other knowledgeable characters in the novel. The interior reflection
on the political uselessness of these elite Danish writers is Elizabeth's;
she is a "coloured" – meaning of mixed race, "part African, part
English" (1974: 15) – South African exile who resents Camilla's
assertions of cultural superiority. Elizabeth has "spent all her life
running away from the type of white person like Camilla" (1974:
77). Camilla "flung information at her in such a way as to make it
totally incomprehensible and meaningless, subtly demonstrating that
to reach her level of education Elizabeth had to be able to grasp the
incoherent" (1974: 76).

The irony here lies in Head's own textual production, which is
far from simple in its exploration of socially produced mental breakdown, its mingling of African and Western mythemes, its generic
disruptions and problematized characters, and its far from naively
utopian political vision. The difference between Head's pioneering
mode of textual production and Moi's examples is that Head's is not
classically modernist in the high European sense; indeed it explicitly
questions the depoliticizing elitist tendency of modernism's insularly
formalist concerns, while producing new postcolonialist modes of
textual and subjective confrontation.

Like Naylor's *Mama Day*, *A Question of Power* locates utopian
possibility in discursive contrasts and displacements. One of the
novel's most poignant moments is also one of its most ideologically

loaded and linguistically complex. At the end of the novel, Elizabeth's
sanity is partly restored through her return to the agricultural project
where before her breakdown she had been working with a local
woman named Kenosi. In Elizabeth's absence, Kenosi has been
struggling to keep the garden going, and the income from its produce
has seriously shrunk. Upon Elizabeth's return, Kenosi

> pulled out of her pocket the garden record book of vegetable sales
> and handed it to Elizabeth. There in a shaky, painstaking handwriting
> was a meticulous record of all she had sold. The spelling, oh, the
> spelling was a fantastic combination of English and Setswana:
> "Ditamati 30c," she wrote. "Pamkin 60c, Dibeetteruti 45c, Dionions
> 25c, Dibeans 20c, Dispinach 15c, Dicarrots 25c, Ditamati 45c. . . ."
> Elizabeth laughed silently. That garden was hallowed ground to
> Kenosi. She could see her over those months sitting at a table in her
> hut at night with a candle, frowning over all the entries she made,
> careful not to lose a cent. The record book looked so beautiful that
> Elizabeth kept quietly turning it over in her head – Ditamati, Dionions,
> Dispinach, Dibeans, Dicarrots – as she and Kenosi walked up and
> down the garden. (1974: 203–4)

The struggle to render in writing mimes the struggle to make the
land grow, which in turn mimes the struggle to speak in the form
of English and Setswana that marks the postcolonial space of the
novel. Kenosi's record book testifies to the garden's vitality in commercial terms. But her language represents a form of accounts
rendered in another sense, in which the linguistic hybridity of Bots-
wanan culture testifies to that culture's postcolonial vitality. The
garden is no longer a pastoral retreat from small capital exchanges,
but small capital exchanges become re-pastoralized by the novel's
celebration of agrarian community. We might describe Kenosi's
account book as a text of her friendship with Elizabeth, their work-
ing-women's partnership in the community. To recycle the last sentence of the novel to describe Kenosi's garden book being offered
to Elizabeth in this way, "It was a gesture of belonging" (1974: 206).

We could describe the whole of Mariama Bâ's *So Long a Letter*
as similarly situated in a discursive space of female friendship. In
pouring out, after her husband's death, her story of abandonment
– a classic case of mid-life crisis, Senegalese style, in which her
husband takes a much younger second wife – the narrator Ramatou-
laye gathers strength from addressing a kind of journal in letters to
her old school friend Aissatou. The whole text of the novel is a
testament to female and feminist solidarity in the face of male betrayal

of emancipatory ideals, once shared by a whole generation of men and women in their radical student days, trying to create democratic socialism in a new nation. We could say of what these two women construct between them, the textual bond between addressor and addressee, what Linda Kauffman says of women's writing in the epistolary tradition as a whole: "The writing is the revolution" (Kauffman 1986: 20–2, 318).

Paradox and the Postcolonial Subject: Hanif Kureishi

But then the postcolonial space is never free of contradictions. Beginning here, we shall use at several points the film *Sammy and Rosie Get Laid* (1987), directed by Stephen Frears and written by Hanif Kureishi, as a test case for some of the difficulties that arise in trying to articulate a multiple politics of identity in the contemporary moment. We might consider the point in the film when the white social worker, Rosie, and her father-in-law, Rafi, a former government official recently arrived in Britain from Pakistan, nearly come to blows in a posh London restaurant over how his fighting against imperialism in Pakistan led to torture of the opposition once his party came to power. His confidence that only *he* knows the real struggle is set contradictorily against her high moral ground, from which his politics has merely added to the "amount of evil in the universe":

> RAFI: (*Furious*) You've never suffered! Never had to make hard political decisions!
> ROSIE: Yes, every day in my work!
> RAFI: You are only concerned with homosexuals and women! A luxury that rich oppressors can afford! We were concerned with poverty, imperialism, feudalism! Real issues that burn people!
> ROSIE: We're only asking what it is like to destroy another life.
> (*Kureishi 1988: 28*)

How can we possibly negotiate the political stakes here? Do not the codes of justice and responsibility and political identity get crossed for good in this scene, however theatrical? Those of us who cannot not identify in some sense with Rosie, at least to the extent that she represents all the new social movements in their most easily commodified, white, downwardly mobile, welfare-state professional, middle-class feminist form: how *can* we simply identify with her here, turning global political issues, the whole legacy of imperialism, into simple schoolgirl morality? Who can dismiss Rafi as the stage villain he is clearly so capable of being, when one is sitting comfortably in a First World scene of reading? On the other hand, who can sit silently through his anathematizing of women and homosexuals as not real subjects of history, as if he knew who and what they were? Who wants to endorse his conscience-free, pragmatic attitude towards torture and murder: they were necessary, so we did them? Isn't this the logic of imperialism and of First World militarism and neo-colonialism chillingly repeating itself?

If *Sammy and Rosie* reveals the catachrestical nature of the name "politically correct subject," then Kureishi's novel *The Buddha of Suburbia* takes that movement towards exposure even further. The multiple but intertwined notions of a post-sixties liberated subject, of a sexually revolutionized subject, of a politically progressive and aware subject, of a feminist male subject, of an anti-racist subject, and of a coherent postcolonial subject are all subjected to subtle critical scrutiny in the novel. Each becomes something of a catachresis. And this effect is even more textually remarkable because the novel consists entirely of first-person, autobiographical-sounding narration: the most intimate narrative domain of the self-knowing subject.

How is this textual effect achieved? First, Kureishi constructs the relations between and among the narrator/hero (Karim Amir) and the eponymous hero (the buddha of the South London suburbs, who turns out to be not Karim but Karim's father, Haroon) through a series of discursive displacements. Then there are the other characters whose social trajectories the novel follows, all of whom become crucially part of the textual makeup of Karim and Haroon. There is Charlie, Karim's schoolmate and sometime lover; Jamila, Karim's cousin and sometime lover; Eva, suburbanite housewife who becomes a new woman through marrying Karim's father, Haroon, and becoming an interior designer in the London economic and cultural boom of the late 1970s. Then there is Changez, Bombay escapee and Jamila's husband by arranged marriage, the native-diasporic other counterposed to Karim's "funny kind of Englishman":

My name is Karim Amir, and I am an Englishman born and bred, almost. I am often considered to be a funny kind of Englishman, a new breed as it were, having emerged from two old histories. But I don't care – Englishman I am (though not proud of it), from the South London suburbs and going somewhere. Perhaps it is the odd mixture of continents and blood, of here and there, of belonging and not, that makes me restless and easily bored. Or perhaps it was being brought up in the suburbs that did it. Anyway, why search the inner room when it's enough to say that I was looking for trouble, any kind of movement, action and sexual interest I could find, because things were so gloomy, so slow and heavy, in our family, I don't know why. Quite frankly, it was all getting me down and I was ready for anything. (Kureishi, 1990: 3)

Karim's story is not "his" alone, not his discursive property, any more than his identity is his, though he wishes he could assume such an heroically integral kind of self. Karim is an effect of "two old histories," the Indian and the English, an effect of his lower middle-class suburban origins – "from the South London suburbs and going somewhere" – and an effect of his historical moment, poised between the social ferment of the 1960s and the newly distributed prosperity of the late 1970s, "restless and easily bored . . . looking for trouble, any kind of movement, action and sexual interest I could find." The chief casualty of this historical moment is Karim's English mother, Margaret, abandoned by Haroon, the civil servant and aspiring buddha, for Eva's more ambitious explorations – artistic, sexual, and social. But this is the 1970s, the moment of high feminism; even the unexotic former doormat Margaret gets a new lease on life. Liberated from gloomy domesticity, she remakes herself and starts again in happier circumstances, with a white English boyfriend.

Although we see everything from Karim's point of view, his continuing discovery of how intertwined everyone's story is with everyone else's means we must compare his developing character with many others' transformations. Even the older generation, Karim's parents and Eva, are capable of enormous changes. Changez's very name situates him as most put-upon by the shifting social order. But it is Jamila whose story most closely parallels Karim's own – the most properly feminist subject of Kureishi's novel as well as the most explicitly politically committed character.

Karim's success as an actor reveals the theatrical quality of social being, its catachrestical status, in which "one's own" gestures and speeches always refer to a something else, an imaginary unity of identity, which can never be an adequately literal referent for all this signification of the fiction of self. But all is not simply a matter of role-playing, let alone of one being free to choose one's roles. "They laughed at my jokes, which concerned the sexual ambition and humiliation of an Indian in England" (1990: 220), reports Karim. Miming the very sexual ambition and humiliation which are his own and not his own, Changez's own and not his own, Karim succeeds in going somewhere, away from the suburbs and into the cultural and social heart of London.

The politics of appropriation prove absolutely crucial to Karim's theatrical career. That is to say, Karim's success as an actor largely depends on his appropriating a character, an identity, more recognizably and comically "Indian" than his own could ever be and marketing that to white audiences. His rise begins with his playing Mowgli in an experimental stage version of *The Jungle Book*. Then he performs a character very like Changez, risking alienating his friend and Jamila's husband in order to have something to sell. Without Changez as a model for his so-called original characterization, he fears his whole career will fall apart. After all, he argues, "Who else could I base my character on? I didn't know any other 'black' people. Pyke [the hip white director] would sack me" (1990: 185). The question of the politics of identity in postcolonial cultural spaces being largely a matter of marketing identities could hardly be more crudely or materially posed.

From radical theatre, Karim's trajectory is an obvious one as the 1970s grind towards a conclusion: he lands a part in a new, politically engaged TV soap opera that sounds very much like *EastEnders*, one that will explore issues of class, race, gender, ethnicity, and sexuality in this postcolonial moment. He sees through the hype of the whole television and media scene, of course, but cannot resist the success and money it offers: "[F]ive minutes told me that these were trashy, jumped-up people in fluffy sweaters. They spoke as if they were working on something by Sophocles. Then they asked me to run around the office in an improvisation set in a fish and chip shop" (1990: 259). The novel closes with a celebration – of Karim's job and of Haroon and Eva's marriage – in an expensive London restaurant, which most, though not all, of the people Karim loves attend: "And so I sat in the centre of this old city that I loved, which itself sat at the bottom of a tiny island. I was surrounded by people I loved, and I felt happy and miserable at the same time. I thought of what a mess everything had been, but that it wouldn't always be that way" (1990: 284). While the champagne flows, Karim feels he is no longer a failure. It is a fairly ephemeral, yuppified epiphany. People will have hangovers in the morning, and Karim will reproach himself for not having felt it all quite deeply enough. But there is so much accumulated irony accruing to the text by this time that it feels like the only appropriate conclusion.

So much for Karim as hero and star. Meanwhile, Jamila gets to represent a kind of political solidity and conviction that Karim can only admire, envy, and feel intimidated by. She deals with her arranged marriage by agreeing to live with Changez provided they can live communally, sleep with whom they wish, etc. She bears a child named Leila Kollontai to Simon, a radical lawyer in the household, then takes Joanna as a lesbian lover. As in *Sammy and Rosie*, the toughest political stance belongs to a woman identified with lesbianism:

> As I watched Jamila I thought what a terrific person she'd become. She was low today, and she was often scornful of me anyway, the supercilious bitch, but I couldn't help seeing that there was in her a great depth of will, of delight in the world, and much energy for love. Her feminism, the sense of self and fight it engendered, the schemes and plans she had, the relationships – which she desired to take this form and not that form – the things she had made herself know, and all the understanding this gave, seemed to illuminate her tonight as she went forward, an Indian woman, to live a useful life in white England. (1990: 216)

In an ironical contemporary idiom, in which depth of feeling is something to be pursued and coveted but rarely achieved – oh wow, is this passion or sentimentality? – this is as good as it gets, as far as praise for feminism and political commitment goes. As in his other works, Kureishi backs off from claiming very much for his straight male heroes. Rafi's anathematized categories, "homosexuals and women," come closer to representing the category of "politically correct subject," but that category remains finally unfilled in his fictions because it is unfillable by anyone. This is principally why we have analyzed his work, however paradoxical the relation may seem, in relation to writing by women of color in the UK.

Writing by women of color in the US and UK has a long way to go before being fully commodified and institutionalized, despite the wild claims being made by rightwing critics about the triumph of leftwing reformulations of the canons taught in schools and universities. As a consequence, the reading of a text written by an African-American woman writer or a postcolonial woman writer of color is likely to carry a potentially heavier critical charge than the reading of white feminist texts in this marketplace, in this historical moment. And Hanif Kureishi can find greater mainstream acceptance for his very probing postcolonial fictions than his female counterparts, though, if we were to take him at his word, he does so partly with undeniable pleasure, and partly to his own chagrin. That is the paradox of being a male feminist fellow traveller these days.

6

History and Poststructuralism

Now any member of a social movement is a social agent, capable of resistance. With all this talk of "decentered" subjects and anti-essentialist identities, how is one to conceive of agency? As Gayatri Spivak observes in an interview: "the subject must identify itself with its self-perceived intention. The fact that it must do so is not a description of what it is. That is the difference between decentered and centered. There is no way that a subject can be anything but centered" (Spivak 1990: 146). Centered, that is, in terms of its intentions. Anti-essentialist theories focus on processes of construction rather than given or fixed essences in their conceptualizations of subjectivity. The important thing to keep in mind is the distinction between "a decentered subject" and a subject continually in the process of *centering* itself. So while the subject is always in process, neither finally centered nor fixed, it is always acting as if it *were* centered, and it must do so in order to act at all.

How, then, do we theorize agency in an anti-essentialist way? For, even more than subjectivity, agency may seem hard to think without the grounding of a unified, self-knowing subject that imagines itself free to act as it chooses. Marxist theories of class subjects in struggle displace the individual agency central to liberal theory but may still be criticized as essentialist in their unproblematical linking of class consciousness with economic determination by the mode of production in the last instance.

In order to arrive at an answer to how to think agency, we shall have to examine the difference poststructuralism has made in thinking about it in at least two academic disciplines, history and literary studies. The white male heterosexual worker of the First World industrial nations just won't do any longer as the alternative or insurgent subject of history, the locus of resistance to ruling-class dominance. In the light of new social and intellectual movements, both historians and literary critics have responded to the challenge of rethinking agency.

Historians, Agency, and Literary Theory

Working within what he calls "the materialist conception of history," the historian R. S. Neale, for example, finds that the Marxist category, mode of production, "actually relates structure to agency in interactive 'un-determined' ways. And the system places at the centre of its discourse human agency of a powerfully creative kind" (Neale 1985: xiii). The materialist conception of history can thus be made to account for agency; but reconstructing its specificities within the historical record requires an analysis of creativity, and thus becomes bound up with certain kinds of "literary" analysis. When Neale reads Vera Brittain's memoir *Testament of Youth* (1933) and her *War Diary* for the years 1913–17 as documents of social history, for example, he invokes literary theory as a means of supplementing materialist history and warding off his discipline's tendencies towards empiricism and economistic positivism:

> I will raise the problem of the "literaryness" of her production, to suggest how much has to be left to the reader, and I will question whether feeling, as a component in agency, can be understood as other than specific to class, time and place, or apart from the historical location and consciousness of readers who have to become writers. That is, I raise again Roland Barthes' notion of the "limpness" of history, and point to the inadequacy of theory as it now is. Yet, I also claim that theory is the best we have. Without it there is only the domination of empiricism and the econometrics of positivism. (1985: 177)

Although the passage is somewhat oblique, it appears that, at this point in Neale's analysis, historical and literary theory necessarily converge in the conceptualization of agency. And they converge specifically around the question of "feeling" as part of the literary constructedness of Brittain's texts, and as the limit of possible historical knowledge. As a materialist, Neale insists on the historical determinations of this effect of feeling: class, time and place, the location and consciousness of readers. Gender is presumably implicit in his list of material determinants, since the passage in Brittain's diary most provocative for his speculations on feeling deals with the construction and regulation of a class-specific female heterosexuality, laden for him "with all the dead weight and inhibitions of privacy and social distance, the chronicle of which is told in *The Civilizing Process*" (1985: 180). The sentence that particularly interests Neale is this comment of Brittain's about her lover: "He took my hand and kissed it again as he did in the train once before – but this time there was no glove upon it" (cited Neale 1985: 179). Neale puts the episode of the glove together with an incident described in a suffragette journal, in which a young woman attempting to speak to a crowd is violently silenced, her clothes ripped down to the waist and her hair torn by angry men. This incident Neale describes as the other, "fearful" side of privacy and social distance, "another kind of response to the strange and alien relation of the sexes nurtured inside the walls of nearly all the houses in the kingdom" (1985: 180–1).

Having thus put these accounts together in a "literary" way, challenging his readers to fill in his admittedly speculative, suggestive analysis of the possible connections between gender, class, privacy, sexuality, power, and fear, Neale explicitly draws back from literary questions:

> I know that I cannot create a new discipline that could convincingly bring all the necessary elements together, and that something must be left to the reader. However, I do believe that such a discipline should not be one with a primary focus on connecting the historical to the literary traditions of scholarship. Rather we should persist in seeking ways of relating economy to culture and to consciousness and to the constricted lives as well as to the creative and human agency of people. (1985: 183)

For Neale, the "literary" is now so firmly on the side of the humanist subject – free to act "creatively" – that it can contribute little to his materialist conception of history. In fact, Neale ends his essay by denying literary studies any theoretical weight at all, relegating them to the realm of empiricism, formerly associated with "non-theoretical" history: "At present, Raymond Williams's cultural materialism, despite the idealism inherent in it, is the best guide there is, at least for the apprentice urban historian dissatisfied with literary or any other kind of empiricism" (1985: 184).

Neale's conclusion is a good example of what another historian, Joan Scott, describes as the oppositional self-representations of the disciplines of history and literary studies. Whenever literary critics talk about history, real historians are likely to find fault with their lack of sophisticated engagement with current debates in the discipline of history. Literary critics tend to recycle old-hat history, history as background or context. Whenever historians talk about literary texts, literary critics are likely to find fault with how the historians use literary sources as windows upon or mirrors held up to historical truth, as if literature either reflected or provided direct access to real social conditions, social relations, and social practices. Literary critics, especially those interested in theory, would call this move "naive mimeticism." Literature is not a mirror of "what's out there," but is produced in relation to its own history, institutions, and conventions. There is such a thing as "textuality," the play of language and signification within a text, to be accounted for. We should thus not be surprised that when literary critics and historians attempt to talk to each other there is frequently trouble:

> Oppositions between text and context, fiction and truth, art and life structure the self-representations of the disciplines of literature and history. Each discipline defines its expertise through a contrast with the other's objects of inquiry and methods of interpretation. Each discipline also resolves the ambiguities of its own project by using the other as a foil. In the process, each articulates the rules and conventions that identify them as discrete fields of knowledge, necessarily emphasizing certain methods and materials. . . . These differences can create obstacles to interdisciplinary work for those who define themselves entirely within disciplinary parameters, but they are less troublesome from the theoretical perspective I have been discussing. (Scott 1988: 8)

The theoretical perspective Scott has been discussing she calls "poststructuralism," including under this rubric the work of Foucault and the analysis of the conflictual processes of knowledge production theorized by Derrida as "deconstruction." By bringing this theoretical perspective to bear on her own work as a feminist historian, Scott attempts to bridge the disciplinary gap between history and literary studies.

One of the most important effects of this rapprochement between the disciplines through the use of "literary" theory is the emphasis it places on agency, reconceived to include the agency of the historian or critic as well as the agency of the historical subjects of investigation. Concern with history writing as knowledge production, as production of knowledge in which the historian is always interested, leads to disciplinary self-reflection on the politics of the historical enterprise itself, and on the question of whose agency and interests are being represented. Spivak, commenting on the work of the Subaltern Studies group who are rewriting the history of colonial India from the perspective of peasant consciousness and insurgency – a history of subaltern agency, in short – concludes:

> When historiography is self-consciously "non-theoretical," it sees its task, with respect to rival historical accounts of the same period, as bringing forth "what really happened" in a value-neutral prose. Since the incursion of "theory" into the discipline of history, and the uncomfortable advent of Michel Foucault, it is no longer too avant-garde to suspect or admit that "events" are never not discursively constituted and that the language of historiography is always also language. (Spivak 1987: 241–2)

What might this self-reflexive disciplinary attention to language mean for theorizing historical agency?

If events themselves are never not discursively constituted, it follows that history, as the accounts of social movements and political struggles of the past and present, is constantly being rewritten. Historians disagree about the meaning of the English civil wars of the 1640s and the interregnum political experiments of the 1650s, for instance. Did they constitute an English Revolution, a rebellion, a series of local uprisings without any coherence of principles or ideas, or another stage in the progress towards constitutional liberties signified by the legal system of the modern British state?

To argue for any of these positions entails a theory of historical process and a method of historical inquiry, a politics deeply embedded in the historian's approach to the empirical records of the period, its many documents and archives, including previous historical accounts. Historians frequently debate the properly historical interpretation of events, arguing from evidence or archival facts, but such an argument always necessitates acts of interpreting and explaining, not least in the definition of what constitutes a fact. Such debates may be conducted quite heatedly, for the political stakes are high. It is not merely the determining of the proper or most adequate understanding of past events alone that is at issue in such debates – however we view the past affects our sense of the political possibilities of the present. The impact of feminism on the historiography of seventeenth-century England, for instance, has begun to change the interpretation of historical evidence in significant ways.

Feminist Politics and Historiography

In *The World Turned Upside Down: Radical Ideas During the English Revolution* (1972), Christopher Hill broke new ground by reconstructing a radical sectarian tradition in mid-seventeenth-century England that constituted a revolt within the Revolution, a potential social revolution more wide-ranging than the political triumphs of men of property secured during the Commonwealth and Protectorate of the 1650s and consolidated with the Glorious Revolution of 1688. "The English Revolution" as a way of thinking about certain events – the civil wars of the 1640s, the execution of Charles I in 1649, the coming to power of the generals of the New Model Army, the emergence of Oliver Cromwell as head of the new Commonwealth and then of the Protectorate, the failure of this experiment with the Restoration of Charles II in 1660 – is largely Hill's creation. Before his work in the 1950s these decades were in no sense seen as comparable with the French, American, or Russian Revolutions. But as an historian working with Marxist categories, even after his break with the Communist Party in 1957, and thus concerned with retrieving a usable radical past for British and Anglophone societies, Hill has been consistently interested in asking not only "what happened?" but "what did it mean?"

As Hill argued in 1949, "If there is any point in studying history at all, its object must be to help us by understanding the past to control the present. Bad history will lead to bad politics" (cited in George 1988: 18). As Hill writes in *The World Turned Upside Down*:

> The object of the present book is to look at this revolt within the Revolution and the fascinating flood of radical ideas which it threw up. History has to be rewritten in every generation, because although the past does not change the present does; each generation asks new questions of the past, and finds new areas of sympathy as it re-lives different aspects of the experiences of its predecessors. . . . We may find that the obscure men and women who figure in this book, together with some not so obscure, speak more directly to us than Charles I or Pym or General Monck, who appear as history-makers in the textbooks. (Hill 1972: 13, 15)

Now, like many historians, Hill has little time or patience for the obscurantist vocabulary of much literary theory. He does not drop Foucault's name or theorize about the textuality of the historical archive. On the other hand, unlike the historian whom Spivak describes, striving for a value-free history and a value-neutral prose, Hill acknowledges that the history we write is dependent upon the questions we ask and that those questions have everything to do with the political present in which we both ask and write.

Published in the early seventies, written with the optimistic revolt of the sixties clearly in mind, *The World Turned Upside Down* implicitly connects the radical sectarians of seventeenth-century England with twentieth-century social and sexual experiments. The sexual revolution, women's liberation, hippie and yippie and black and gay liberation – such social movements towards general emancipation, towards true democracy, have historical predecents in the English Revolution of the seventeenth century, according to Hill. When Hill, writing reconstructively about a radical tradition, discusses the activities of sectarian women, he emphasizes connections between the symbolic significance of their gestures and the "uninhibited speculation" of the revolutionary decades, "which included the relation of the sexes among many other themes" (1972: 253). Women's participation in revolutionary speculation and protest, while important, is only one strain among many in his analysis. And he interprets women's activities, which had no official political sanction in the period, with some skepticism about their motives, asking questions about whether their more outrageous gestures constitute rebellious, gender-specific, and possibly sexual exhibitionism or "serious" propaganda:

> It would have been difficult at the time, and is impossible now, to assess the relative importance of repressed exhibitionism and serious symbolic propaganda. In 1652 a lady stripped naked during a church service, crying "Welcome the resurrection!" The incident was remarkable principally because it took place in the chapel at Whitehall; such occurrences were less rare at Ranter and Quaker meetings. (1972: 256)

Women form part of the spectacle of "uninhibited speculation" but the relation of their gestures to the "serious propaganda" of political protest remains unclear.

Now notice what happens to the same event in the hands of a feminist literary historian:

> Other female radicals might not have claimed to be deities themselves, but their activities were still seen as dangerously subversive, and many attacks on them were published. *A List of Some of the Great Blasphemers*, for example, records that many women asserted that they were pregnant with the new Christ of the Second Coming. David

Brown's *The Naked Woman*, 1652, was written in outrage after a woman had stripped naked in Whitehall to mock a sermon delivered by Peter Sterry on the theme of Resurrection. Brown was furious that the minister had failed to reprimand the woman or have her arrested, believing that this kind of rebellious behaviour was symptomatic of a more general rejection of the new government's authority. She should have been closely questioned, he asserts, in a manner which would make her proper, submissive role clear to her.

> She ought to have been demanded . . . 4. With what company she walketh? 5. How long? 6. Whether or not she was sent by them? 7. If not, then by whom? 8. If by none at all, then did she not run unsent? 9. What her name was? 10. If she hath a husband? 11. If yea, what his name was? 12. Where he dwelleth? 13. And if he and she live together? (Hobby 1988: 28)

In Elaine Hobby's analysis, the political context and motives of the woman's stripping naked at Whitehall are foregrounded. Hobby notices the connection between the woman's ironical pronouncement "Welcome the resurrection!" and the possibility of popular rejection of the new parliamentarian government's authority. Was it really to be accepted as a government of the godly, "the kingdom of the saints?" For Hobby, women's agency within the radical sects was a matter of both religious commitment and political commitment. Self-governing within their groups, though guided by God's authority speaking directly to and through them, such women prophesied, wrote pamphlets and petitions, participated in debates, and hoped for revolutionary transformation of both government and society on these radically egalitarian terms. Hill's thesis of "the revolt within the Revolution" as a moment of "uninhibited speculation," and the naked woman's possible exhibitionism as an instance of breaking through repressive sexual protocols, gives way in Hobby's analysis to an historical investigation explicitly of "how the women's activities present a case for their right to be involved in matters of national government" (Hobby 1988: 27).

This comparison need not persuade us simply to substitute Hobby's account for Hill's. Indeed Hobby's account in many ways presupposes Hill's, thus allowing her to focus on *women's* "revolt within the Revolution." In terms of reconstructing *women's* histories in the period, Hobby's more developed account of this incident is undoubtedly of greater interest than Hill's, but Hobby recognizes that a history of women cannot be fully constructed without some reference to what men were also doing. Otherwise, we risk writing histories of women as if they occupied a separate space in an entirely female ghetto. Hill's uninhibited speculation and experiment on the road to radical democracy; Hobby's women refusing obedience to husbands and governments and, while invoking God's authority, acting for themselves: with these different agendas for both past and present, Hill's and Hobby's accounts of the same event suggest the inevitably political and constantly shifting stakes of historical representation.

We might notice too that although neither Hill nor Hobby shies away from what Neale ruled out of bounds as "the literary" – matters of sexuality and affect, questions of textual construction and interpretation – neither ventures very far into this territory either. Both Hill and Hobby keep their arguments firmly focused on the political, and in order to do this they do not dwell for long on either sexuality or textuality. There is no discussion of literary form, of the play of rhetoric within the documents they are reading. The language of the reporting of the incident at Whitehall is represented by both as more or less transparent, not as "language" in Spivak's sense. It is as if those literary questions presented enormous problems for the conducting of political analysis, even for historians willing to examine the stakes of historical representation, to ask not only "what happened?" but also "what did it mean?"

Feminist Politics and Literary History

If the discipline of history can be said to be openly political, replete with arguments that have some bearing on the present, the discipline of literary history may appear relatively untroubled by such concerns. When the empirical materials upon which a discipline is based consist more explicitly of texts and artifacts than of events, formal matters pertaining to the kind of cultural practice under investigation tend to be foregrounded. Literary historians may describe the history of various genres or kinds of writing as narratives of succession or progress, one poem or novel succeeding another, one author building upon another's achievement. Cultural historians construct similar chronological or developmental narratives, or they may focus on the interrelatedness of various art forms in a particular historical moment. The political character of specific interpretations of literary or other texts may thus easily be obscured. Questions of genre, form and aesthetics, the principles of beauty and the generation of affect within particular art forms, can seem quite removed from the field of political debate.

But seeming is not the same as being; the writing of literary history entails a politics of historical inquiry and explanation. Alastair Fowler, for example, develops an analysis of genre, or kinds of literary text, as a systematic way of understanding literary works from their original appearance in the world through our contemporary reading, a way of interpreting them and determining their aesthetic value. He discusses the succession of literary genres not in terms of "classes" of literary works but in terms of "family resemblances": "What produces generic resemblances, reflection soon shows, is tradition: a sequence of influence and imitation and inherited codes connecting works in the genre. As kinship makes a family, so literary relations of this sort form a genre" (Fowler 1982: 42). Once we attend to the language in which it is constructed, we cannot avoid noticing how Fowler's project makes literary history seem like a family affair. And, in Fowler's family histories, tradition and inheritance are emphasized, not rebellion and independence.

One of Fowler's reasons for establishing his generic system is that he believes that a certain "overextension of political iconoclasm" has invaded literary studies, an iconoclasm "inappropriately directed against legitimate authorial privilege" (1982: 266). In one sense, this is an argument for taking into account an author's historical context and intentions as best we can reconstruct them. In another sense, however, this language of family resemblance, inheritance, and legitimacy is ideologically loaded in terms of gender and class relations. Fowler argues that his generic notion of legitimate, patrilineal literary history is not conservative or hierarchizing (1982: 35–6), and he grants that expansion of the canon or curriculum in the name of something called Women in Literature "may be justified" on ethical grounds. Yet he cannot resist returning to a distinction between " 'the best that is known and thought in the world' " and "political studies of low culture" (1982: 10).

The best that is known and thought turns out to be what the fathers think and pass on to their sons. And these fathers and sons are men of property, possessors of intellectual property as part of their birthright within the property-owning educated classes. What women and the lower classes write may be of "political" interest but it is "low culture." Fowler worries that academics may be depriving the people of "the best" because of a political interest in this low culture: "Shall we in the name of antielitism deprive the people of their legitimate inheritance? Is their literature to be less than the best?" (1982: 10). We might well ask, how can "we" be so sure that we know what "the best" is? Is it only "antielitism" that would question such judgements? By what criteria are "we" to determine what should be passed on to "the people"? Fowler assumes that "the best" is self-evidently better than works by women, the working class, or culturally marginal groups of all sorts. But how are we to make such a judgement once we have recognized the political character of both representation and aesthetic judgement, as Michèle Barrett and others have demonstrated?

Mary Jacobus, drawing upon Derrida's essay, "The Law of Genre" (1980), has shown how Fowler's paternalistic preoccupation with cultural legitimacy is both gendered and embedded in a conservative politics: "By consecrating genre as part of the order of nature while simultaneously emphasizing the gradual evolution of genre in response to historical change, Fowler reveals himself to be a conservative rather than revolutionary not only in the realm of genre-theory, but in the realm of theory itself, where 'farouche structuralists' are said to be at work . . . " (Jacobus 1984: 56). On the one hand legitimate authorial privilege leads to a literary history based on legitimate inheritance. On the other, there are politicizing kinds of iconoclastic theory, notably "farouche structuralism," that threaten this narrative of legitimate literary inheritance. And there would appear to be complicity between a defense of authorial and high-cultural privilege and resistance to certain literary theories. We are now up against the question of agency once more.

If for historians the question of agency tends to be posed in terms of what happened and who acted in the past, for literary critics agency arises most often as the critic's own agency in matters of interpretation and judgement. And nothing foregrounds the literary critic as agent more than the question of theory.

Theory and Literary-Historical Studies

During the past twenty years especially there has been vehement debate within the institutions of literary and cultural studies in Britain, North America, Western Europe, Africa, the Subcontinent, Australia, and elsewhere, debate about the theory and method and implicit politics of the disciplines of literary criticism, literary history, and social and political history. The term "theory" itself has come to have a privileged place in these debates.

To analyze an academic discipline, like history, or a particular instance of a disciplinary practice, like a piece of work by a particular historian representing a certain school of history writing, can constitute a theoretical reflection on that kind of history if the analysis takes certain forms. A theoretical analysis considers its object as a rule-governed activity subject to certain constraints regarding what counts as evidence, what constitutes an argument, what appeals are to be made to empirical truth, explanatory adequacy, rhetorical effectiveness, or any other standard of judgement. An abstract or scientific consideration of the disciplinary practice being analyzed: this is what is usually meant by "theory" in the technical sense.

But a theoretical analysis may also consider the piece of historical writing as a text, as a narrative construction that tells the story it tells, and not the others it might have told, and that may contain moments within itself that work against its ostensible argument, that undermine the cover story. To take apart some historical representation and reveal its constructedness as a text, as writing, subject to disciplinary procedures and other unvoiced assumptions, ideologically contradictory and necessarily poised on the edge of the particular insoluble logical difficulty, excess, hole, or aporia that marks the limits of the text's logic, is to engage in theoretical reflection as well.

This second kind of theoretical analysis owes a great deal to what the literary critic and theorist of editorial practice Jerome McGann, among others, would call the poststructural problematic. McGann's situation as a textual editor and theorist of bibliographical as well as critical practice makes his attempts to promote connections between Marxist, feminist, and poststructuralist work strategically significant for literary studies because the field of bibliography and textual editing has been both under-theorized and particularly resistant to feminist and other forms of political critique. As materialist feminist critics and literary historians, we could well locate our own theoretical position within the broad "commitment to explore the social and historical dimensions of literary works" which in 1985 McGann characterized as representing an important shift within literary studies. He associates this commitment with an extreme (some might say postmodern) self-consciousness among scholars about their sociohistorical interests and a general project that is "antithetical, in several respects, to the (equally various) tradition of formal, structural, and text-centered literary studies which have been so influential in the academy for two generations" (McGann 1985: 3).

One of McGann's timely contributions to the theory of historically based literary studies is his assertion of the commensurability of

Marxist and feminist theory with the poststructuralist displacement of referentiality. "Marxist and Marxist-influenced criticism," he writes, "has been an especially important factor in" the development of recent "sociohistorical critical work":

> largely . . . because the questions it poses are founded in a powerful and dynamically coherent tradition of critical enquiry. Feminist studies have also done much to expose the sociohistorical dimensions of literary work. Because both of these critical approaches necessarily practice a hermeneutics of a repressed or invisibilized content, both have found no difficulty in assimilating the basic poststructural programmatic. (1985: 4)

This is a provocative move, since many critical theorists are eager to point out that a rigorous poststructuralism will insist on the priority of discourse and thereby deprive the materialist historian of access to the "real." Robert Holub, for example, accuses Derrida of calling "for the annihilation of history itself" (Holub 1984: 160; see also Felperin 1987). And, as we have seen, there has been no easy or necessary rapprochement between feminists and Marxists. Yet for McGann the fact that both groups often displace ostensible for "invisibilized" content links them in their suspicion of simple referentiality.

The problem of referentiality, of language as "constitutive" rather than merely "mimetic" of what must be taken as reality, has occupied many students of the human sciences this century. As McGann admits, "To the extent that traditional forms of historical criticism have not been able to assimilate or refute such a view, they have been moved to the periphery of literary studies" (McGann 1985: 4). It is arguable that historians too, like Neale and Scott, have claimed certain forms of disciplinary power for themselves by addressing such theoretical issues. McGann would clearly like to make certain critically and theoretically informed kinds of historical work central, not peripheral to literary studies.

We should notice that McGann here does not elucidate the grounds upon which any Marxist or feminist critics have addressed themselves to language as constitutive, but rather describes their practice as hermeneutic or interpretative. According to him, Marxists and feminists uncover a necessarily "repressed or invisibilized content" (class struggle or gender oppression) and, to the extent that such content is not obvious, their decoding of it is not locked into the commonsensical view of language as transparently referential. This does not take us very far, however, from a commonsensical view of language as unproblematically referring to something else, of texts as containing a certain fixed content waiting to be made visible, even if that something else or that content, like class or gender struggles, has to be made to reveal itself to the reader by means of a little critical or interpretative work. For the poststructuralist displacement of referentiality puts the whole system of hermeneutics, of decoding a certain hidden meaning that will exist as the privileged truth of the text, in question. And not all feminists or Marxists would see their projects as hermeneutic ones. While we share McGann's desire to bring together certain kinds of Marxist, feminist, and poststructuralist historically informed analyses of literary texts and archival documents, we do not think that the conditions for this encounter are obvious or immediately given. The ground for such an encounter must be prepared with more attention than McGann pays here to the heterogeneity, both textual and institutional, of these critical practices.

Poststructuralism and Historical Agency

More precisely, what is meant by the poststructuralist displacement of referentiality? In the wake of developments in linguistics, anthropology, psychoanalysis, and Marxist theory that depend upon the analysis of cultural phenomena as systems with determining structures, as in the work of Saussure, new attention is being paid to the operations of language, writing, and textuality as signifying practices. In the first decade of this century, Saussure established that language does not name things: "The linguistic sign unites, not a thing and a name, but a concept [signified] and a sound-image [signifier]" (Saussure 1972: 70). He argued that the bond between the signifier and the signified was arbitrary, in the sense that there was no natural connection between them, only a conventional, socially constructed one, and he suggested that linguistics could provide a paradigm for a much wider study of semiology, the science of signs, in all forms of cultural activity:

> In fact, every means of expression used in society is based, in principle, on collective behavior or – what amounts to the same thing – on convention. . . . Signs that are wholly arbitrary realize better than the others the ideal of the semiological process; that is why language, the most complex and universal of all systems of expression, is also the most characteristic; in this sense linguistics can become the master-

pattern for all branches of semiology although language is only one particular semiological system. (1972: 72–3)

If the first phase of this systematization of the study of cultures after Saussure is generally known as structuralism, the focus on language and writing as productive of signification and social value in ways that put the neutral scientificity of systems and structures into question is often referred to as poststructuralism.

As sociologists will be quick to point out, the undermining of referentiality characteristic of poststructuralism is also the cornerstone of Karl Mannheim's sociology of knowledge. The critique of foundationalism and the emergence of anti-foundationalism are thus neither new nor confined to literary and historical studies. But, as some sociologists of knowledge have recently argued, the anti-foundationalist critique could be said to be newly timely, given the linkage of widespread debates about poststructuralism with new modes of knowledge and information in the postmodern era (Fraser 1989, Hekman 1990, Dant 1991).

As McGann indicates, a poststructuralist approach to the study of literary or historical texts puts in question any easy reference to an outside world – represented in the text, yet still outside it. Texts signify; they function to produce and proliferate meaning within culturally specific practices of representation. There is no simple "inside" or "outside" of a text, no decipherable meaning outside the historically and culturally specific signifying codes that make the text legible to a particular reader, who is also always historically situated as well as inscribed within practices of signification. And there is no decipherable "world" not also inscribed by specific cultures and historical practices. The world to which we refer must be inscribed, must itself become a text, in order to be thought about or lived in. We are thus, however unwittingly, constantly engaged in processes of textuality and reading in all aspects of our social lives.

This recognition of the necessarily textual condition of all practice, especially the recognition of inevitable investigative interest and complicity, no matter what one's commitment to the search for truth, is a recognition which historians in particular have resisted. We might recall the split between discourse and history or "the real" so often invoked by those anxious to debunk poststructuralism as apolitical theorizing that merely gets in the way of real blood-and-guts politics.

Let's consider a different meaning of "discourse," one put in play by both Derridian deconstruction and Foucault's discourse theory, a definition that has proved crucial for both imagining the articulation of new social movements, as Ernesto Laclau and Chantal Mouffe have argued, and for the construction of new identities without essences. What if we argue, as Laclau and Mouffe do, that history and the real *are* discursive, that discourse consists of more than simply linguistic phenomena?

> The fact that every object is constituted as an object of discourse has *nothing to do* with whether there is a world external to thought, or with the realism/idealism opposition. An earthquake or the falling of a brick is an event that certainly exists, in the sense that it occurs here and now, independently of my will. But whether their specificity as objects is constructed in terms of "natural phenomena" or "expressions of the wrath of God," depends upon the structuring of a discursive field. What is denied is not that such objects exist externally to thought, but the rather different assertion that they could constitute themselves as objects outside any discursive condition of emergence. (Laclau and Mouffe 1985: 108)

In these terms, proposing a split between the real and discourse, or arguing that a deconstructive attention to matters of textuality and metaphoricity necessarily precludes addressing history and politics, can be seen to be "ideological" in the bad sense, an act of mystification and disavowal. Such acts of ideological reinscription frequently owe their potency to disciplinary distinctions and defenses of turf. But if we accept that, in the broad sense noted above, events are never not discursively constructed, and that the language even of history writing is always also language, we will have taken some politically useful critical distance from such disciplinary ideology.

We therefore think that there can be no truly radical critical or political practice that is not attentive to history, but we must also recognize that history is itself always discursively constructed from "documents" that " 'process' or rework 'reality'," as intellectual historian Dominick LaCapra puts it (LaCapra 1985: 19). The invocation of history too often precludes any investigation of the concept itself, let alone its material specificities or its politics in a strategic sense, and it is often accompanied by a fetishization of the past and the archive. As Denise Riley comments, justifying her discursively historical essay on the category of women in history:

> Foucault has written, "The purpose of history, guided by genealogy, is not to discover the roots of our identity but to commit itself to its dissipation." This is terrific – but, someone continues to ask, whatever does feminism want with dissipated identities? . . . It is the misleading

familiarity of "history" which can break open the daily naturalism of what surrounds us. (Riley 1988: 5)

The "daily naturalism" of the effects of sexuality, race, and imperialism, as well as class and gender, will be examined in subsequent chapters. Deconstruction, a politically useful but not foundational moment of poststructuralist thought, will be crucial to the efforts to break open, historicize, and de-naturalize these categories.

Part III

The Politics of Contemporary Theory

7

The Politics of Essence

If deconstruction cannot found a political program, if anti-essentialist theories put identities into question, how is a poststructuralist identity politics possible? And yet the proliferation of new social movements and new politicized identities testifies to the continuing power of identity as a mobilizing term, even in this postmodern moment. What we can see at work over and over, in many globally dispersed locations, is what Biddy Martin and other critics have called the project of undoing identity on the grounds of identity:

> Our task is to deconstruct, to undo our own meanings and categories, the identities and the positions from which we intervene at any given point so as not to close the question of woman and discourse around new certainties and absolutes. We cannot afford to refuse to take a political stance "which pins us to our sex" for the sake of an abstract theoretical correctness, but we can refuse to be content with fixed identities or to universalize ourselves as revolutionary subjects. (Martin 1988: 16)

Our final chapters will address the seeming, but only seeming, paradox of a contemporary identity politics of undone identities, focusing on some of the most powerful forms such thinking has taken, both inside and outside the high-theoretical discourse of academic institutions.

Remember that in 1977 the Combahee River Collective of Boston identified their project as struggling against "interlocking" systems of oppression – racial, sexual, heterosexual, and class oppression. What happens when we begin to take each of these categories apart in an anti-essentialist vein? Has the advent of poststructuralist theory made the analysis of such interlocking and possibly contradictory systems of oppression easier, or more difficult, or just different from the way it looked in 1977? We might begin by looking again at Michèle Barrett's 1988 Introduction to *Women's Oppression Today*. It appears that the difficulty Barrett has had articulating feminism with Marxism, and subsequently with critiques of racism and hetero-sexism, has something to do with Barrett's own disciplinary commit-ments to sociological analysis. Criticizing her 1980 book for being insufficiently attentive to questions of race and ethnocentrism, Barrett admits:

> the general area of ideology, culture and subjectivity has proved a far more fertile ground for new work around issues of ethnic difference and racism than has been the case with the traditional economic and social concerns of socialist thought and the academic social sciences. This is principally because existing theories of social structure, already taxed by attempting to think about the inter-relations of class and gender, have been quite unable to integrate a third axis of systemic inequality into their conceptual maps. Theoretical perspectives using the more flexible vocabulary of subjectivity and discourse have made it possible to explore these issues without being constrained by the need to assign rank in what is effectively a zero-sum game of structural determination. Hence the proliferation of interesting work on these themes in literary criticism and cultural studies generally, and the paucity of advances in sociology and macro-economic thought. (Barrett 1988: xii)

If Barrett is right, then a poststructuralist vocabulary will make the task of articulating multiple forms of oppression easier than it had been previously. The new identity politics, if it puts identity into question and refuses to essentialize its categories, will be better equipped to deal with social and subjective complexity than its more strictly Marxian or sociological predecessors. This more flexible vocabulary of subjectivity and discourse will provide the principal terms around which the chapters in Part III will be organized.

Essentialism: What's the Fuss About?

But what is essentialism, and why must exponents of anti-essentialist feminism or of the new identity politics around race, gay sexuality, and postcoloniality have such a highly charged and often contested relation to it? Let's take the case of feminism and essentialism/anti-essentialism first. This debate sometimes appears as a perceived split between theory and experience in feminist debates. Sometimes, not

always, this split lines up with a generational division identified by
Alice Jardine (1989): women's formulations of, and engagement with,
feminism which date from the late 1970s and afterwards, as opposed
to what went before. We could call the later, more self-consciously
theoretical, versions of feminism anti-essentialist in that they tend
to problematize categories founded on philosophical essences by
showing them to be constructed relationally, discursively.

As Diana Fuss puts it in *Essentially Speaking*, a book devoted
entirely to providing a good, clear introduction to this particular
debate, we could describe the two camps who pride themselves
on their identification with experience and theory, respectively, as
essentialists versus constructionists:

> Essentialism is classically defined as a belief in true essence – that
> which is most irreducible, unchanging, and therefore constitutive of
> a given person or thing. . . . In feminist theory . . . essentialism can
> be located in appeals to a pure or original femininity, a female essence,
> outside the boundaries of the social and thereby untainted (though
> perhaps repressed) by a patriarchal order. . . . Constructionism,
> articulated in opposition to essentialism and concerned with its philo-
> sophical refutation, insists that essence is itself a historical construction.
> Constructionists take the refusal of essence as the inaugural moment
> of their own projects and proceed to demonstrate the way previously
> assumed self-evident kinds (like "man" or "woman") are in fact the
> effects of complicated discursive practices. (Fuss 1989: 2)

Fuss's own project is to expose the way constructionism precisely
depends upon essentialism rather than being purely in opposition to
it. As a poststructuralist feminist who takes her cues from Derrida,
Lacan, and Foucault as well as Monique Wittig, Luce Irigaray, and
Gayatri Spivak, Fuss wishes not to repudiate essentialism but to
study it deconstructively, to analyze its deployment in various discourses. Her position is akin to what Spivak describes as a belief
"that one shouldn't throw away things but use them, strategically"
(Spivak 1990: 10).

This double-take on the question of essence distinguishes Fuss's
work from some earlier attempts to expose and root out essentialisms
as inherently reactionary forms of thought. Making a Fuss, as it
were, means acknowledging that anti-essentialism itself can become
a reactionary position if it is allowed to freeze into an orthodoxy,
to lose a sense of its own strategic deployments: "To insist that
essentialism is always and everywhere reactionary is, for the construc-

tionist, to buy into essentialism in the very act of making the charge; *it is to act as if essentialism has an essence"* (Fuss 1989: 21).

A frequently cited text that takes up an anti-essentialist position explicitly is Denise Riley's *"Am I That Name?" Feminism and the Category of "Women" in History* (1988). For Riley,

> the risky elements to the processes of alignment in sexed ranks are never far away, and the very collectivity which distinguishes you may also be wielded, even unintentionally, against you. Not just against you as an individual, that is, but against you as a social being with needs and attributions. The dangerous intimacy between subjectification and subjection needs careful calibration. (1988: 17)

That careful calibration requires a recognition of the material effects of discourses within which the shifting category of "women" has its being. As Riley suggests, quoting Marx on the concept of labor, "even the most abstract categories . . . are nevertheless, in the specific character of this abstraction, themselves likewise a product of historical relations, and possess their full validity only for and within those relations" (Marx 1973: 105; cited in Riley 1988: 16).

Difficult as this sounds, the tension that Riley proposes between "women" as a foundation of and "women" as a stumbling block to feminism is, from an anti-essentialist position, a necessary and productive tension that populist appeals for a return to real women ignore at their peril. From this position, it is no longer acceptable to situate oneself merely "as a woman." Those who would do so run the risk of being read as speaking from and for First World, Euroamerican, class, race, and heterosexual privilege. According to younger feminist critics like Biddy Martin and Chandra Mohanty, older feminisms which generalize about women unproblematically, uncrosshatched by the multiple differences between women, are not even adequate "to the task of articulating the situation of white women in the West," let alone other women, elsewhere (Martin and Mohanty 1986: 193).

This valorization of feminist critique only insofar as it is anti-essentialistically committed to differences between and among women, and to articulating the concrete specificities of particular historical and cultural contexts rather than generalizing about women, is by no means a dominant position within feminism. Indeed, many of the most eminent feminist critics on both sides of the Atlantic continue to define their positions in relation to the category of women, relatively unspecified and uncrosshatched by other axes of difference.

Feminism without Women?

In the same 1986 volume in which Martin and Mohanty's essay appears, Tania Modleski criticizes Jonathan Culler's would-be deconstructive male-feminist framing of the question of "reading as a woman." She challenges Culler's "'hypothesis' of a woman reader" by arguing for the importance of feminist criticism's empowering of real women readers, represented by, or, rather, "actual-"ized in, the "female feminist critic" (Modleski 1986: 132–4). Thus, on the one hand, Modleski's essay gestures towards a democratizing, populist notion of real women's experience – feminist criticism is *for* women, it's a political tool we can use to resist our oppression, it's not simply a theoretical approach like any other. On the other hand, she does not problematize the category "women" in terms of material differences like differences in class, race, sexuality, or culture; she places it in an antagonistic relation to "men," including would-be male feminists like Culler.

These real female readers of an unspecified variety do in fact become rather quickly grounded in Modleski's essay, not through their specifically class-, nation-, and race-inflected, gendered, and sexually and ethnically identified subject positions, as Martin and Mohanty might wish, but through their location in an institution, as feminist critics. The populist gesture gives way to a return to academic discourse, as Modleski substitutes an "*actual*" female reader for Culler's hypothetical one, in the person of the female feminist critic. Thus Modleski replaces the open-ended category of the woman reader with the discursively positioned category of the feminist critic in order to insist on the inseparability of interpretation and power, and her essay concludes with a stirring call to feminist action on behalf of women, again undifferentiated among themselves: "the ultimate goal of feminist criticism and theory is female empowerment" (1986: 136).

It is not that Modleski perceives there to be no material differences among feminists. Far from it, since in the penultimate paragraph of her essay, she implies that she has written her essay to intervene in feminist debates with women, to criticize certain moves made by anti-essentialist and deconstructive female feminists as much as to take on Culler. Modleski clearly sees that the implicit feminist taboo on disagreeing with other feminists in public has to be violated. Although "sisterhood" is a "laudable" feminist "emphasis," she observes, "we may gain more by acknowledging the power struggles that go on among us than by perennially disavowing them" (1986: 136). And so Modleski resuscitates the categories of real women readers and female experience, against the current of anti-essentialist problematization and the proliferation of differences within and among feminisms.

Now the anti-essentialist, crosshatched-by-other-axes-of-difference, subject-positions-position might well ask of Modleski's essay, how are we to reconcile her populist emphasis on empowering women readers, presumably both inside and outside academic institutions, with her rather too homogeneous categories of real women and their experience? Commenting on Modleski's essay, Fuss asks, "Why . . . do I find Modleski's concluding invocation of 'female empowerment' so distinctly *disempowering*?" (Fuss 1989: 28). Predictably, Fuss argues, because Modleski has not accounted for which women she is speaking for, to, and about. Fuss queries, "Does she propose to rescue *all* female readers, including 'third world' readers, lesbian readers, and working-class readers? Are not some female readers *materially* more empowered than others, by virtue of class, race, national, or other criteria? For that matter, are not *some* female readers more empowered than *some* male readers?" (1989: 28). According to Fuss, although Modleski's essay "presents itself as a materialist investigation of 'reading as a woman,'" her argument ends up re-essentializing "the category of Woman" because it neglects to address the "real, material differences between women" (1989: 28).

One of the consequences of this unlimited divisibility model most feared by critics like Modleski, who wish to maintain the right to employ "women" as a relatively undifferentiated category, is that under all this pressure from other axes of difference women will once again disappear. Unlimited divisibility might in the end produce ultimate invisibility. This is the burden of Modleski's recent critique of Denise Riley's book. In *Feminism Without Women* Modleski observes, "It is not altogether clear to me why women, much more so than any other oppressed groups of people, have been so willing to yield the ground on which to make a stand against their oppression" (1991: 15). Could it be that the hostile reaction the notion of woman produces in many women, who have taken up the banner of anti-essentialism so enthusiastically, repeats a patriarchal and misogynist phobia?

Citing Teresa de Lauretis's important 1989 article on the essentialism debate, Modleski advises us to "hold onto the category of woman while recognizing ourselves to be in the *process* (an unending one) of *defining and constructing the category* (which, as noted earlier, includes very disparate types of people)." And Modleski goes on to celebrate the contributions of "women of various sexualities, classes, ethnicities, and races" who without benefit of anti-essentialism per se "have strenuously resisted efforts of white middle-class women to colonize them" (1991: 20).

We think that this, Modleski's most recent word on the subject, should be understood in the context of a strategic, not an uncritical, deployment of essentialism. We agree that we should be suspicious of postfeminist moves, suspicious of suggestions that we give up on feminism, or on the notion of mobilizing as women and feminists against patriarchal institutions and relations, just when a deafening antifeminist backlash ought to be signaling to us what good work we're doing.

Leaky Distinctions

Believing, then, that we should use things rather than throw them away, let's look at the uses that can be made of *both* anti-essentialist arguments and strategic essentialisms in negotiating new forms of identity politics today. We will examine how the concept of the split or non-self-identical subject and the concepts of discourse and historical genealogy enable a critical rethinking of the categories of sexuality, race, imperialism and ecology through which their combined articulation becomes possible.

If Lacan and Foucault have authored these principal terms of the subject and discourse, new bodies of work on race and the history of sexuality have pushed psychoanalysis and discourse theory further in the direction of a radical, self-critical identity politics than this list of theoretical masters might lead one to expect. The multiple identities explored by radical women of color, the poststructuralist-inflected, anti-essentialist critiques of race performed by African-American theorists, and the historical genealogy of sexuality undertaken primarily by critics in gay and lesbian studies, have so destabilized easy assumptions about sexuality, gender, race, class, and their various intersections and permutations within concrete cultural situations, that these bodies of work have had enormous impact on what can be said about categories of identity in theoretical contexts today.

It also will not do to confuse anti-racism with anti-imperialism, though the movements are related. Critics of colonial and postcolonial discourse have caused more local notions of identity politics to be rethought in the light of the history of imperialism. And the global movements of multinational capital that have supplemented the older political forms of imperialism, often in the form of neo-colonial economic relations, frequently do not respect national boundaries or the sovereignty of nation-states. In both global economic relations and information technologies since the microelectronic revolution, notions of citizenship, nationality, and cultural identity are being challenged. And this is happening at the same moment, and along the same networks of power, that have forced us to recognize a pending ecological crisis of global proportions.

Borders national, human, technological, and animal are being simultaneously questioned. The age of the "leaky distinction," in Donna Haraway's phrase, is upon us (Haraway 1991: 152). The need for anti-essentialist critiques of essentialist thinking – like "people are people, and animals are animals," implying that there is a firm line between the two, and that the first category thus should always, self-evidently, take priority over the latter – has never been greater. If any materialist or feminist project is to survive, it had better be a *green* materialism in this historical moment.

8

Identity and Sexuality

What Derrida, after Saussure, has done for language and textuality, Lacan has done for subjectivity: he has provided a necessary beginning for thinking about models of the self as founded in difference and not identity. If "in the beginning" there is difference or relationality rather than identity, even the search for *an* origin becomes problematical. The lack of any natural link between signifiers and signifieds, between signs and their referents, posits a generative difference, not a founding identity. Linguistic meaning is seen to be produced by differences between signifiers themselves, and by the unstoppable chains of signification which constitute any signifying practice, any example of linguistic or other cultural production.

The Lacan Story

In his essay "The Agency of the Letter in the Unconscious," Lacan appropriates for his rereading of Freud Saussure's notion of the structure of the signifier by attributing to Saussure a certain algorithm:

$$\frac{S}{s}$$

which is read as "the signifier over the signified, 'over' corresponding to the bar separating the two stages" (Lacan 1977: 149).[1] Because the units of this structure are subjected to the double condition "of being reducible to ultimate differential elements and of combining them according to the laws of a closed order" (1977: 152), Lacan argues, we can see simultaneously both the localized structure of the signifier, what he calls the "letter," and the linear way in which signifiers combine along signifying chains: "For the signifier, by its very nature, always anticipates meaning by unfolding its dimension before it. . . . From which we can say that it is in the chain of the signifier that the meaning 'insists' but that none of its elements 'consists' in the signification of which it is at the moment capable" (1977: 153). Lacan concludes, "We are forced, then, to accept the notion of an incessant sliding of the signified under the signifier" (1977: 154).

This problematization of our ability to control meaning, intention, and signification has become one of the hallmarks of the poststructuralist critique of humanist presuppositions about language. Readers of David Lodge's novel *Nice Work* are treated to satirical repetitions of this recognition of the perpetual sliding of the signified under the signifier, a recognition disturbing to would-be masterful subjects, like the managing directors of failing manufacturing plants in deindustrialized Britain, and white, upwardly mobile men generally, who are unaccustomed to "reading in" the exhausting signification of heterosexual sex throughout Euroamerican culture. As Lodge's satirically feminist heroine Robyn Penrose points out, advertising is a particularly powerful locus of signification, a veritable repository of examples of signifieds sliding under signifiers:

> "Somebody in an advertising agency dreamt up the name 'Silk Cut' to suggest a cigarette that wouldn't give you a sore throat or a hacking cough or lung cancer. But after a while the public got used to the name, the word 'Silk' ceased to signify, so they decided to have an advertising campaign to give the brand a high profile again. Some bright spark in the agency came up with the idea of rippling silk with a cut in it. The original metaphor is now represented literally. But new metaphorical connotations accrue – sexual ones. Whether they were consciously intended or not doesn't really matter. It's a good example of the perpetual sliding of the signified under the signifier, actually." (Lodge 1989: 221–2)

If we cannot control our own acts of signification, what can we control? If sexual difference is constantly being signified whether we wish it to be or not, how are we to avoid confronting the implications of sexism and oppressive power relations once we have recognized how signification works? This is a discomfiting analysis for Vic Wilcox, managing director and proud smoker of Marlboros, the ads for which don't disturb a naive faith in the stability of the signified, as Robyn points out.

Since the Marlboro ads establish not a metaphorical but a metonymical connection between smoking that brand and a life of cowboy macho and independence, the ads still signify in excess of any simply literal notion that "a cigarette is just a cigarette," but they do so apparently without doing so. In the substitution of one thing for another, metaphors forge a relation of similarity between apparently unlike or discrete objects. Metonymic substitutions, on the other hand, depend upon relations of contiguity, by substituting some part, attribute, association, cause, or effect of an object for the object itself.

Lacan attempts to organize the mechanics of the entire apparatus of signification, including Freud's model of the unconscious and the mechanics of dreamwork, through the interplay of metaphor and metonymy. Transposing the structuralist critique from Saussurean linguistics to the study of subjectivity, Lacan argues not only that "the unconscious is structured like a language," but that the

$$\frac{S}{s}$$

algorithm of signifier/signified can serve as a model for the individual subject, who is, of course, constructed in and through language.

Lacan proceeds to elaborate on this algorithm by producing his infamous equations, so offputting to students of literature and anyone who suffers from math anxiety that they represent a principal stumbling block for Lacan's prospective readers. As Jane Gallop comments, "The violence of Lacan's style is its capacity to make the reader feel nonidentical with herself as reader, or, in other more psychological terms, to make the reader feel inadequate to her role as 'the man to whom Lacan addresses himself,' that is, inadequate to Lacan's style" (Gallop 1985: 117). One of these equations or glosses on the algorithm

$$\frac{S}{s}$$

is the equation for metonymy, which Lacan symbolizes as:

$$f(S \dots S')S \cong S(-)s$$

Lacan describes this formula as representative of metonymic structure in the following way:

> that is to say, [this symbolizes] the metonymic structure, indicating that it is the connexion between signifier and signifier that permits the elision in which the signifier installs the lack-of-being in the object

relation, using the value of 'reference back' possessed by signification
in order to invest it with the desire aimed at the very lack it supports.
The sign — placed between ( ) represents here the maintenance of
the bar — which, in the original algorithm, marked the irreducibility
in which, in the relations between signifier and signified, the resistance
of signification is constituted. (1977: 164)

Here certain similarities between Lacan's thinking and Derrida's may
be discerned.

We could say that the signifying chain operates according to the
logic of the supplement, and that Lacan's notion of the subject in
founded on lack, the lack that the supplement shows to have been
implicit in the first term it is supplementing. The critique of identities
and origins proceeds according to a supplementary logic, not beginning with a self-identical subject or origin, but in difference – the
signifying chain, marked by ellipsis and elision, by the lack of fit
between signifiers and signifieds, and by the differences between
signifiers themselves. The chain is constructed relationally along an
axis of displacements; there is a lack-of-being in these very *relations*,
a lack of identity between signifier and signified and between subjects
and their desired objects, that generates both signification and desire.
Both signification and desire thus "originate" not in a self-identical
subject but in a relation of lack, or lack-of-being, "using the value
of 'reference back' possessed by signification," the logic of the supplement as it applies to signification, "in order to invest it with the
desire aimed at the very lack it supports." A desire founded on lack
is an alienated desire, a desire that can never be satisfied, the product
of a self who is not self-identical, but rather split, constructed in
difference, in the relation between the S and the s, the bar between
which symbolizes the irreducibility of the resistances that mark the
constitution of both signification and the subject.

One of the difficulties of Lacan's style lies in his use of such
"mathematical" formulae in his remodeling of the subject of psychoanalysis. What purposes might this strategy serve? Using mathematical equations, as in the example above, defamiliarizes our sense of
such otherwise literary figures as metonymy. These figures become
newly strange and newly scientific-seeming. The new scientificity of
linguistic concepts applied to Freud's theory of the unconscious
heightens both our sense of Freud's scientificity and the scientificity
of Lacan's reading of Freud. Indeed, Lacan wants to argue that
Freud's psychoanalytic theory had already recognized the importance
and material agency of the signifier before Saussurean linguistics had

come into being, and that Freud's theory in fact paved the way for Saussure's "before the formalizations of linguistics for which one could no doubt show that it paved the way by the sheer weight of its truth" (1977: 162). Thus Lacan represents Freud as a structuralist "before the letter," one who has recognized the materiality of the letter or signifier all along, so that Lacan is performing no radically revisionist reading of Freud's texts but merely allowing us to see what was already there: a linguistically inflected, structuralist Freud awaiting a (post)structuralist reading.

The relation between Lacanian "mathematical" equations and his discursive explanation of them also works in another way. The equations may render the discourse scientific, but those very non-verbal equations need a discursive explanation in order to be intelligible. Lacan not only explains his equations verbally by reading them discursively, as in the example above; he demonstrates by doing so that we cannot read mathematical formulae at all without in some sense discoursing about them, translating them back into verbal signifying systems. Once again, the insistent agency of the *letter* is insisted upon. And Lacan not only insists upon it explicitly in his discourse, but reveals it to be indisputably true by offering us gnomic non-verbal formulae in need of legible lettering. As with Freud's anticipation of Saussurean linguistics, so with the material agency of the letter: the letter as agent of discursive signification comes to dominate non-discursivity. Even the seemingly non-discursive concept of the unconscious is shown to be discursive. Lacan writes, "The unconscious is neither primordial nor instinctual; what it knows about the elementary is no more than the elements of the signifier" (1977: 170). This recognition thus paves the way "by the sheer weight of its truth" for a model of the subject that is constructed in and through language.

Lacan builds his model of the split subject in opposition to Descartes's *cogito*: "*Cogito ergo sum*; I think, therefore I am." For Lacan, the self's "radical ex-centricity to itself" (1977: 171) prevents such self-presence within consciousness, such self-identity and autonomy, from being possible. Lacan's radical revision of the *cogito* goes like this: "I am not wherever I am the plaything of my thought; I think of what I am where I do not think to think" (1977: 166). This splitting of the subject can be exemplified by the scene of writing, where the "I" who writes and the "I" who is represented in writing remain irreducibly different. The "I" who is represented takes on the character of an Other, in some sense an object of desire, simultaneously mirroring and alienated from the subject who writes: "For this subject, who thinks he can accede to himself by designating himself in the statement, is no more than such an object. Ask the writer about the anxiety that he experiences when faced by the blank sheet of paper, and he will tell you who *is* the turd of his phantasy" (1977: 315). There is an Other, or an "it" within the "I." It is in this sense that Lacan speaks of the discourse of the unconscious as the discourse of the Other, "in order to indicate the beyond in which the recognition of desire is bound up with the desire for recognition" (1977: 172). The subject is thus founded on a radical alterity, an otherness within, which makes the subject ex-centric to itself, decentered though constantly misrecognizing itself as centered, self-identical, and autonomous. Such misrecognitions are irreducible fictions, not mistakes to be corrected. The fiction of a unified self, of an identity which is unproblematically self-identical, is as inescapable as, for Althusser, one's being hailed or called into being by ideology, or, for Derrida, the constant efforts at centering necessary for any act of thinking, any theoretical or practical activity.

So for Lacan the originary moment of subjectivity is a moment of misrecognition, of fiction and illusion. In "The Mirror Stage," Lacan traces the development of the subject in order to account for this founding illusion. The concept of the mirror stage, that fundamental misrecognition in the mirror, was most influential for Althusser's theory of how ideology works through hailing subjects into being, or interpellation. And Lacan's discussion here of the Imaginary, the Symbolic, and the Real, organized around the phallus as the trancendental signifier, has proved most influential for feminist theorists of subjectivity. Some time between the ages of six and eighteen months, says Lacan, the infant experiences an identification with its own image in the mirror, a moment of jubilation, of mastery in excess of what it is capable of in terms of motor coordination or physical autonomy:

> This jubilant assumption of his specular image by the child at the *infans* stage, still sunk in his motor incapacity and nursling dependence, would seem to exhibit in an exemplary situation the symbolic matrix in which the *I* is precipitated in a primordial form, before it is objectified in the dialectic of identification with the other, and before language restores to it, in the universal, its function as subject. (1977: 2)

Feminist readers of Lacan such as Jane Gallop gender this infant differently in order to construct an identification with Lacan's text, though it is worth remembering that for Lacan, as for Julia Kristeva in "Stabat Mater" (see Kristeva 1986), the paradigmatic infant is always male. And if this passage sounds like Lacan writing as a developmental psychologist, we should resist the desire to read simple linear development, temporal or subjective, into his model. Making the paradigmatic infant female, and drawing attention to the connection between a dialectic (non-linear notion) of temporality and a constitutive fiction, Gallop comments:

> The jubilation, the enthusiasm, is tied to the temporal dialectic by which she appears *already* to be what she will *only later become.* . . . This moment is the source not only for what follows but also for what precedes. It produces the future through anticipation and the past through retroaction. And yet it is itself a moment of self-delusion, of captivation by an illusory image. Both future and past are thus rooted in an illusion. . . . Since the entire past and present is dependent upon an already anticipated maturity – that is, a projected ideal one – any "natural maturation" (however closely it might resemble the anticipated ideal one) must be defended against, for it threatens to expose the fact that the self is an illusion done with mirrors. (Gallop 1985: 78–83)

So while the chronological progression is not a simple one, because the mirror stage both anticipates the future and organizes the past, this stage called the Imaginary does prepare the ground for the infant's entrance into language, culture, and subjecthood by way of confronting castration and the Law of the Father. This process Lacan describes as entering the Symbolic order, though, since the phallus is the privileged signifier for the joining of language and desire, as well as the organizing site of sexual difference, men are presumed to enter the Symbolic more fully and constitutively than women.

As soon as one has said "language," from a feminist point of view, the likelihood of that language being the language of patriarchy is very strong indeed. And this is certainly the case with Lacan, who has proven to be of interest to feminists precisely because he addresses the relation between patriarchy and language or the Symbolic order so explicitly. But the languages of patriarchy are not strictly universal either as semiotic systems or as the discursive organization of social differences. Historically and materially, languages – even in their symbolic inflections – are inseparable from social and economic systems and practices that, in political terms, cast the question of language in terms of national and cultural differences as well as gender differences.

To put it simply, there is a certain structure to the subject identified

by Lacan which might translate across cultural and linguistic difference, but it can easily be exaggerated and abused as a universalism,
another colonizing gesture. Speaking as a postcolonial critic and a
Third World intellectual operating in the First World, Spivak formu-
lates the crucial thing about Lacan's theory of the subject like this:

> When one thinks about the unconscious as the positing of radical
> alterity, the positing of an It in the I, doesn't matter if it's Chinese
> or from the Andaman islands. . . . You see, the thing is when you
> say it's structured like a language, when it's structured like metaphor
> and metonymy, everything begins to go astray. (Spivak 1990: 150)

The notion of radical alterity has proved useful for theorists of the
new identity politics because of the way it situates the self-as-subject
and the Other in an inseparable relation. Not only to recognize
"othering" – the projection of foreign others in relation to oneself
– but to break down the imperial relation that has historically
accompanied this practice: that is the political task of deploying the
concept of radical alterity. We would argue, however, that when
Lacanian psychoanalysis comes to stand for a total analysis of subjectivity and sexuality this is another instance when "everything begins
to go astray." One of the problems with the existing feminist debate
on sexuality has been a relentless focus on psychoanalysis as *the*
language of sexuality and the family as *the* ground of identity. Such
a focus not only familializes sexuality but also heterosexualizes it.
Recent work by gay and lesbian critics has proved crucial to challenging a strictly psychoanalytic, family-based paradigm for understanding sexuality. They have insisted instead that sexuality must be
understood historically.

The Family Romance

The family: it is hard to consider this term in the nineties without
assuming a self-conscious tone, either reverent or irreverent, for the
family is far from a neutral category. Appeals to family values have
been mobilized by the right in their efforts to shut down everything
from abortion clinics to AIDS research. The breakdown of the
family has been held responsible for every social problem from
unemployment to drug trafficking and street crime. Neither countercultural alternatives to the nuclear family nor childcare, welfare,
and free healthcare can be encouraged, we are told, if the sanctity

of the family is to be preserved. As many feminists of color have made clear, however, sometimes the family is one's only buffer against a hostile and racist state.

Signs of an anti-feminist backlash in the media and popular culture include the contrast between a Technicolor version of family values and the crazed single woman, as in the film *Fatal Attraction*. If the vengeful single woman is fatally excluded from the family's charmed circle, she has only her own selfishness to blame, while according to popular representations, because of her there is also an army of forlorn, forsaken men out there, desperately seeking the family as the fulfillment of all longing, as in Christopher Lasch's notion of the family as a "haven in a heartless world" (1977).

Above all, perhaps, the family is rich in clichés. The family is always being celebrated, and it is always in danger. This endangered species is crucial to the New World Order, American-style, but, as American television testifies night after night, the nineties sit-com requires not the happy nuclear family of the fifties but rather the ironically functioning dysfunctional family. So, even when the family is shown to be a social form which doesn't work, we are not encouraged to think of alternatives.

Freud used the term "the family romance" to describe the popular fantasy that one is not really the child of one's mother and father, but rather the offspring of parents of a higher social standing. We use it here to describe a fascination with the family as the final explanation of social phenomena. We will argue that the notion of the family has itself been the site of so many false starts and so much confusion for both Marxism and feminism that it has a lot to answer for, or, if you prefer, it bears a great deal of theoretical responsibility for the particular dilemmas in which we currently find ourselves. One of the most divisive of these dilemmas is the split over the status of psychoanalysis among feminists doing self-professedly materialist work. Ideology or psychoanalysis? Marxism or Lacanianism? What does this divide between the social and the psychic mean for a materialist feminism? Framing the question depends decisively on how we think about the family, whether it becomes the province of psychoanalysis and therapy, or of social theory and social policy.

Oedipus Rex: Gayle Rubin

Two of the most useful attempts to read the concepts of kinship and the family critically are Gayle Rubin's essay "The Traffic in Women"

(1975) and Rosalind Coward's chapter, "The Concept of the Family in Marxist Theory" in her book *Patriarchal Precedents* (1983). Both begin by taking the Marxist tradition seriously; both end up with psychoanalysis as the place for feminists to be doing their work. Rubin is a US feminist, Coward a UK feminist. Like her historical materialist predecessors Marx and Engels, Rubin uses anthropological data to problematize the naturalness of contemporary Euroamerican kinship arrangements, attempting to understand both the seeming variety of and the persistently male-dominated structuring of kinship relations across periods and cultures through the concept of the historically and culturally specific construction of "sex/gender systems." She wants to add a feminist supplement to Marx's analysis of class relations that would use his and Engels's historical method to theorize a "political economy of sex."

Coward, influenced by Foucault, attempts to historicize the concept of the family by analyzing the various discourses and academic disciplines through which it has been not only studied but ideologically constructed. For Coward, assumptions about men and women within a universalizing history of the family have too often prevented any proper analysis of sexual division or antagonism, let alone any explanation of women's subordination. The same assumptions about the family have limited the potential of both Marxist and psychoanalytic theories to tackle head-on the problem of women's oppression. Both Rubin and Coward agree that women's seemingly universal subordination is crucially linked with their construction as gendered (for Rubin) and sexually identified (for Coward) subjects within systems of signification in which the social meanings given to anatomical difference are seen as prescribing asymmetrical gender destinies in a most oppressive way.

Both Rubin and Coward, then, begin with a commitment to seeing women's oppression as crucially bound up with other forms of social and economic relations, though not reducible to them. Both begin with the assumption that Marx and Engels's historical materialism provides the best theoretical lever for exposing the social and ideological, not the natural, constitution of human activities. Yet the fact that gender and sexuality are not so much addressed within Marxist theory as subsumed within the analysis of class relations drives both Rubin and Coward to psychoanalysis as the place where sexuality can be studied and not assumed. In the course of both their enterprises, we end up with a fascinated reflection on the radical potential of psychoanalytic theory. Rubin goes so far as to claim that "Psychoanalysis is a feminist theory *manqué*" (Rubin 1975: 185).

By wanting to save psychoanalysis from its previous misuses, from its mishandling by a sexist institution and from the residues of misogynist gender ideology contaminating it in the hands of its founders and practitioners, Rubin and Coward claim to be unleashing its radical potential. But in trying to save psychoanalysis for feminism, we argue, both end up re-privileging certain psychoanalytic assumptions that might well be seen as in themselves ideological residues. The reinvention of a Marxist project sufficiently pressured by feminist concerns, or feminist interruptions, gets postponed once again in favor of a psychoanalytic project, as if that were feminism's proper home – women being offered again for therapy, talking their way out of "their" problems, rather than changing history and social relations, as Swindells and Jardine put it (1990: 78, 165, 4, 24). Rather than rescuing the radical potential of psychoanalysis, therefore, Rubin and Coward may have been sucked into a less than radical fascination with psychoanalysis itself. A psychoanalytic reinscription of the family romance can be seen to be subtly undermining the radical potential of their own critiques. Let's look in more detail at what this process entails.

Gayle Rubin's principal contribution to feminist theory is the notion of a "sex/gender system," by which the ahistoricity of patriarchy and its heterosexual presumptions may be avoided. Rubin's position is particularly noteworthy for having been formulated as early as the mid-1970s, since it addresses questions of gay liberation as well as feminist liberation and never takes heterosexuality for granted (unlike Coward's, whose sexual difference terminology implicitly insinuates a certain heterosexual division of the world into "women" and "men," couple-able subjects constructed through "sexual division"). Rubin wants to imitate Marx in his critique of bourgeois political economy by reading Lévi-Strauss and Freud because "they provide conceptual tools with which one can build descriptions of the part of social life which is the locus of the oppression of women, of sexual minorities, and of certain aspects of human personality within individuals." She calls that part of social life the "'sex/gender system,' for lack of a more elegant term" (1975: 159). This system determines what counts as sexuality and gender in a particular society; it is "a set of arrangements by which the biological raw material of human sex and procreation is shaped by human, social intervention and satisfied in a conventional manner, no matter how bizarre some of the conventions may be" (1975: 165). Taking from Lévi-Strauss the idea of "the exchange of women" as "an initial step toward building an arsenal of concepts with which sexual systems can be described" (1975: 177), Rubin goes on to link feminism and gay liberation as two forms of rebellion against a sex/gender system equally oppressive to straight women, lesbians, and gay men:

> Gender is not only an identification with one sex; it also entails that sexual desire be directed toward the other sex. The sexual division of labor is implicated in both aspects of gender – male and female it creates them, and it creates them heterosexual. The suppression of the homosexual component of human sexuality, and by corollary, the oppression of homosexuals, is therefore a product of the same system whose rules and relations oppress women. (1975: 180)

Thus, even when what we might consider specific forms of homosexuality are encouraged, as in some New Guinea men's groups or the institutionalized transvestism of the Mohave, "the rules of gender division and obligatory heterosexuality are present even in their transformations" (1975: 182).

In order to understand how these rules of prohibition and of what counts as sex get transmitted, argues Rubin, we need to return to Freud, but not just through any old reading because "the radical implications of Freud's theory have been radically repressed" (1975: 184). Hence the way psychoanalysis, especially in the US, has been used to oppress straight women, gay men, and lesbians, and hence the attacks on Freud by the women's and gay movements. No, we will proceed to examine "The Oedipus Hex" by means of a Lacanian structuralist reading that will de-biologize Freud and make it possible for women to "Unite to Off the Oedipal Residue of Culture," according to Rubin's section headings, all in the interests of eventually theorizing that Marxian "Political Economy of Sex," the section with which her essay ends.

What happens in the course of this critical return to Freud via Lacan, however, is something different from what Rubin seems to want to be arguing. We might well rewrite her section "The Oedipus Hex" as "Oedipus Rex," because she ends up re-enthroning Freud's Oedipus rather than offing him. There is a tension in Rubin's argument between setting up the psychoanalytic notion of the Oedipus complex as a mere mechanism with no specific content – it simply marks the individual subject's acquisition of a socially specific gender and a sexuality – and falling back on Freud's own description of the Oedipus complex. For Freud's presentation, far from being cross-culturally applicable, is quite culturally specific regarding what the

Oedipus complex entails in terms of gender identity and what counts as (hetero)sexuality.

Thus Rubin's own language shifts from page 189 when she argues, via Lacan, "When the child leaves the Oedipal phase, its libido and gender identity have been organized in conformity with the rules of the culture which is domesticating it," a deliberately open phrasing in which there is nothing self-evident about what it means to have been gendered "male" or "female." We "Revisit" Oedipus in the next section – not being able to leave him alone – and arrive at the call for women to "Off the Oedipal Residue" on page 198, where we find that Rubin is proposing not a revolutionary overthrow but Oedipal reformism, "reorganizing the domain of sex and gender in such a way that each individual's Oedipal experience would be less destructive." A "revolution in kinship" (1975: 199) should be feminism's goal, because if there were no "obligatory sexualities and sex roles" (1975: 204), if "men did not have overriding rights in women (if there was no exchange of women) and if there were no gender, the entire Oedipal drama would be a relic" (1975: 199). If it were a relic, would it crumble and disappear? Or would it remain, whether as symbolically loaded, though anachronistic, residue or as simple cross-cultural mechanism? How have we moved very far beyond the psychoanalytic establishment, if the revolution is purely a revolution in kinship, in the family, independent of other social and economic relations?

Rubin does not answer these questions. She ends, rather perfunctorily, by insisting that sex/gender systems need to be seen in relation to other social systems, such as state formation, in order to be fully understood: "Eventually, someone will have to write a new version of *The Origin of the Family, Private Property, and the State*, recognizing the mutual interdependence of sexuality, economics, and politics without underestimating the full significance of each in human society" (1975: 210). *Someone else* needs to carry on with Engels's worthy project. She, Gayle Rubin, is apparently too exhausted to go beyond reforming Oedipus, rewriting his significance to make it less disastrous for women and gay liberation.

Treacherous Hearts: Rosalind Coward

For Rosalind Coward, psychoanalysis is a necessary wedge with which to pry open the concept of the family so important in Marxist theory and so awkward for feminism. It is "precisely the weight which the family came to bear in marxism which has prevented adequate understanding of the relations between the sexes" (Coward 1983: 131). Engels's *The Origin of the Family* is the most useful text for revealing "the political theory by which the woman question became such a problematic area in marxism while at the same time being absolutely central to it" (1983: 141). Engels's account of the division of labor in the family and the relation of this to class division is, according to Coward, "very suspect" because it is built on "presuppositions about the relations between the sexes which have made their theorisation difficult." These are: "a natural division of labour between the sexes; a male psychologistic motivation to ensure transmission of property to genetic offspring; and finally, the capacity and desire of the male to submit the female to these exigencies" (1983: 152–3). Thus, although Engels was trying to account for the emergence of the "'modern family,'" he writes in such a way that certain features of that family – the subordination of women, male sexual privilege – are treated as assumptions intrinsic to the family universally and transhistorically. And women disappear ideologically into the marital unit never to be heard of again except as familial participants in class relations: "The analytic priority of the family subsume[s] any separate consideration of the division between the sexes as an antagonistic division" (1983: 160).

Psychoanalysis is the terrain for understanding this sexual antagonism or, as Coward sometimes puts it more neutrally, "the specificities of sexual relations" (1983: 187). Since Marxism on its own remains oblivious to these specificities, Coward, like Rubin, thinks that Freud's discoveries have enormous radical potential for investigating sexuality as not consisting of self-evidently "given" fixed identities. Unfortunately, this radical tendency has usually lost out to another tendency within psychoanalysis, one which presents an intellectual stumbling block not so different from Marxism's, though it would prove even more coercive, "an apparently entirely reactionary commitment to the universality of the nuclear family" (1983: 222). A psychoanalytic theory geared to enforcing the nuclear family cannot recognize the radical potential of its own insights about sexuality.

In its discovery that a coherent or homogeneous notion of the subject is only a fantasy, that "not only is identity a construct, but it is also continuously and precariously reconstructed" (1983: 265), and that anatomical difference only takes on meanings within particular cultures, psychoanalysis provides what Coward praises as a "nonessentialist theory of sexuality" (1983: 256). And such a theory can explain how men are able to exercise power over women in our and other societies by showing how ideology works to merge all the terms, and all the lived possibilities, pertaining to the domain of sex and organize them into the self-evidently heterosexual polarities of masculinity and femininity:

> A closer examination of the differences between these terms [sex, sexuality, sexual identity, sexual division, sexual relations] will reveal that there has been an ideological work to merge these terms to work coherently on the combined axis of anatomical division and sexual instinct. It is the fact that *sexed* groups are constructed on anatomical division and our sexual identities are enmeshed around these divisions which is the primary mechanism by which men are able to exercise power over women. (1983: 279–80)

Now the funny thing about Coward's argument is that, although she seems to be trying very hard to break out of that conventional hetero-notion of how sexuality should be organized, she keeps pre-supposing it as the shared condition of her audience.

The last page of her book reinscribes that old heterosexual pre-sumption at the same time that her ostensible argument is protesting against it: "Because our culture privileges sexual identity as the truest part of our beings, we are secured voluntarily in a social unit which subordinates women" (1983: 286). We? Are secured? Voluntarily? We are all straight women? All of us are married? We all live in familial units in which our oppression as women is most directly felt? Cultural representations and social-structural relations are less important as sites of subordination than our individual sexed subjec-tivities?

Of course it follows from this assumption that the chief motor of women's oppression, the chief mechanism by which men's power is secured, is constituted in and by sexual division itself. Have we not then returned to a psychoanalytical version of gender as the primary oppression upon which others are constructed? And isn't this radical feminist view an idealist position rather than a materialist one? This mechanism for securing men's power assumes women's internaliz-ation, however precarious, of femininity and men's of masculinity. Or as Coward, still striving for a more materialist formulation than a strictly psychoanalytical one will allow, phrases it, what women and men internalize is the ideological "equation between anatomical division and sexual identity": "Sexual identity has been constructed as flowing from anatomical identity and on this have been built ideologies of appropriate desires and orientations" (1983: 286).

If this equation were as totalizing and definitive as it sounds, then the reconstruction of sexed subjectivities through a radical psychoanalysis alone would indeed revolutionize contemporary cultures and societies. If this equation were an adequate explanation of women's oppression, then, as the French materialist feminist Monique Wittig has argued, lesbianism would constitute a revolution in itself. For, Wittig declares, if lesbians refuse heterosexual desire and subordination to men, then lesbianism by definition disrupts the whole oppressive polarization of culture into simply two sexes: "for 'woman' has meaning only in heterosexual systems of thought and heterosexual economic systems. Lesbians are not women" (Wittig 1980: 110).

Yet political lesbianism is quite clearly not the direction in which Coward's argument takes us. We conclude rather with a reinscription of that very equation between anatomical and sexual difference, a final reiteration that the part played by "sexual identity [note the singular usage once again] in women's subordination" has been much misunderstood and now "feminist investigations" have laid a foundation for "understanding and changing this structure" (1983: 286). Besides Coward's own, what feminist investigations? Presumably the kind of Lacanian or structuralist feminist psychoanalysis going on in the work of Juliet Mitchell, Jacqueline Rose, and the members of the *m/f* group, especially Parveen Adams and Elizabeth Cowie (cited Coward 1983: 310, n. 13).

Back to the Couch: Jacqueline Rose

To produce psychoanalysis as the inevitable end of Marxist analysis seems to us at best problematical. Perhaps the purest proponent of this strategy is Jacqueline Rose, who argues in *Sexuality in the Field of Vision* (1986) that any politics will founder which does not recognize the unconscious and its ability to sabotage even the best-intentioned political program. According to Rose, "the political case for psychoanalysis" rests on the following two insights, which distinguish it from a functionalist account:

> Like Marxism, psychoanalysis sees the mechanisms [whereby ideological processes are transformed, via individual subjects, into human actions and beliefs] . . . as determinant, but also as leaving something in excess. If psychoanalysis can give an account of how women experience the path to femininity, it also insists, through the concept of the unconscious, that femininity is neither simply achieved nor is it ever

complete. . . . The difficulty is to pull psychoanalysis in the direction of both of these insights – towards a recognition of the fully social constitution of identity and norms, and then back again to that point of tension between ego and unconscious where they are endlessly remodelled and endlessly break. (Rose 1986: 7)

The difficulty of pulling psychoanalysis towards political action is what Marxists complain of over and over. Rose finds the placement of psychoanalysis within political discussion to be crucial. Is psycho-analysis to be introduced on its own terms or on Marxism's? Rose writes, "Thus it will have crucial effects, for instance, whether psychoanalysis is discussed as an addition or supplement to Marxism (in relation to which it is then found *wanting*), or whether emphasis is laid on the concept of the unconscious" (1986: 89).

Rose worries that whenever psychoanalysis is discussed as an addition or supplement to Marxism it is "found *wanting*." We have not exactly found this to be so, in either Rubin's work or Coward's. Rather, the reverse has been true. Derrida would argue that the theory of the supplement entails that whatever supplements that which has gone before supplants it, points up its lack. It is not the supplement that is found wanting, but that which is supplemented/-supplanted by it. However, since, as we shall see, Rose goes to great lengths to distinguish her loyalty to Lacan from any engagement with Derridian deconstruction, we should not expect her to apply a Derridian definition here or elsewhere.

For Rose, a supplement is likely to be found wanting, and when psychoanalysis is that supplement it must not be allowed to look inadequate. The psychoanalytical corrective to this Marxist mis-reading lies in properly emphasizing the concept of the unconscious:

For while it is indeed correct that psychoanalysis was introduced into feminism as a theory which could rectify the inability of Marxism to address questions of sexuality, and that this move was complementary to the demand within certain areas of Marxism for increasing attention to the ideological determinants of our social being, it is also true that undue concentration on this aspect of the theory has served to cut off the concept of the unconscious, or at least to displace it from the centre of the debate. (This is graphically illustrated in Michèle Barrett's book, *Women's Oppression Today*, in which the main discussion of psychoanalysis revolves around the concept of ideology, and that of the unconscious is left to a note appended at the end of the chapter). (1986: 89)

Now it seems to us that there is a great deal of difference between cutting off a concept and "displacing it from the centre of the debate." Rose's language seems to vacillate between defending the unconscious as a crucial factor in political theorizing, knowing it will otherwise be overlooked, and insisting that all political theorizing be centered on the unconscious itself – a politics of the unconscious rather than a social political program.

Although Rose regularly invokes Marxism as the appropriate theory with which to address social issues, one wonders whether her terms for political discussion would ever allow any straying into the social, *any movement outside* the unconscious. Or are we always to be, as it were, on the couch, exploring sexual difference "as one of the most fundamental, if not *the* most fundamental, of human laws," and thus *privileging* it "in political understanding and debate" (1986: 7)? When Rose writes, "To understand subjectivity, sexual difference and fantasy in a way which neither entrenches the terms nor denies them still seems to me to be a crucial task for today" (1986: 23), the claims for psychoanalysis seem modest and absolutely necessary. But what would it mean to be always centering and privileging the unconscious, to the exclusion of any extended consideration of ideology? Wouldn't that in fact constitute "an entrenchment" of these terms?

Two or Three Things about Freud: Michèle Barrett

Let's look at Barrett's note, to which she confines the unconscious rather than letting it seep into her chapter. And let's notice that Rose herself parenthesizes her reference to Barrett's note, hedging away from an argument with Barrett rather than taking her on, having it out over what the relations between ideology and the unconscious should be. In fact we might think from Rose's parenthesis that Barrett appended her note on the unconscious to a chapter on ideology, but that is not the case. The note, on "Freud's Account of Psychosexual Development," is a four-page discussion appended to a chapter on "Femininity, Masculinity, and Sexual Practice." So the note forms a sort of bridge between the discussion of gender and sexuality in one chapter and the discussion of "Ideology and the Cultural Production of Gender" in the next.

Why does Barrett choose this strategy? She implies she does because there is a difference between using particular insights from a body of work and accepting its internal consistency as a theory.

If you like, this is the kind of distinction that impels Barrett to respond critically to other people's eclecticism, their failure to make such a distinction. With comically catty disregard of the sensitivities of the feminist champions of psychoanalysis, Barrett writes:

> I am not . . . sufficiently convinced of the internal coherence of Freudian psychoanalytic theory to argue that fundamental reservations on crucial stages of his account invalidate his work entirely. On the contrary, I shall be arguing later in this chapter [in the note] that some of his observations are of great interest and can be useful. (Barrett 1980: 58)

Unlike Marxism, psychoanalytic theory has yet to prove itself as a coherent intellectual system, according to Barrett. Hence the anecdotal character of her inclusion of some of Freud's "observations" in a note. Thus, while some of Freud's insights may be useful in that they "relate to some common features of psychosexual development in capitalism" (1980: 60), Barrett remains particularly skeptical of Freud's tendency to universalize rather than historicize and suspicious of psychoanalysis's relation to history.

On these grounds alone, she fails to see how Marxism, feminism, and psychoanalysis can be theoretically reconciled (1980: 60). And here she holds those feminist champions who insist on psychoanalysis's importance for a materialist analysis largely responsible for this lack:

> What perhaps, would be convincing on the question of historical specificity versus universalism would be accounts of psychic structures, psychosexual development and familial relations drawn from comparative studies. Whilst the problems of undertaking such work are obvious, both for the historical and for the cross-cultural possibilities, it would presumably be feasible for some progress to be made towards research that could demarcate the limitations (or otherwise) of the applicability of psychoanalytic theory to other kinship structures. Yet feminists arguing for the compatibility of psychoanalysis with some form of materialism have tended to explore other areas (reworking of Freud's cases, general theoretical discussion of capitalism and patriarchal psychic structures, the application of psychoanalysis to cultural analysis, for example) and hence have left their claims unsubstantiated. (1980: 59)

Here Barrett cites three articles in *m/f*, one each by Rose, Cowie, and Adams. They have not begun to answer her questions about psychoanalysis; why then should she devote more than a note to its usefulness?

Barrett does not exactly caricature Freud's observations when she writes her note. His concept of the unconscious, and his theory of heterosexuality as not instinctive but tortuously (and incompletely) achieved, merit the comment, "The radical implications of this view should not be overlooked" (1980: 80). But, adds Barrett a bit later, "For the purposes of this book" – which is, after all, an analysis of women's oppression – "it is worth noting his conclusions in the essays on female sexuality and the adult feminine personality" (1980: 82). She then rehearses some of Freud's most misogynist moments: women's passivity, if not their total lack of libido; women showing less sense of justice than men, being less ready to submit to "the great exigencies of life," and being more influenced in their judgments by affection or hostility, etc. This is Barrett's form of letting the record show that Freud's writings are deeply embedded in the very gender ideology so crucial to securing women's oppression. Such moments clearly complicate, though they do not invalidate, Freud's usefulness for feminism. In Barrett's terms, we may be inclined to make use of the concept of the unconscious or of an anti-essentialist view of sexuality, but we should remember that the founding texts of psychoanalysis are not unproblematical in their representation of women.

So much for Barrett's arguments. There remains something excessive about their presentation, about their existence as and in textuality. If we were to draw back from the book's closely argued status and consider it as a text, then there is something distinctly odd about the note on Freud. It is one thing to treat him anecdotally, another to cut off the discussion by subordinating it in a note, rather than, say, a section of a chapter, as happens with other figures in *Women's Oppression Today*. Barrett's note has the effect of an apotropaic gesture, a gesture warding off some anticipated evil. It is as if any extended consideration of the unconscious in relation to theories of sexuality or of ideology in the body of her text would undermine Barrett's position in some way, seep in perhaps "unconsciously" to muddy the limpid waters of her analysis.

Feminism and Deconstruction, Again

Barrett's desire to separate the discussion of psychoanalytic concepts from the body of her argument repeats a separation in feminist debates identified by Swindells and Jardine. Citing a 1982 interview with Mitchell and Rose in *m/f*, Swindells and Jardine claim that "the gap between Mitchell's political feminism and Rose's deconstructive Lacanianism (true to Lacan, but unhelpful for Mitchell's enterprise) is clearly visible – an omen of things to come" (1990: 83). If we apply Swindells and Jardine's opposition of "deconstructive Lacanianism" and "political feminism" to Barrett, we can see her siding with Mitchell, politics, and ideology, rather than with Rose, psychoanalysis, and the Lacanian unconscious. This opposition has made it difficult to think about ideology *and* the unconscious together at all, as we have seen, though the two remain shadowy partners on the Marxist feminist agenda. But what is the significance of that term "deconstructive" in Swindells and Jardine's comments on Rose?

Rose herself not only disavows any alliance with deconstruction; she criticizes Derrida roundly for his failure to break with pre-feminist gender ideology and argues against the usefulness of deconstruction for feminism because Derrida is himself a kind of essentialist when it comes to questions of subjectivity. Hers is very much a Lacanian argument but not a deconstructive one. Not surprisingly, Spivak has responded to this challenge in "Feminism and Deconstruction, Again: Negotiating with Unacknowledged Masculinism," by "defending a sort-of-Derrida against Rose defending a sort-of-Lacan," a project which she recognizes to be fraught with absurdity, but necessary nevertheless (1989a: 207). We think the most telling point in Spivak's critique of Rose is the way she hits upon the moment when Rose, as it were, refuses the deconstructive predicament. In this sense, Rose, like Rubin and Coward, falls back from the radical instabilities posed by the "political case for psychoanalysis" in the very act of putting that case. We read Rose as refusing the deconstructive predicament precisely when she finds herself trying once more to introduce psychoanalysis into Marxist political discussion and in that moment falling back on a liberal discourse of "rights," thus implicitly confirming what all the Marxists in the audience had been suspecting about feminism and psychoanalysis all along.

The moment which Spivak pinpoints is Rose's formulating of women's relation to femininity as "the right to an impasse." While not celebrating notions of a decentered model of the subject – for such pure fragmentation "would be as futile as it would be psychically unmanageable for the subject" – Rose nevertheless insists that "only the concept of a subjectivity at odds with itself gives back to women the right to an impasse at the point of sexual identity, with no nostalgia whatsoever for its possible or future integration into a norm" (Rose 1986: 15). Spivak comments:

> This desire for an impasse is not unlike the desire for the abyss or infinite regression for which deconstruction must perpetually account. I do, of course declare myself bound by that desire. The difference between Rose and myself here is that what she feels is a right to be claimed, I am obliged to recognize as a bind to be watched. (1989a: 208)

The notion of claiming "a subjectivity at odds with itself" as a *right* strikes us as more than a little problematical. Negotiating with an enabling double bind is one thing. Staking a claim on one's split subjectivity, on the final unfixity of sexual identity, is another. What would it mean in terms of a politics of class, race, or even sexuality, for that matter? But Rose does not want to recognize the psychoanalytic predicament as a deconstructive predicament, as a double bind with which to negotiate while getting on with whatever political issue is on the agenda, such as family policies or the institutional choice of a literary-critical method. Rose wants to stake her claim on her right to that anti-essentialist subjectivity over and over. That *is* her political platform. Psychoanalysis must be continually reintroduced to the center of the debate. And women must be allowed their right to a problem with femininity that will never be resolved, in spite of all the family policies and feminist theories in the world.

As Spivak argues, Rose tries to turn Derrida's version of deconstruction merely into a narrative about the "decentered" subject, rather than recognizing that his is a critical posing of the theoretical limits of all practice, an exposure of how the subject is not decentered but rather always in the process of centering itself in order to act, write, or think. Deconstruction in itself cannot found a political program, yet a failure to recognize the limits to which it points can lead to political fundamentalism. This is the enabling double bind of deconstruction that Spivak retrieves from Rose's dismissal.

We would argue that Rose's dismissal of deconstruction occurs at the moment when her appropriation of psychoanalysis for feminism turns into psychoanalytical fundamentalism. That is the secret of the family romance, and why feminists should resist it, without giving up on the particular tools psychoanalysis provides for thinking about sexuality, gender, or the family in anti-essentialist ways.

Sexuality: Beyond a Single Theory

The alternative anti-essentialist way of thinking about sexuality has been the province of gay and lesbian critics. The place of lesbianism within psychoanalytic feminist discussions has been particularly problematical and will constitute our focus here. So think of the rest of this chapter as paradoxical, for that is often the status of lesbian identity today. Think of leather, lace, and lipstick, of clones versus butch–femme relationships, of lesbian bars as changing scenes in the fifties, the sixties, the seventies, of the gay scene of the eighties devastated by AIDS. Think of the difference between an insurgently political newspaper, *off our backs*, and the glossy magazine *On Our Backs*, with its erotic lesbian stories, contact ads, and features on lesbian s/m. Whereas once lesbianism was "feminism's magical sign of liberation," as Katie King has argued (1986), with the possibility that any woman could be a lesbian, or at least exist knowingly on Adrienne Rich's "lesbian continuum" (1980), now simply political lesbianism, or lesbianism for feminism's sake, is frowned upon. The question of sexual identity politics, and of sexuality itself, has become a much more hotly contested and highly therorized terrain than it was in the seventies.

Consider the irony of feminist theorist Gayle Rubin's taking the stage at the Barnard College conference on the politics of sexuality in 1982, dressed in full leather gear and brandishing either – we have heard both versions – Jeffrey Weeks's Foucauldian *Sex, Politics, and Society: The Regulation of Sexuality Since 1800* (1981) or Michel Foucault's *The History of Sexuality*, Volume I (1978). A feminist and a lesbian takes her stand with the sex radicals, with gay men and some straight "pro-sex" women, as well as fellow lesbian sadomasochists, against the "anti-sex," anti-porn feminist contingent. Such complications have called for the kind of precise and highly contextualized remappings of the sexuality debates or sex wars of the eighties, and of the new alliances which have emerged from them, carried out by Katie King (1990, 1992).

The Foucault Story

The name of Michel Foucault is synonymous with poststructuralism and gay theory. More than any other single thinker, Foucault has influenced the debates about identity politics, particularly the debates about sexuality. For Foucault, each term of contemporary discourse provides a site of historical excavation – what he calls genealogy. What is sexuality? What is its history? What are the discursive origins of homosexuality? When was heterosexuality invented? How are the discourses in which these terms circulate also fields of power?

Foucault is a particularly paradoxical figure within identity politics because he challenges the very grounds upon which identity can be constituted. According to Judith Butler, it is crucial to remember the way in which "Foucault points out that juridical systems of power *produce* the subjects they subsequently come to represent" (Butler 1990: 2). Thus the question of a gay subject or a feminist subject must be complicated by the recognition that such a category of political identity "turns out to be discursively constituted by the very political system that is supposed to facilitate its emancipation" (1990: 2). This leads Butler to reject identity as the grounds for feminist politics, "if the formation of the subject takes place within a field of power regularly buried through the assertion of that foundation." She concludes, "Perhaps, paradoxically, 'representation' will be shown to make sense for feminism only when the subject of 'women' is nowhere presumed" (1990: 6).

For Foucault, the body and sexuality are not sources of transgression or liberation in any simple sense. Both the body and sexuality, in their long histories of shifting practices and pleasures, are constructed within discourses, within institutional networks of power and knowledge. If the discovery of children's masturbation as "an appalling sickess" in the nineteenth century establishes a system of control, of corporealization and punishment of sexuality, then the twentieth-century "revolt of the sexual body" represents for Foucault "the usual strategic development of a struggle" in which

> sexuality, through thus becoming an object of analysis and concern, surveillance and control, engenders at the same time an intensification of each individual's desire, for, in and over his body. . . . The revolt of the sexual body is the reverse effect of this encroachment. What is the response on the side of power? An economic (and perhaps also ideological) exploitation of eroticisation, from sun-tan products to pornographic films. Responding precisely to the revolt of the body, we find a new mode of investment which presents itself no longer in the form of control by repression but that of control by stimulation. "Get undressed – but be slim, good-looking, tanned!". . . One has to recognise the indefiniteness of the struggle – though this is not to say it won't some day have an end. (Foucault 1980: 56–7)

An activist as well as an intellectual, before his death in 1984 Foucault often engaged in confrontational politics on behalf of oppressed groups – prisoners, rape victims, homosexuals. He was not unwilling to be seen as a gay activist, yet he found the project of gay liberation at best problematical, at worst a dangerous repetition of official forms of identification that tighten the grip of structures of domination over individuals in the name of representing or emancipating them.

He is an even more paradoxical figure for feminists because gender plays so little part in his analyses. Note the unqualified use of the formulation above about "each individual" and "his body." When women are mentioned in Foucault's work, they tend to appear only as the hystericized bodies of the new legal and medical regime that discursively elicits and regulates modern sexuality. But in itself, this relative inattention to gender in the interests of historically investigating sex can be an enabling recognition of an elsewhere, of a world not already saturated by gender.

Biddy Martin, Judith Butler, and other lesbian feminist theorists have found Foucault's suspension of our most familiar categories to be very useful for the project of anti-essentialist feminist work. Taking Foucault's strictures on juridical systems of thinking to heart, Butler reverses the conventional feminist distinction between "sex" and "gender" in which the latter gets "culturally inscribed" on the anatomical body of the former. Following Foucault's notion of a history of sexuality, Butler concludes that "sex" is as culturally contructed as "gender," and – surprise! – it seems to have been constructed exactly *within* and according to the cultural duality of gender:

> Gender ought not to be conceived merely as the cultural inscription of meaning on a pregiven sex (a juridical conception); gender must also designate the very apparatus of production whereby the sexes themselves are established. As a result, gender is not to culture as sex is to nature; gender is also the discursive/cultural means by which "sexed nature" or "a natural sex" is produced and established as "prediscursive," prior to culture, a politically neutral surface *on which* culture acts. (Butler 1990: 6–7)

Butler is writing in the interests of a proliferation of configurations of sex and gender. She is particularly keen on camp, drag, and other parodic forms of cultural representation within the gay community that give the lie to any notion of a natural heterosexuality by emphasizing gender identity as performance. Such a sex-radical feminist position is enabled by an anti-essentialist, anti-foundationalist critique. Butler claims that the "deconstruction of identity is not the deconstruction of politics; rather, it establishes as political the very terms through which identity is articulated" (1990: 148). Only then can a politics which does not mistake emancipation for a recycled representation of the same old thing become possible.

Foucault's ground-breaking theoretical work in *The History of Sexuality*, Volume I, has an added advantage of which Butler makes almost nothing, however. Foucault himself seems to have thought that this aspect of his work was unduly neglected, yet fundamental: "Yes, no one wants to talk about that last part. Even though the book is a short one, but I suspect people never got as far as this last chapter. All the same, it's the fundamental part of the book" (Foucault 1980: 222). What is fundamental for Foucault is the question of racism within the deployment of the whole discursive apparatus of sexuality associated with the triumph of bourgeois culture and imperial consolidation in the later nineteenth century:

> Racism took shape at this point (racism in its modern, "biologizing," statist form): it was then that a whole politics of settlement (*peuplement*), family, marriage, education, social hierarchization, and property, accompanied by a long series of permanent interventions at the level of the body, conduct, health, and everyday life, received their color and their justification from the mythical concern with protecting the purity of the blood and ensuring the triumph of the race. (Foucault 1978: 149)

Nazism was, according to Foucault, "doubtless the most cunning and the most naïve" combination of eugenic state policy with a whole mythology of the imperial master race (1978: 149–50).

Thus politically inflected work on the history of sexuality, which takes up Foucault's interrelation of issues of racism and eugenics with issues of sexuality and its regulation, can be particularly crucial for the undoing of multiply oppressive identities. This seems to us potentially the most politically productive moment in Foucault's project, because his attention to the articulation of sexuality with nationalism, race, imperialism, and eugenics reveals in a particularly concentrated way the far from unproblematically liberating history of the uses to which sexuality can be put. Far from being a ground of emancipation outside the social, then, or a "prediscursive" terrain, for Foucault sexuality is a field of power that cannot be analyzed in isolation from other social categories and contingencies.

Coming of Age in English Departments: Eve Sedgwick and Gay Studies

If the rise of sexuality as a category of historical investigation, with its recent watershed in gay and lesbian studies, owes a great deal to Foucault in the general sense, in the US context, within English departments, the figure of Eve Kosofsky Sedgwick is cited with almost equal frequency. The irony here is that Sedgwick deals with masculinity, with a homosocial/homosexual continuum of desire from which women are excluded except as counters in an exchange between men. Lesbianism does not much figure in Sedgwick's work. Her best-known book, *Between Men* (1985), has singularly legitimated work on male bonding, repressed homosexuality, and the possibility of homophobic paranoia and homosexual panic as crucial to both English literature and culture since the early modern period. But of lesbianism in that book Sedgwick has only this to say: "The absence of lesbianism from the book was an early and, I think, necessary decision, since my argument is structured around the distinctive relation of the male homosocial spectrum to the transmission of unequally distributed power" (Sedgewick 1985: 18), and that, like male homosocial "(*including* homosexual)" desire, "(Lesbianism also must always be in a special relation to patriarchy, but on different [sometimes opposite] grounds and working through different mechanisms)" (1985: 25). In this sense, *Between Men*, with its wide influence in gay studies and its marginalization of lesbianism, repeats the positioning of lesbianism generally within US feminism.

The Lesbian Squeeze

Two 1980s anthologies which purport to deal with the question of sexuality from a radical-pluralist-left perspective metonymize the relative exclusion of lesbianism from left discourses on sexuality. The lesbian difference might here be thought of as the lesbian squeeze. This squeezing out of the lesbian position is a regrettable inversion of the interventionist vision offered by such forms of cultural protest as the album *Lesbian Concentrate: A Lesbianthology of Songs and Poems* (Olivia Records, 1977), which countered the homophobic "Save Our Children" campaign mounted by singer and orange-juice promoter Anita Bryant in the late 1970s (see King 1987: 32).

When lesbianism figures in *Powers of Desire* (Snitow, Stansell, and Thompson 1983), it figures principally as a "sexual silence in feminism," to paraphrase the subtitle of Amber Hollibaugh and Cherríe Moraga's article, "What We're Rollin Around in Bed With: Sexual Silences in Feminism" (1981). Joan Nestle, who in *A Restricted Country* (1987) gives us powerful fusions of autobiography, polemic, and theory, is here represented only by "My Mother Liked to Fuck" (1981), an anguished three-page plea for the acceptance of female sexual desire, whether lesbian or heterosexual, politically correct or potentially humiliating.

In the book of collected papers from the Barnard College conference on "The Scholar and the Feminist IX: Towards a Politics of Sexuality" held in New York City, April 24, 1982, but not published until 1984, both Amber Hollibaugh and Joan Nestle appear again as lesbian spokespeople, still impassioned and embattled (Vance 1984: 401–10, 232–41). Cherríe Moraga appears as a lesbian and Chicana poet (Vance 1984: 417–24). Gayle Rubin's essay "Thinking Sex: Notes for a Radical Theory of the Politics of Sexuality" (Vance 1984: 267–319) is by far the longest essay in the volume, and the most ambitious and heavily footnoted. Constituting itself as a work of high theory, much informed by Foucault's work and other gay work on the history of sexuality, it is also a full-frontal attack on anti-porn, anti-sex feminists, for squeezing out anything from the sexual scene that doesn't conform to a puritanical or "vanilla" notion of political correctness. In the notes on contributors, Rubin declares herself to be a "sex radical"; she seems to have joined forces with the gay male leather community, about whom she is writing a dissertation (Rubin 1984: xiv).

Thus it would seem that within left feminism, as within mainstream Euroamerican culture, lesbianism is repeatedly marginalized. And within lesbian discourse itself further marginalizations and self-marginalizations take place. Even within the texts in these anthologies and other writings that take up lesbianism as a position, or seek to explore various lesbianisms, the silencing and often violent marginalization of lesbianism itself is a major theme. We might notice how Nestle criticizes this tendency by characterizing lesbian feminism as a butch–femme relationship: "I suggest that the term *Lesbian-feminist* is a butch–femme relationship, as it has been judged, not as it was, with *Lesbian* bearing the emotional weight the butch does in modern judgment and *feminist* becoming the emotional equivalent of the stereotyped femme, the image that can stand the light of day" (Nestle 1987: 106–7). Lesbianism or, more accurately, lesbianisms appear as particularly incapable of theorization. When a writer like

Rubin dons the guise of high theorist, she does so in full leather gear, locating herself not as a lesbian, but as a sex radical, for that is where the theoretical as well as the political action is.

Is there in fact an absence of sufficiently theoretical, or anti-essentialist, lesbian theory that justifies its underrepresented status on the agenda of theorizing sexuality? If that might have once been the case, the later 1980s have seen a flourishing of lesbian theoretical work. The anthologies of 1983 and 1984 would presumably look quite different if they were being compiled now, in the wake of books like Butler's; Fuss's *Essentially Speaking* (1989) and the recent collection she has edited, essays by many hands entitled *inside/out: Lesbian Theories, Gay Theories* (1991); recent special issues of the journals *Signs* and *differences* (US) and *Feminist Review* and *Textual Practice* (UK); and important studies by Terry Castle (1990), Teresa de Lauretis (1989), Elaine Hobby (1991), Katie King (1988), Biddy Martin (1991), and Christine White (1990), among others. One could argue that much of the action in feminist literary studies these days is centered on uncovering the history of lesbianisms in literature, turning Sedgwick's work on its head to find "lesbian counterplots" in fiction, as Castle has begun to do (Castle 1990), or proposing a "'pro-sex' history of lesbianism" that runs counter to previous lesbian-feminist theories, such as Lillian Faderman's, of women's romantic (i.e. non-sexual) friendships traced in literature, which is White's project (White 1990: 206).

Since this portion of this book has been devoted to rethinking the essentialist/anti-essentialist dichotomy, King's analysis of AIDS activisms could well stand as an emblem of what we think the debate should look like now. As King observes:

> Within particular political movements [the essentialist/anti-essentialist dichotomy] is a dichotomy often shorn of strategic meaning and used ahistorically to process and categorize political identities, struggles, and literatures. Charges of essentialism and counter charges of anti-feminism, for example, functioned temporarily to manage political alliances and maintain boundaries in U.S. academic feminism. The political alliances emerging from AIDS art-theoretical activism cannot be managed within this framework. And indeed we need such theoretical activism to overflow in these messy ways, as suggested by Eve Sedgwick's analysis of the essentialist/constructivist dichotomy as always already structured within a genocidal "Western project or fantasy of eradicating [individual gay] identity." (King 1992: 86; citing Sedgwick 1990: 41, 43)

Learning from poststructuralist theory, with its constant scrutiny of one's own terms, yet returning to politics as a ground upon which newly undone identities can be provisionally constituted: far from being under-theorized, such contemporary lesbian work is exemplary of the best materialist feminism. The lesbian difference as the lesbian squeeze, being squeezed in, in order to be squeezed out, has begun to give way to the profound difference lesbian theory can make to both feminist and materialist theory.

Notes

1   Jane Gallop has observed, "Although Lacan attributes this formula to Saussure, it differs in several significant ways from any of Saussure's formulations, and so is actually, in letter if not in spirit, Lacan's creation." See Gallop (1985: 120); Nancy and Lacoue-Labarthe (1973: 38–40).

9

The Theory "Race," Imperialist Fractures, and Postcolonial Subjects

As we suggested in our original schematic history in Part I, the experience of radical alterity within feminism has been most strongly acted out around the question of racial difference. The Combahee River Collective and Barbara Smith in the late seventies articulated multiple positionalities and split identities without reference to post-structuralist theory. In 1981 neither Angela Y. Davis, in *Women, Race & Class*, nor bell hooks (Gloria Watkins), in *Ain't I A Woman: Black Women and Feminism*, needed anti-essentialism to problematize the history of racially exclusionary practices typical of white middle-class feminism.

In 1984, in an important article published in the British journal *Feminist Review*, Valerie Amos and Pratibha Parmar cite hooks in their critique of the racism and ethnocentrism operating within "imperial feminism" in Britain: "Because [white feminists] are not acquainted with traditions outside of their own cultures and histories, the ideological and the theoretical legacies that they write from inevitably deny as valid any modes of struggle and organization which have their origins in non-European philosophical traditions" (Amos and Parmar 1984: 8). In particular, Amos and Parmar locate white feminist chauvinism in feminist theories and practices concerning the family, sexuality, and the women's peace movement. To summarize their important arguments briefly:

1 White feminists' race- and class-blind focus on male violence against women, especially rape, has often led to racist attacks and police repression in black communities.
2 White feminist critiques of the patriarchal or nuclear family ignore crucial differences between black and white familial structures, such as the predominance of female-headed households in many

black communities; or, if the difference is noted, it becomes the
source of a romantic or sentimental misrecognition of black
women's power, as in the myth of the "black matriarch."

3 White feminists have failed to acknowledge that the ways in which
they organize around sexuality exclude black women, for whom
sexuality and, in particular, heterosexual pleasure and abortion
rights may not seem so crucial or problematical as economic survival, homophobia, and political coercion in matters of reproductive rights; forced sterilization, poverty, and poor healthcare
are likely to loom larger on the horizon than reproductive freedom
exercised as abortion.

4 White feminists involved in the peace and anti-nuclear movements
fail to recognize the implicit racism of their politics when the
preservation of the planet for future generations is given precedence
over daily struggles for survival at home and abroad, and no
connections are made between poverty and the arms race or
between the privilege of non-violent protest and the armed
repression by the state that obtains in the ghetto and in many
Third World countries.

5 White feminists wishing to enter into dialogue with black feminists
tend to expect continued servicing from them in the form of
enlightenment and exculpation; this is yet another version of white
feminists' making gains at the expense of black and Third World
women.

In such ways, at least since 1852, and Sojourner Truth's speech at
the second annual convention of the women's rights movement, in
Akron, Ohio, the difference that race makes in a racist society has
audibly interrupted feminist theory and practice. But what happens
if we cease to take race and racial difference at face value, if we
question what racism might lurk in an unexamined history in which
race itself has been constructed as a category to serve particular
ideological, political, and economic needs?

Race without Essence

A recent essay by an African-American historian published in the
British *New Left Review* puts the case for race as an ideology having
a specific history (if we step outside the US context, of course, it
will have more than one history). Since Barbara Jeanne Fields argues
the US case more elegantly than we can hope to do, we will quote

from her at some length. In "Slavery, Race and Ideology in the United States of America," Fields writes:

> Race is not an element of human biology (like breathing oxygen or reproducing sexually); nor is it even an idea (like the speed of light or the value of π) that can be plausibly imagined to live an external life of its own. Race is not an idea but an ideology. It came into existence at a discernible historical moment for rationally under- standable historical reasons and is subject to change for similar reasons. The revolutionary bicentennials that Americans have celebrated with such unction – of independence in 1976 and of the Constitution in 1989 – can as well serve as the bicentennial of racial ideology, since the birthdays are not far apart. During the revolutionary era, people who favoured slavery and people who opposed it collaborated in identifying the racial incapacity of Afro-Americans as the explanation for enslavement. American racial ideology is as original an invention of the Founders as is the United States itself. Those holding liberty to be inalienable and holding Afro-Americans as slaves were bound to end by holding race to be a self-evident truth. Thus we ought to begin by restoring to race – that is, the American version of race – its proper history. (Fields 1990: 101)

This description of a project could also describe the project of anti- essentialist work on race within literary studies – not to deny that in racist cultures an ideology of racial difference operates in oppressive ways, but to expose the very constructedness of that ideology.

Exposing the history, the constructedness, of something opens it up to the possibility of change. Thus Henry Louis Gates, Jr, intro- duces an anthology of essays by a number of critics on "race," writing, and difference, by writing in his introduction, "Writing 'Race' and the Difference It Makes":

> Race, as a meaningful criterion within the biological sciences, has long been recognized to be a fiction. . . . Nevertheless, our conversations are replete with usages of race which have their sources in the dubious pseudoscience of the eighteenth and nineteenth centuries. . . . Race has become a trope of ultimate, irreducible difference between cultures, linguistic groups, or adherents of specific belief systems which – more often than not – also have fundamentally opposed economic interests. Race is the ultimate trope of difference because it is so very arbitrary in its application. (Gates 1986: 4–5)

Not only has race become a code through which to mystify various forms of economic oppression, but, Gates argues, "Scores of people are killed every day in the name of differences ascribed only to race" (1986: 6). In this light, although the gesture of publishing essays in the journal *Critical Inquiry* may seem only "local and tiny," for Gates it remains nevertheless a gesture of some political importance:

> This slaughter demands the gesture in which the contributors to this volume are collectively engaged: to deconstruct, if you will, the ideas of difference inscribed in the trope of race, to explicate discourse itself in order to reveal the hidden relations of power and knowledge inherent in popular and academic usages of "race." (1986: 6)

In "Talkin' That Talk," a conclusion to the same volume, he adds that part of the project of deconstructing race lies in "the necessity of undermining the habit, in the West, of accounting for the Other's 'essence' in absolute terms, in terms that *fix* culturally defined differences into transcendent, 'natural' categories or essences" (Gates 1986: 402).

Strategic Essentialisms?

Not all African-American critics share Gates's and his contributors' enthusiasm for anti-essentialist thinking. We have already noted how Barbara Christian, for one, has remained not only skeptical of but openly hostile to the project of writing about race in the light of any political project, particularly if that entails a heavy dose of theory. To Diana Fuss, it seems that African-American feminist critics have been particularly resistant to subjecting the idea of race or blackness to anti-essentialist critique. Fuss asks, "What accounts exactly for the apparent resistance on the part of many minority women critics to what Barbara Christian has labeled 'the race for theory'? . . . [I]s it possible that there might be an order of political necessity to these more essentialist arguments advanced by black women?" (Fuss 1989: 95).

Barbara Christian's 1987 essay, "The Race for Theory" (Christian 1989), is probably the best-known example of this tendency, but a celebrated exchange also took place in the journal *New Literary History* in 1987, during which a black feminist, Joyce A. Joyce, challenged two of the male masters of African-American theory in the US, Gates and Houston Baker, on the grounds that their commitment to poststructuralist theory constituted a racist and ethnocentric selling-out of African-American thinking to white European hegemony (Joyce 1987a, 1987b). Joyce is worried that, by buying into an elitist critical discourse, black critics distance themselves from their own community, which lacks the educational resources to disseminate such privileged intellectual vocabularies. Both Gates and Baker reply forcefully and dismissively; for them, Joyce has missed the point, which is to revolutionize the discipline of African-American literary studies. Baker accuses her of not having done her homework on black poststructuralism, and targets the fact that the whole exchange is taking place in a white high-theoretical journal like *New Literary History* as evidence of "a combination of white ignorance, black willingness to tread conservative/minstrel paths, and a multi-ethnic fear in the academy of new and difficult modes of critical and theoretical study" (Baker 1987: 368).

The charge lurking here is one of black feminist anti-intellectualism. From a feminist point of view, Gates and Baker come off sounding rather arrogant and paternalist, like Big Daddy when some uppity female talks back. Yet Joyce's choice of black *poststructuralist* theory as her target may seem misplaced. Why did she not address, rather, the resistance to feminism in some highly celebrated African-American work? Or the many forms of institutional privilege and elitism that can so often get covered over by intellectual labels which turn out not really to be the issue at all? One might think from reading Joyce that there were no black feminist critics simultaneously committed to theoretical and political radicalism for whom poststructuralism had proved as useful an intellectual strategy as it has for Gates and Baker.

US Third World Feminism

Let's look at some work on race by feminists that, in different ways, makes use of arguments we could call anti-essentialist. For Gloria Anzaldúa, who with Cherríe Moraga edited *This Bridge Called My Back*, modeling the subject means figuring the radical woman of color, who is neither First World nor Third World. In *Borderlands/La Frontera* (1987), Anzaldúa meditates upon that feminist subject of international and cultural borders, "the new mestiza." And Anzaldúa does this in linguistic as well as residually biological terms. The question of blood, of cultural difference as genetically related, cannot be entirely bypassed, for mainstream US culture with its imperial and racist history will not allow that. But if the marginality of the new mestiza – the woman of mixed blood, of mixed

race and culture, who takes up a radically oppositional stance to
whatever is oppressive in the cultures in which she participates – is
conceived of in linguistic terms, as a matter of what Lacan would
call radical alterity, we have entered an anti-essentialist theoretical
domain for thinking about race and marginality:

> Ethnic identity is twin skin to linguistic identity – I am my langu-
> age. . . . Until I can accept as legitimate Chicano Texas Spanish, Tex-
> Mex and all the other languages I speak, I cannot accept the legitimacy
> of myself. Until I am free to write bilingually and to switch codes
> without having always to translate, while I still have to speak English
> or Spanish when I would rather speak Spanglish, and as long as I
> have to accommodate the English speakers rather than having them
> accommodate me, my tongue will be illegitimate.
>
> I will no longer be made to feel ashamed of existing. I will have
> my voice: Indian, Spanish, white. I will have my serpent's tongue –
> my woman's voice, my sexual voice, my poet's voice. (Anzaldúa 1987:
> 59)

The desire for a legitimate identity that knows neither native authen-
ticity nor pure colonial power-wielding, an identity constructed out
of differences and impurities, can best be thought through in linguistic
terms. And it is a model in which the question of race and the question
of imperialism and decolonization cannot be finally separated, a
point to which we shall return.

Another Chicana feminist, Chela Sandoval, wishes to generalize
beyond the figure of the new mestiza to a theory of "U.S. Third
World feminism" as a model of "differential oppositional consciousness" (Sandoval 1991). Tracing some of the same movements by
women of color within and against white US feminism which we
have already discussed, Sandoval proposes an anti-essentialist model
of marginal identities within US culture. According to her, US Third
World feminism figures within itself oppositional tactics derived from
and articulated with other social movements, and as such provides
a model for a wide-sweeping oppositional movement within the US
today:

> U.S. third world feminism represents a central locus of possibility,
> an insurgent movement which shatters the construction of any one of
> the collective ideologies as the single most correct site where truth
> can be represented. Without making this move . . . any liberation
> movement is destined to repeat the oppressive authoritarianism from
> which it is attempting to free itself and become trapped inside a
> drive for truth which can only end in producing its own brand of

dominations. What U.S. third world feminism demands is a new subjectivity, a political revision that denies any one ideology as the final answer, while instead positing a *tactical subjectivity* with the capacity to recenter depending upon the kinds of oppression to be confronted. (1991: 14)

If we detect here a kind of deconstructive logic informing political activity, the need for complex political and social articulations of a discursive kind, and a focus on the subject as the locus of these transformations, we will be reading in Sandoval's formulations the legacy of poststructuralism within the new identity politics.

According to Sandoval, her theory derives most directly from feminist activism, but it is a theory crucially informed by Althusser's theory of ideology and Fredric Jameson's theory of postmodernism as "the cultural logic of late capitalism" (Jameson 1984). Where she differs most sharply from Jameson, whose influence on and support of her work she acknowledges, is in finding a certain utopian potential in the "historically unique democratization of oppression" which characterizes late capitalist social relations and postmodern cultural conditions and contains the possibility "for the emergence of a new historical moment – a new citizen – and a new arena for unity between peoples" (Sandoval 1991: 22, n. 50). Here Sandoval appears to be calling for a model of revolutionary agency on the part of new social agents identifiable within the new discursive political spaces of postmodernism, the very project which Ernesto Laclau and Chantal Mouffe have theorized (see Landry and MacLean 1992).

The Future is Unwritten: Hortense Spillers

If we turn more directly to literary studies, the work of Hortense J. Spillers offers the most sustained account of an articulation of poststructuralism with work on gender and race. In two important articles, we can see Spillers challenging the Oedipal and imperialist dynamics of Judaeo-Christian historiography, on the one hand, and conventional thinking about slavery, gender, and subjectivity, on the other. Writing about Toni Morrison's novel, *Sula* (1973), in an essay originally published in *Feminist Studies* in 1983, Spillers offers at once a materialist critique of fictional representations of black femininity, a feminist and materialist critique of Harold Bloom's "anxiety of influence" model of literary history, and a poststructuralist, materialist, and feminist critique of the origin stories and salvation paradigms implicit in much writing about slavery, whether it be fiction or history. In an essay published in *Diacritics* in 1987, Spillers establishes a new paradigm for thinking about gender and slavery in the American context, turning upside-down the racist assumptions of much official US discourse on the subject. How often have we heard that the problem with the black community lies in the "matriarchal" black family, a view well represented by the infamous Moynihan Report of 1965? What happens if we address both the economic and semiotic history of slavery in America, in order to understand the difference that "race" makes in these contexts?

Spillers's style is a model of how to work within numerous critical languages at once, rendering moments from black vernacular and various hip colloquialisms into the problematics of deconstructive philosophy and out again. The opening of "A Hateful Passion, A Lost Love" skillfully models how a deconstructive materialist feminism might inscribe its own position of enunciation in the very moment of announcing its argument.

> Toni Morrison's *Sula* is a rebel idea, both for her creator and for Morrison's audience. To read *Sula* is to encounter a sentimental education so sharply discontinuous from the dominant traditions of Afro-American literature in the way that it compels and/or deadlocks the responses that the novel, for all its brevity and quiet intrusion on the landscape of American fiction, is, to my mind, the single most important irruption of black women's writing in our era. I am not claiming for this novel more than its due; *Sula* (1973) is not a stylistic innovation. But in bringing to light dark impulses no longer contraband in the black American female's cultural address, the novel inscribes a new dimension of being, moving at last in contradistinction to the tide of virtue and pathos that tends to overwhelm black female characterization in a monolith of terms and possibilities. I regard Sula the character as a literal and figurative *breakthrough* toward the assertion of what we may call, in relation to her literary "relatives," new female being. (Spillers 1987a: 181)

The tension between "rebel idea" and "new female being," the two figures upon which the argument turns, is considerable. A rebel idea figures and tries to call into being the possibility of a new form of social being. This new female being is a materialist concept, not a psychological "feminine self" or a liberal "new woman." So the celebration of rebelliousness in "rebel" is perhaps more qualified by the status of "idea" than it might seem at first glance. Spillers's point is that the book as agent of change operates discursively, makes a difference to those who read it, figures a *breakthrough* in contemporary gender ideologies, so that that which exists as possibility, this new female being, might be able to emerge.

The conditions of her emergence in Spillers's argument are complex, and we shall only look at two of them here: a new take on literary history and a new take on history, especially African-American history, as a grand narrative. In the first place, Spillers displaces Harold Bloom's model of literary history as Oedipal struggle over paternal inheritances as inappropriate for the fiction she examines by subjecting his famous "anxiety of influence" theory to a gender-conscious and materialist critique:

> Harold Bloom's by-now familiar revision on the Freudian oedipal myth in relation to the theme of literary successions and fortunes is not applicable to the community of black American women writers, even as a necessary critical fable. Bloom speaks for a powerful and an *assumed* patriarchal tradition, posited by a dominative culture, in the transmission of a political, as well as literary, wealth; in the case of black women's writing (and women's writing without modification) the myth of wealth as an aspect of literary "inheritance" tends to be sporadic. (1987a: 205, n. 3)

"Sporadic" here has all the force of arch understatement. If women have frequently been men's legal property, slaves were literally and materially the property of their owners. Inheritances are property, or are modeled on property, and only legal and material subjects can inherit them; the objects of exchange, those properties themselves, cannot.

The notion of a "sporadic" as opposed to a continuous or divinely sanctioned history carries over into Spillers's critique of Judaeo-Christian metaphysics as it informs some black women's writing, though distinctly not the rebel idea of *Sula*. Margaret Walker's *Jubilee* (1966), for instance, depends upon what Spillers calls "God terms" (1987a: 188). Walker's "theonomous" view of history, and the consequent heroism of her characters, implicate her in a paradigm of Judaeo-Christian salvation history dependent upon a metaphysics of presence such as Derrida critiques. Spillers does not defer, or even refer, to Derrida; she engages in her critique of the metaphysics of presence as it applies to the mythology of "roots" in the tradition of black writing. What happens when history, like "inheritance," is a matter of sporadic rather than divinely orchestrated events? If there is no necessary heroism or eventual salvation attached to the sufferings of slavery, what attitude ought we to have regarding African-American origins and roots?

Recuperating Zora Neale Hurston's *Their Eyes Were Watching God* (1937) as a partial predecessor of Morrison's *Sula*, Spillers posits a necessary historical rupture from a disfiguring past, when "the roots of experience are poisonous" (1987a: 195), and the God terms are seen as the signifiers of an oppressive metaphysical tradition as often used to justify slavery as to undermine it. The very character of Sula herself is a material figure for a self-determination willing to break with the past, for Sula "is a matter of her own choices" (1987a: 184). "Sula's outlawry may not be the best kind, but that she has the will toward rebellion itself *is* the stunning idea. This project in liberation, paradoxically, has no particular dimension in time, yet it is for all time" (1987a: 204).

In "Mama's Baby, Papa's Maybe: An American Grammar Book" (1987b), Spillers sets out to establish a syntax or recoding of gender and familial relations that will set the record straight regarding the legacies of slavery in the contemporary black community in the US. Well aware of the difficulty of her project, she nevertheless does not hesitate to employ difficult subject matter or difficult formulations. "[I]f rigor is our dream," she writes, we cannot afford not to address the difficult, even the repellent when the historical record demands it (Spillers 1987b: 68).

Within chattel slavery, the name of the father goes missing. Children inherit their mother's name and their mother's enslaved status. From Moynihan's point of view, the resulting absence of black male agency in the family is the fault of the daughter, or the female line. As texts like the Moynihan Report glaringly illustrate, this "stunning reversal of the castration thematic, displacing the Name and the Law of the Father to the territory of the Mother and Daughter, becomes an aspect of the African-American female's misnaming" (1987b: 66). And Spillers attempts "to undo this misnaming in order to reclaim the relationship between Fathers and Daughters within this social matrix for a quite different structure of cultural fictions" (1987b: 66).

This undoing of raced and sexed identities on the grounds of identity will mean focusing on the experience of enslavement, deracination, and captivity, on the Middle Passage from Africa across the Atlantic to the New World, and on the fact that captive bodies, properties in the making, are thus de-gendered in ways unthinkable within a nineteenth-century white framework of gender ideology. "Even though the captive flesh/body has been 'liberated,' and no

one need pretend that even the quotation marks do not *matter*,"
Spillers writes, "dominant symbolic activity, the ruling episteme that
releases the dynamics of naming and valuation, remains grounded in
the originating metaphors of captivity and mutilation." What is more
obvious in the Moynihan Report than its repetition, *without much
difference*, of the semiotics of slavery? Spillers argues:

> And I would call it the Great Long National Shame. But people do
> not talk like that anymore – it is "embarrassing," just as the retrieval
> of mutilated female bodies will likely be "backward" for some people.
> Neither the shameface of the embarrassed, nor the not-looking-back
> of the self-assured is of much interest to us, and will not help at all
> if rigor is our dream. We might concede, at the very least, that sticks
> and bricks *might* break our bones, but words will most certainly *kill*
> us. (1987b: 68)

Once again, the opening and concluding moments of the essay are
devoted to figuring a certain rebellious possibility in the difference
that a raced history makes for African-Americans. The problematizing of gender resulting from the exigencies of slavery requires, in
particular, making a place for a different social subject "*out of the
traditional symbolics of female gender*": "In doing so, we are less
interested in joining the ranks of gendered femaleness than gaining
the *insurgent* ground as female social subject. Actually *claiming* the
monstrosity (of a female with the potential to 'name'), which her
culture imposes in blindness, 'Sapphire' might rewrite after all a
radically different text for a female empowerment" (1987b: 80).

If "race" is a theory, its insurgent moments are some of the most
empowering within both the feminist and materialist traditions, for
people of color, and for those who would identify with radical
critical practices and anti-racism. And yet the resistance to "theory"
is more widespread in black feminist writing than one might guess
from reading Spillers. What happens when we take this problem to
the movies?

bell hooks Goes to the Movies

Under the sign of race and anti-racism, the US black feminist bell
hooks, for instance, registers her unease with the ironic mode of the
film, *Sammy and Rosie Get Laid* (1987). Can we trust audiences
with irony when such delicate yet important matters as shades of

racism are at stake? Her chief reservation about the film concerns
the relative absence of, indeed the deliberate disappearing of, black
women from the narrative, beginning with the opening sequence, in
which a black woman is shot by the police while trying to shield
her son from arrest, and continuing through the central scene, in
which three men of color are shown in bed with three white women
while black male Rastas sing the Motown song by the Temptations,
"My Girl." Hooks comments:

> As a black female watching this scene, I was struck by this use of a
> song which emerged from segregated African-American culture as an
> expression of possessive love between black female and black male,
> evoked here to celebrate this inter-racial spectacle of non-white men
> with white women. I found this scene very amusing. It graphically
> exposed contradictions. However, when I stopped laughing I found
> its message to be potentially frightening and even threatening, because
> it did not overtly promote critical reflection about the absence of
> black women, and could easily be seen as making light of the disposing
> of women of color, of sexual and racial violation of women of color
> by white women and men. (hooks 1990: 161)

Hooks also objects to the featuring of the black male character
Danny/Victoria, while a black woman and black male child – his
girlfriend, his child? – simply appear and disappear momentarily
within the script. Hooks observes, "Well, none of this should have
been surprising; let's face it, the black woman as mother was wiped
off the planet in the very first scene" (1990: 161). For hooks, this
means that the film endorses a kind of genocide.

Then there is the problem of the lesbians. Hooks wants to ask why
Rani, the character "who has radical political beliefs," is "portrayed as
'hysterical,' one might even say as monstrous" (1990: 160). Hooks
writes, "She and her black woman lover are 'into' confrontation;
they want to hold Rafi [Sammy's father, a former Pakistani politico
in a repressive, revolutionary regime, now hiding out in Britain]
responsible for his actions." For hooks, this means that Rani and
Vivia are "uptight and uncool" (1990: 160). Since they are the only
important women of color in the film, one Pakistani, one Afro-
Caribbean, hooks rightly considers their treatment to be crucial. In
his published account of the making of the film, Kureishi himself
records how he got into trouble with a white female New York
script consultant, who wanted to know why he had developed their
characters; far from finding them negligible, she thought they had
become too important (see Kureishi 1988: 85–6).

Yet why, if hooks is searching for strong characterizations of black women, does Vivia's blackness count for so little; is it because she is not a mother but a lesbian lover? And why does Vivia and Rani's confrontational politics strike hooks as "'hysterical'"? Another reading might see them as having the courage of their convictions, and thus as being able to voice what Rosie, the white feminist and would-be radical, keeps trying to avoid facing, the contradictions in her father-in-law's politics and how they, in their intersections with the contradiitons in her own, figure some of the more awkward legacies of imperialism in the postcolonial moment:

ROSIE: (*To* RANI *and* VIVIA) Please, not now.
RANI: But you do know who you have living in your flat?
ROSIE: I don't hate him.
RANI: Typically of your class and background. Your politics are just surface.
ROSIE: What do you want to do?
RANI: We want to drive him out of the country. (*To* VIVIA) This is liberalism gone mad!
         (VIVIA *and* RANI *look pityingly at* ROSIE.)

(Kureishi 1988: 38).

Whether Rosie's politics "are just surface" is not only a question the film keeps asking over and over; it is also the question which feminists of color have asked of white feminists again and again. The difficulty of reading Rosie finds its productive tension in the passionate clarity of Rani and Vivia's erotic and political self-determination. The politics of race does not map easily onto the politics of sexuality, especially when it comes to the differences lesbianism might make. And the politics of race is not simply another name for the politics of imperialism.

The Critique of Race is not the Same as the Critique of Imperialism

If "challenging imperial feminism" is to remain a useful metaphoric strategy, as it was in the hands of Valerie Amos and Pratibha Parmar, some necessary distinctions between the critical and political movements for anti-racism and anti-imperialism need to be maintained.

Gayatri Spivak's example of the contradictions thus posed is as follows: "Anti-racism is yearly brought to crisis by anti-imperialism when we begin to see that even the most disenfranchised US black person can get a US passport, which is an incomparably superior thing to, say, an Indian passport" (Spivak 1990: 139). How or whether the "most disenfranchised US black person" could ever take advantage of this potential documentary superiority, Spivak does not address. So the need to maintain distinctions works both ways; anti-imperialism as a theoretical project is no substitute for anti-racism.

The difficulty in the US context is at once the anti-racist need, on the part of both whites and blacks, to address anti-black racism at home, and a complementary desire to project what is happening in the US onto the world at large. In this respect, the best intentions of leftwing radicals mime the worst tendencies of US foreign policy. Fighting racism in South Africa is no substitute for fighting it in Detroit. But neither is what is happening in Detroit's Pan-Africanist circles necessarily analogous or even much related to what is happening in Nigeria or Senegal, or within the African diaspora in other international locations.

The Said Story

The difficulty of thinking through such distinctions has been one of the impetuses behind the development of postcolonial theory. Thinking "radical alterity," or the problematic of the Other, in an international context has proved so difficult as to have produced many highly contested positions. One of the ground-breaking texts in this regard has been Edward W. Said's *Orientalism* (1978), which in many ways has established the most widely influential paradigm for thinking about European imperialism, the colonialist science of Orientalism, and its role in fashioning Europe's colonial others. Employing Foucault's notion of discourse, Said writes:

> My contention is that without examining Orientalism as a discourse one cannot possibly understand the enormously systematic discipline by which European culture was able to manage – and even produce – the Orient politically, sociologically, militarily, ideologically, scientifically, and imaginatively during the post-Enlightenment period. . . . This is not to say that Orientalism unilaterally determines what can be said about the Orient, but that it is the whole network of interests inevitably brought to bear on (and therefore always involved in) any occasion when that peculiar entity "the Orient" is in question. How this happens is what this book tries to demonstrate. It also tries to show that European culture gained in strength and identity by setting

itself off against the Orient as a sort of surrogate and even underground self. (Said 1979: 3)

Thus the very notion of the Orient emerges as an ideological construction that gains its coherence from its structural relation to a Europe, an Occident, unthinkable in any other way.

It is the peculiar exteriority of the representation of the Orient, with which we in the West are all too familiar, and of which we are almost certainly unconscious, that concerns Said. The first epigraph to *Orientalism* is a sentence from Marx's *Eighteenth Brumaire* which echoes back and forth throughout the discourse of postcolonial criticism: "They cannot represent themselves; they must be represented." This sentence occurs in the passage in which Marx characterizes the French peasantry as incapable of class consciousness and thus susceptible to seeing themselves as politically represented by a Napoleon or Louis Bonaparte, despots who appeal to the peasants' self-congratulatory patriotism and narrow self-interest. Such a class is reactionary in its inability to conceive of itself as a class, and thus to represent itself as a class (see Tucker 1978: 608).

For Said, Marx's description of the French peasantry aptly characterizes the European imperialist attitude towards its colonial Others. It is the exteriority of the representation that is at stake, that allows Orientalism to do its work of subjection and subjugation. Said observes: "The exteriority of the representation is always governed by some version of the truism that if the Orient could represent itself, it would; since it cannot, that representation does the job, for the West, and *faute de mieux*, for the poor Orient. 'Sie können sich nicht vertreten, sie müssen vertreten werden,' as Marx wrote in *The Eighteenth Brumaire of Louis Bonaparte*" (1979: 21).

What is crucial about Marx's use of "represent" in this much-cited passage, according to Spivak, is its double meaning. For if we were to extend the quotation from Marx we would find him playing not only on representation in the political sense (*Vertretung*), but on representation in its more aesthetic sense of a restaging (*Darstellung*). Spivak argues, "My view is that radical practice should attend to this double session of representations rather than reintroduce the individual subject through totalizing concepts of power and desire." Those theorists who would avoid repeating in their own work the very totalizing gestures they seek to critique "must note how the staging of the world in representation – its scene of writing, its *Darstellung* – dissimulates the choice of and need for 'heroes,'

paternal proxies, agents of power – *Vertretung*" (Spivak 1988: 279).
In an interview, she spells out the distinction even more clearly:

> First, about *Vertretung*, stepping in someone's place, really. *Tritt*
> (from *treten*, the second half of *vertretung* [*sic*]) has the English
> cognate *tread*. . . . *Vertretung*, to tread in someone's shoes, represents
> that way. Your congressional person, if you are talking about the
> United States, actually puts on your shoes when he or she represents
> you. Treading in your shoes, wearing your shoes, that's *Vertretung*.
> Representation in that sense: political representation. *Darstellung–Dar*,
> there, same cognate. *Stellen*, is to place, so "placing there." *Rep-*
> *resenting*: proxy and portrait. . . . Now, the thing to remember is
> that in the act of representing politically, you actually represent your-
> self and your constituency in the portrait sense, as well. You have to
> think of your constituency as working class, or the black minority,
> the rainbow coalition, or yet the military-industrial complex and so
> on. That is representation in the sense of *Darstellung*. So that you do
> not ever "simply" *vertreten* anyone, in fact, not just politically in the
> sense of true parliamentary forms, but even in political practices
> outside of parliamentary forms. (Spivak 1990: 108)

Once again, the political stakes are what is at issue here in the debate
over representation. Spivak concludes:

> Unless the complicity between these two things is kept in mind, there
> can be a great deal of political harm. The debate between essentialism
> and anti-essentialism is really not the crucial debate. It is not possible
> to be non-essentialist. . . . The real debate is between these two ways
> of representing. (1990: 109)

For if one were to pretend actually to tread in the other's shoes,
without acknowledging the aesthetic or imaginative displacement –
the "portraiture" – involved, then one would be complicit in a new
form of authoritarianism or fundamentalism. And it would be a
fundamentalism constructed precisely on the grounds of, and in the
place of, a supposedly radical or liberationary practice.

Some Problems in Postcolonial Theory

Here the difference between the Lacanian notion of a self-consolidat-
ing Other, an "it" within the I, which serves imperialist purposes
by casting the native *as* an Other, and the existence of actual others,
native peoples, within the circuits of imperialism or in decolonized

terrain, should be kept in mind. The tyranny of unacknowledged representation, the pretense that no substitution was, in fact, necessary to constitute a proxy, would replicate the imperialist gesture of silencing the Other once again, while seeming to allow the other to speak directly, in an unmediated way, a way free of any interference from representation as restaging. This time, there would be a fiction in circulation that no pretense was necessary; the representation would seem utterly transparent and truly representative of the other: "Now they can represent themselves; they just have to be represented by one of their own."

Ironically, although she has gone to great lengths to expose the fundamentalist perils of precisely this argument, along with Said and Homi K. Bhabha, Spivak has been criticized for simply silencing the other in her work. Whether problematizing the conditions of the other's emergence, through the Other, constitutes yet another neo-imperialist act of silencing remains to be seen. Benita Parry has suggested that Spivak's and Bhabha's theories end up "downgrading" the "anti-imperialist texts written by national liberation movements," and their notions of "epistemic violence" and colonial hybridity "have obliterated the role of the native as historical subject and combatant, possessor of an-other knowledge and producer of alternative traditions" (Parry 1987: 34). To throw off the legacy of imperialism, for Parry, will require something more than arguing that there is no "outside" to imperialist discourse, no authentically native other untouched by the history of imperialism. This task, according to Parry, "rests with those engaged in developing a critique from outside [imperialism's] cultural hegemony, and in furthering a contest begun by anti-colonial movements" (1987: 55). Whether such a task is possible at all, in the terms in which Parry represents it, or whether she has misrepresented Spivak's and Bhabha's projects, can only be adjudicated by some examination of their theories of colonial discourse and postcolonial identity.

The story of imperialism for Spivak and Bhabha unfolds as follows. Across the fractured semiotic field of colonized native cultures, Spivak argues, the narrative of imperialism writes itself, installs itself proleptically as law. A prolepsis is a representation of a future act as having already been accomplished. For example, the British Raj projected its authority by behaving as if there had never been a time when it hadn't been in command. The imposition of imperial codes and practices upon the colonized, this fracturing of all indigenous sign-systems, Spivak terms a process of "epistemic violence." The cultural effects of this violent rupture are complex, but they include

the effective silencing of authentic native cultures as such. Spivak
concludes, in "The Rani of Sirmur":

> "great works" of *literature* cannot easily flourish in the fracture or
> discontinuity which is covered over by an alien legal system masquer-
> ading as law as such, an alien ideology established as only truth,
> and a set of human sciences busy establishing the "native" as self-
> consolidating Other ("epistemic violence"). (Spivak 1985: 130)

This project assures that the other will speak to the imperial subject
only in the alien language, not be able to "'answer one back,'" as
Spivak puts it (1985: 131), in any "native" language uncomplicated
by imperial contact.

The planned epistemic violence of the imperialist project silences
the native speaker while constituting her as a native informant, a
potential source of knowledge/power for the imperialist subject. Thus
it happens that we may only glimpse the other through the interstices
of the colonialist text. Commenting on the work of the Subaltern
Studies group, who are re-writing the history of colonial India from
the point of view of peasant insurgency, Spivak notes that the historians in the group themselves reiterate the efforts of construction
they must make to build their case from the kind of evidence available:

> Another note in the counterpoint deconstructing the metaphysics of
> consciousness in these texts is provided by the reiterated fact that it
> is only the texts of counter-insurgency or élite documentation that
> give us the news of the consciousness of the subaltern. "The peasants'
> view of the struggle will probably never be recovered, and whatever
> we say about it at this stage must be very tentative." (Spivak 1987:
> 203)

That which is truly "subaltern," most truly marginalized, cannot
"speak." If the subaltern could speak, he or she would no longer
occupy the place of the subaltern.

In this regard, Parry seems not quite to have grasped the point of
Spivak's critique. Writers of "anti-imperialist texts" are clearly not
"outside" the field of imperialism as a discourse, imperialism as a
discursive field, since they address it directly. And those positioned
to engage in a critique of colonial discourse, or to provide alternative
traditions to imperial Western ones, can hardly themselves occupy
the place of the subaltern. The subaltern is a name for those who,
precisely, cannot speak or represent themselves. The postcolonial
critic writes in the hope that the subaltern as such will eventually
disappear.

Once the history of imperialism has begun, no previously existing indigenous culture remains completely outside its circuits. When the native informant is *forced* to speak, when the native informant can speak and be understood, that is, it is of course most likely to be in the language of the imperialist. How reassuringly subjected the native is, in producing this speech which is not native, but is an imitation of the imperial word! Thus the native heard is a native mimic. The native-effect, as it tends to be received by imperialist audiences, is in fact a form of mimicry, and an effect of colonial hybridization.

Bhabha has theorized "hybridity" as *the* culturally specific effect of colonialism – operating within what Spivak calls a fractured semiotic field and producing a discourse that doubles, doubly displaces, and disrupts the self-proclaimed "authoritative" representations of the imperialist power:

> If the effect of colonial power is seen to be the *production* of hybridisation rather than the hegemonic command of colonialist authority or the silent repression of native traditions, then an important change of perspective occurs. It reveals the ambivalence at the source of traditional discourses on authority and enables a form of subversion, founded on that uncertainty, that turns the discursive conditions of dominance into the grounds of intervention. (Bhabha 1985: 97)

For Bhabha, native mimicry embodies cultural and political resistance to imperialism, rather than abject capitulation to it:

> To the extent to which discourse is a form of defensive warfare, then mimicry marks those moments of civil disobedience within the discipline of civility: signs of spectacular resistance. When the words of the master become the site of hybridity – the warlike sign of the native – then we may not only read between the lines, but even seek to change the often coercive reality that they so lucidly contain. (1985: 104)

Thus, rather than a nostalgia for lost traditions, or a desire for re-establishing authentic native origins, the project of postcolonial criticism consists of analyzing the workings of ideology in the complex texts that make up the scenes of colonial and decolonized space.

Spivak Goes to the Movies

The critique of race, however important, cannot alone undo the work of imperialism. Spivak's take on *Sammy and Rosie Get Laid*, for instance, reverses a number of bell hooks's arguments and reservations. Reading the film deconstructively, but according to a rather "old-fashioned" and "didactic" grid (Spivak 1989b: 80), Spivak finds it politically exciting and potentially mobilizing because of the way it situates characters both allegorically and within a kaleidoscopic network of discourses (Amnesty International-style fact-finding, photo-journalism, Indy Pop and Motown, Punjabi abuse boringly subtitled, Colin MacCabe lecturing on Derrida): "To put it in code, signifying practices move on a scale of materiality" (1989b: 84). According to her, we don't quite know how to read Rosie, and that indetermination figures the situation of the subject of radicalism in the UK today. Rosie's being "white, deliberately downwardly class-mobile, a social worker, heterosexual," a woman who "loves all the right people" – lesbians, blacks – and "is in an interracial marriage," comes close to figuring what Raymond Williams described as "The Bloomsbury Fraction," a long tradition of very class-marked criticism of imperialism from within a certain fraction of the British elite (see Williams 1980: 148–69). "And it just seemed to me that," Spivak writes, "given our general unpreparedness for knowing what is and is not radical, that beleaguered position is seen today as the white ideological subject-position of reactive welfare-state socialism" (1989b: 81). In the scene in the posh restaurant, in which Rosie and her father-in-law Rafi have a shouting row, Rosie in her "very sharp weapon-like earrings" looks "as though a sort of caged beast has been cornered":

> And that to an extent is the beleaguered position of the civilised conscience for whom torture is bad under any circumstances. . . . And the reason that one can't read Rosie is that she dramatises this confrontation between radicalism and an old fashioned simple morality based on rather simple ethics. And that is the great unreadable at the moment in terms of genders. (1989b: 82)

In case you think Spivak has managed to forget about race and heterosexuality in her desire to tell us how (not) to read Rosie, we should add that her other crucial points seem to be how politically valuable and complex Kureishi's treatment of the lesbians, Rani and

Vivia, is, and how important the undoubtedly problematical treatment of African blackness, represented by Danny, is.

What links these points is a deconstructive refusal to seek, as
hooks seems to want to do, unqualifiedly positive images of the
other, a project which, according to Spivak, "is, in the long run,
deeply insulting" (1989b: 86). If *King Lear* is not to be read as
"giving you a formula for running about mad in storms," then one
must attend to certain complexities of representation. In this light,
the fact that Rani and Vivia are both "the gay couple" – repeating
Kureishi/Frears's earlier focus in *My Beautiful Laundrette* (1986),
where the gay couple was interracial and male – and "much more
than the gay couple," in their association with multiple discourses,
languages, and the film's stylistic transformation away from realism,
strikes Spivak as interesting and important (1989b: 83). Danny/Victo-
ria she locates as "a kind of referent for radical innocence," typical
of the "unquestioned admiration" which subcontinental postcol-
onials, like Kureishi and Spivak, often feel for "the underclass of
black African extraction" whose history of imperialism, deracination,
and slavery gave them "much less entry, much less access, into
the culture of imperialism. Whereas our access into the culture of
imperialism was more the epistemic violation, the mind-fucking and
this, of course, was not altogether a non-collaborative affair" (1989b:
86–7).

Such are the contradictions of our historical moment. It is not a
question of trashing hooks via Spivak, nor of insisting on the racism
or (hetero?)sexism lurking in Spivak's "unquestioned admiration" of
the underclass of the African dispora via sexy Danny (played by
MTV icon Roland Gift, of the band Fine Young Cannibals). Rather,
let us keep our codes of reading clear. Anti-racism is not the same
as anti-imperialism. Spivak's work is particularly valuable in the way
it makes such distinctions, while also insisting on forging connections,
often of a difficult global kind.

Some Global Connections

For Winifred Woodhull, in "Unveiling Algeria" (1991), it is
important not to confuse the desire for solidarity with Arab feminists
with the desire for solidarity with various Arab national and anti-
imperialist struggles, which have so often called for the suppression
of Arab feminism. We must come to terms with, rather than cover
over, or "veil," if you will, a frequently "fundamental contradiction

between the demands of North African feminists and the Maghreb's affirmation of its Islamic identity" (Woodhull 1991: 126). Citing Mai Ghoussoub (1987), Woodhull writes:

> If Ghoussoub is right – that is, if in Arab countries where there exists an oppositional socialist movement, women are again subordinating the women's struggle to the supposedly "larger" class struggle; and if, throughout the Arab world, women are bowing to Islamic fundamentalism's antifeminism in the name of nationalism or Arab unity – then it is essential to renew the effort to dismantle modes of cultural-political analysis that ignore or rationalize the suppression of Arab feminism by national and anti-imperial struggles. . . . Above all, this implies, at every moment, guarding against what Ghoussoub calls "the contemptuous anti-Arab racism of American society, and its hypocritical indignation at the fate of Arab women" (18). (1991: 127–8)

Memories of Western-Allied coverage of the 1991 Gulf War with Iraq should provide no end of examples of these dangers. Thinking identity differently in the postcolonial scene increasingly requires such difficult, and precise, formulations as Woodhull gives us here.

For Julia V. Emberley's work on feminism and decolonization in Canada, the following comment of Spivak proves enabling:

> If the peasant insurgent was the victim and the unsung hero of the first wave of resistance against territorial imperialism in India, it is well known that, for reasons of collusion between pre-existing structures of patriarchy and transnational capitalism, it is the urban sub-proletarian female who is the paradigmatic subject of the current configuration of the International Division of Labor. (Spivak 1987: 218)

Emberley comments: "Though Spivak's critique is directed toward women living in India, her analysis of the effects of marginalization and dispossession are relevant to, though not necessarily representative of, the position of Native women in Canada" (Emberley 1990: 23, n. 4). In taking off from Spivak, Emberley is able to work through a difficult archival problem, the narrative and historical status of the eighteenth-century Chipewyan woman translator, "Thanadelthur," and how she figures "for Canadian history an idealized and contradictory representation of the Native woman as heroic proxy and sacrificial victim" (1990: 22).

In the trade in stories about this figure, one can see the situation of contemporary Native women in Canada very much in play. If one constructs them as Emberley does, as neither heroic proxies nor sacrificial victims, but as agents who can resist both high-intensity imperial violence and "low-intensity coercion – assimilation" (1990: 50), then one is deploying the figure of the Native woman "as an insurgent, an intervention destabilizing the meaning of imperial totalization – a reading of Native women working within the circumstances with which history has confronted them" (1990: 50).

As we move closer to the notion of women in the international division of labor, we begin to enter that new microelectronic territory in which "women in the integrated circuit" function ambiguously for multinational capital. This phrase of Rachel Grossman's (1980), picked up by Donna Haraway in her "Cyborg Manifesto," names "the situation of women in a world so intimately restructured through the social relations of science and technology" (Haraway 1991: 165). These are the women of the so-called "clean industries" of California's Silicon Valley, as well as the women of the urban sub-proletariat in some far-flung Export Processing Zones (EPZs) around the globe. And the boundaries they disturb, while related to neo-colonial capital flow and decolonized space, cannot be fully contained under the heading of imperialism or postcolonial subjects. These boundary-cases are the subjects of the next chapter.

10

Towards a Green Cultural Criticism

Historically, the construction of social differences within the pores of capitalism has taken many forms. The set of new relations which Rachel Grossman's term, "women in the integrated circuit," signifies could be described as a blurring of boundaries. Economically, multinational capital flows are disturbing traditional notions of national sovereignty. Technologically, the microelectronic revolution and what Donna Haraway has labeled the "informatics of domination" are altering previous category-distinctions such as natural and artificial, human and animal.

Increasingly sophisticated techniques for artificially producing life and prolonging it, artificial intelligence research and robotics, the dissemination of computer technology and computer literacy on a global scale: all these developments raise questions about the natural, about distinctions between humans and machines. And, as a sense of impending ecological crisis deepens, new relations between humans and animals have become possible. A critique of "anthropocentric" ways of thinking has been mounted by radical ecologists at the same moment that the sovereign subject of ideology, or the coherent subject of liberal discourse, has been shown to be a fiction by feminist and poststructuralist theorists. How have these changes come about?

Capital It Fails Us Now

Since the Second World War, we have seen a growing integration of a world system of production based on new relations between the less developed and the highly industrialized countries. The 1950s and 1960s saw the continued dominance of the core industrial countries that maintained their power as sources of innovative research and design, technological expertise, and financial outflows, with the capitalist periphery and semiperiphery emerging as the place for specialized assembly operations. As June Nash and María Patricia Fernández-Kelly suggest:

> Aided by the consolidation of the multinational corporation since the end of World War II and by the accentuated fluidity of capital investments, this new global division of labor is upsetting previous conceptualizations of politics and economics as core and periphery. Decaying industrial cities of the United States and Europe have in the last decade become characterized by breakdowns of municipal services, marginalization of large segments of the work force, and the atrophy of democratic operations of trade unions and community interest groups. The workforce of these increasingly marginalized "core" economies is shouldering a growing tax burden to support the military hegemony of multinationals that no longer have a base in any nation. (Nash and Fernández-Kelly 1983: vii)

The first important shift to notice is that the place of the so-called underdeveloped countries has changed, from sources of exploitable raw materials and cheap labor to sites of manufacturing, often shorn of protective legislation, worker benefits, and labor restrictions. This new phenomenon of "offshore" work-sites of multinational corporations has paralleled what Nash and Fernández-Kelly describe as "the proliferation of export-processing zones (EPZs) throughout the world":

> More than a uniformly defined or geographically delimited concept, the export-processing zone provides a series of incentives and loosened restrictions for multinational corporations by developing countries in their effort to attract foreign investment in export-oriented manufacturing. This has given rise to new ideas about development which often question preexisting notions of national sovereignty. (1983: viii)

According to the United Nations Industrial Development Organization, there are at present almost 120 export-processing zones in areas as far distant from one another as East and Southeast Asia, Latin America, Africa, Western Europe, and the United States. Nash and Fernández-Kelly state that "[a]lmost two million people are currently employed in EPZs throughout the world and many more are directly or indirectly affected by their existence. In Asia alone more than three hundred thousand women labor in electronics plants located in EPZs" (1983: viii). Preferred to male workers for their so-called innate manual dexterity and ability to perform repetitive activities, not to mention the expectation that they will be less likely than men to organize into trade unions, these young women workers trade their eyesight for cash, often as the sole income-earners for entire families.

These are pre-eminently the women of the integrated circuit, but, with the dispersion of EPZs continuing, their situation is prophetic of what is also materializing more slowly elsewhere. For women in the electronics industry in the Silicon Valley of California, for instance, the predominant issues may be deskilling, the piecework, part-time, or homework economy, and the way women are perceived as a reserve army of labor who do not require job security or the benefit packages that are corporate America's answer to welfare-state socialism in the European countries. They may not be expecting to trade their sight for employment and income, but they are undergoing exploitative proletarianization nevertheless. The feminization of poverty continues apace.

This new attitude towards identifying ever more exploitable labor forces is one result of what Nigel Harris has called "the end of the Third World" as an ideology. By this, Harris does not mean that the countries and people of the Third World are disappearing, but rather that a certain argument about connections between development, liberation movements, and national reform is disappearing:

> Third Worldism began as a critique of an unequal world, a programme for economic development and justice, a type of national reformism dedicated to the creation of new societies and a new world. . . . [A]n increasingly integrated world system lays down narrower and narrower limits to the possibility of local eccentricity, including reform. In a competitive system, holding down the price of labour takes precedence over protecting it, and the domestic economy becomes increasingly a spin-off of a wider order. (Harris 1987: 200–1)

Thus the prospects for exploitation and immiseration within the New World Order increase as economic growth appears increasingly random. And yet, Harris argues, there is another side to the story that is considerably more optimistic. We might see a global system, were it to replace the existing competition between sovereign nation-states, as decreasing the likelihood of war, eventually eliminating poverty and starvation, and offering opportunities for rational and humane social organization on a global scale:

> The process of dispersal of manufacturing capacity brings enormous hope to areas where poverty has hitherto appeared immoveable, and

makes possible new divisions of labour and specializations which will vastly enhance the capacity of the world to feed everyone. Above all, the realization of one world offers the promise of a rationally ordered system, determined by its inhabitants in the interests of need, not profit or war. Of course, it will not be won by waiting. (1987: 202)

That last sentence is surely an understatement. And whose rationale will define need and its satisfactions, allocate resources, administer global justice? What is the status of those "inhabitants?" Are they abstract citizens of a New World Order – a theme developed by US President George Bush to drum up support for military intervention in the Gulf, with the US and its allies seen as "peacekeeping" police forces – or members of local communities devoted to relative self-sufficiency and ecological soundness?

Harris's optimism that a globalized economy can be peacefully achieved is undercut by Raymond Williams's skepticism about precisely the same issues. Favoring decentralization, a politics of locality and community that he calls "'green socialism'" (Williams 1989: 237), Williams worries about diminishing resources and the lengths to which members of rich societies accustomed to a high degree of consumerist consumption will be willing to go to control them. In an essay entitled "Socialism and Ecology," Williams observes:

> For we are bound to notice – and the people from the poorest parts of the world do increasingly notice – that the world economy is now organized and dominated by the interests of the patterns of production and consumption of the highly industrialized countries, which are also in a strict sense, through all the different political forms, the imperialist powers. This is shown most dramatically at the moment in the case of oil. (1989: 222–3)

Although not collected until 1989, this essay was written in 1982. Williams seems to have predicted the Gulf War of 1991 with uncanny precision. While praising the "alternative current" that seeks to develop more ecologically sound kinds of production and livelihood – "notably the renewed interest in agriculture and forestry, in new forms of energy production and of transport, and in various kinds of more locally based, non-exploitative and also renewable and non-obsolescent kinds of work" – Williams is quite clear that this current will not be suffcient to solve any immediate problems that may develop in relation to the whole existing economy:

> The problem of resources – the pressure point on the whole existing capitalist mode of production – will become the problem of war or

peace. This problem will be presented, through all the powerful resources of modern communications, as a problem of hostile foreigners who are exercising a stranglehold over our necessary supplies. Opinion will be mobilized for what will be called "peacekeeping"; in fact wars and raids and threatening interventions to ensure supplies or to keep down prices.

   Thus the continuation of existing patterns of unequal consumption of the earth's resources will lead us inevitably into various kinds of war, of different scales and extent . . . because we are not willing to change the inequalities of the present world economy. (1989: 224)

Thus the legacy of imperialism prescribes a future in which multiple flash-points of violent conflict seem likely to ensue. And within a global ecological perspective the whole project of unlimited growth and development, in which the Third World countries are encouraged to aspire to Western patterns of consumption, becomes not only a wrongheaded and wasteful vision but an impossible one.

   Williams also puts his finger on another node of potential conflict, one between multinational economic interests and the interests of nation-states. What happens when national foreign policy comes into conflict with corporate economic interest? Take, for example, the following self-congratulatory advertisement for *Forbes* magazine, standard reading matter for US businessmen, a magazine that archly promotes itself as a "Capitalist Tool." Featuring a headshot of Iraqi leader Saddam Hussein, the ad reads: "Forbes attacked Saddam Hussein last December." During the autumn of 1990, as the military build-up for war in the Gulf intensified, the ad appeared in a number of magazines, including the November 1990 issue of the satirical *Spy*. Across Saddam Hussein's portrait run quotations from ostensible stories that have appeared in *Forbes*: "Why is Washington befriending this tyrant?" "The Saudis and Kuwaitis need no reminding that Hussein used the pretext of a border dispute to start his war with Iran." "He still hopes to ride on a barrel of oil to leadership of the Arab world." We are invited to think that US corporate intelligence is superior to US political intelligence, that economic issues literally fuel political disputes, and that the US government has been slow to wake up to the need for war with Iraq, while the business community has long seen that war with Saddam Hussein was inevitable because of the question of oil, of who controls "our" necessary resources. "[E]asy cheap credit, easy cheap petrol": Williams identifies these as crucial conditions for the unthinking consumption, and the mobile, privatized selves, to which we have grown accustomed as contemporary citizens of the Western industrialized countries (see Williams 1989: 172).

Some Green Solutions

It follows that radical ecologists and exponents of Green politics should be proposing a total reorganization of economic, political, and social life on a global scale. Andrew Dobson, who provides an excellent general introduction to the terrain of Green politics, usefully distinguishes between shades of green. If consumers in search of less polluting or wasteful products to purchase might be described as "'green'" (Dobson 1990: 5, 140–2), there is also an important difference between "light-green" reform environmentalism and "dark-Green" radical ecologism (1990: 73, 89, 206–13). According to Dobson, the difference depends on one's attitude towards the environment and its implications for our current modes of production and consumption. Do we seek "a cleaner service economy, sustained by cleaner technology and producing cleaner affluence" (1990: 9)? Dobson describes this "light-green" attitude as "'managerial,'" since it assumes that humans remain anthropocentrically in charge and that environmental problems "can be solved without fundamental changes in present values or patterns of production and consumption" (1990: 13). "Dark-Green" or capital-"G" "Green" radical ecologism, on the other hand, argues that care for the environment "presupposes radical changes in our relationship with it, and thus in our mode of social and political life" (1990: 13).

One of the positions frequently taken up from this perspective is the need for small, relatively self-sufficient communities, in which the quality of social life and the relation between life and work would more than compensate for a greatly reduced and altered standard of consumption. One of the important exponents of the self-reliant commune as the way of the future is Rudolf Bahro, whose political trajectory has led him from East German Marxism to the West German Green Party, and then to a break from the Greens in June 1985 over the issue of animal experimentation, which he opposed absolutely for what Dobson calls "recognizably deep ecological reasons" (1990: 70). In the book in which Bahro marks the greening of his long commitment to socialism, he argues for a cultural revolution against industrial expectations – "industrial disarmament" (Bahro 1984: 145–9) – a contraction of mobility and consumption within small, self-reliant communities, and replacement of the world market

by world communications, a "world-market informational structure"
(1984: 180):

> The old industrial system is at an end: the increase in material consump-
> tion and production, with the inbuilt waste, pollution and depletion
> of resources, has reached its *non plus ultra* and is enough to destroy
> us in a few generations. Here in Bremerhaven we unload cars from
> Japan and load cars for America. The amount of material consumed
> per capita is now ten times higher than it was in the time of Schiller,
> not because individuals consume so much more but because of the
> massive material infrastructure of the world market. We must now
> enter into a phase of contraction, which in the first instance has to
> be economic. (Bahro 1984: 179)

According to Bahro, "there will certainly be practical compromises
with the eco-industry or bio-industry, and we will probably still
have the computer" (1984: 178), but countries like Germany should
strive for relative self-reliance, if not complete self-sufficiency, "without having to import apple juice from Morocco and without all this
EEC agricultural policy" (1984: 181). Bahro also advises considerably
reduced expectations of travel: "Perhaps it will be adequate if we
travel to Italy twice, as Goethe did" (1984: 222).

The important thing is to come to terms with the limits of the
earth's resources, and the fact that our First World, capitalist systems
of production and consumption cannot be maintained. Once this is
recognized, the goal becomes one of developing new modes of integrating social and economic life:

> Human development requires a basic security, a sense of being shel-
> tered by a community, where you don't have to think of your old-
> age pension at the age of twenty, where individuality can be expressed
> and enjoyed in communication with others, where self-realization can
> take place in a different sense from that of European individualism. . . .
> Certain things are obvious: that a solution to problems is best found
> in small groups, that human companionship for the satisfaction of
> mutual need requires a certain minimum number, and that some access
> to the wider world must be possible. (1984: 222)

But not, adds Bahro, if this access means that we have to see "all
the countries in the UN and to fly around the world twenty-seven
times," for this kind of access for everyone would not be possible
(1984: 222). Here Kant's universal imperative – that which is just is
that which is just for everyone – joins with the recognition of rapidly
diminishing resources.

The Problem of Eco-Feminism

Accompanying such an ecological vision of a reconstructed social and economic order, we frequently find a certain homage to feminism and to women. Bahro is no exception in this regard. For him, feminism is polarized between a post-French Revolutionary, "bourgeois" logic of emancipation, which "still lies *within* the logic of the civilization which has to be overcome," and a more radical challenge to patriarchal domination that could result in the "peaceful dissolution of this earliest crystallization of the power structure" (1984: 217). Not so much displacing as rewriting the Marxist notion of the proletariat as having a special world-historical mission to bring about revolution, Bahro speculates that "it is entirely possible that women have something like a general mission in this respect" (1984: 217).

Where have we heard this before? Women as saviors of the human race, women as having a civilizing mission, women as representing a reconstituted, value-laden family in tune with the new times, women as providing what Swindells and Jardine have labeled "moral realism" for the men? Symptomatically, in Swindells and Jardine's terms, Williams makes the connection between William Morris and this new brand of radical ecology plus socialism explicit: "The writer who began to unite these diverse traditions, in British social thought, was William Morris" (Williams 1989: 215). We are back with Swindells and Jardine's cautionary tale about the appropriation of women by the male left, the way women get used up in representing the moral side of politics.

One of the problems for feminism with this proposed rapprochement with Green politics is that the radical male ecologists' notion of what feminism is, and of what women are, is as subject to pre-feminist distortions as is any other politics. There is, to be sure, a strand of feminism that identifies itself as "eco-feminism" and seeks to address issues of environmental and ecological importance from a feminist perspective. But what is its relation to a materialist feminism, as concerned with human social relations as with relations between the human and non-human worlds? If eco-feminists position themselves in such a way that women have a special mission to save the planet because they are naturally more nurturing or closer to nature than men, haven't they fallen prey to gender ideology once again? And if, in their rush to replace capitalist industrial society with ecologically sound alternatives, ecologists and eco-feminists argue for a return to pre-industrial modes of production, to a more organic society, where will this leave feminism and other new social movements?

These questions plague Donna Haraway, among other critics of eco-feminism including some eco-feminists themselves, especially those whose Third World or anti-imperialist perspectives necessitate a focus on material problems and tying "together the analysis of race, class, gender, and speciesism" (Salleh 1991: 209; see also Shiva 1988). Haraway wants to address radical social transformation and issues of global ecological significance, but she wants to do it on materialist feminist terms. No return to irrational nature-worship, bogus spirituality, or the natural affinity of the feminine and the non-human for her! Haraway insists that we need to come to terms with technology rather than repudiate it in the name of a so-called return to some presumably organic past. Remember that there will still be computers and microchips in Bahro's Green alternative world-informational structure.

Enter the Cyborg

Enter, therefore, Haraway's model of the cyborg, who occupies a border territory between human and machine. Cyborgs break up traditional grand narratives, such as those of Judaeo-Christian historiography. They have neither natural parents nor patrimony. They stand outside the Oedipal family romance. Like Hortense Spillers's "rebel idea" – that Toni Morrison's character Sula might be a figure for new female being outside strictly patriarchal and Oedipal narratives – we find that the "cyborg incarnation is outside salvation history" (Haraway 1991: 150).

Not surprisingly, Haraway dismisses the spiritual tendencies of some versions of eco-feminism, particularly those that would put us back in touch with the goddess, with some spirit of the earth, or with the planet conceived as "Gaia," in the hypothesis of James Lovelock – understanding the earth itself as a living organism, within which other living organisms exist symbiotically in such a way that they keep the planet fit for life (see Dobson 1990: 42–7). Such wishful thinking will not get us very far, according to Haraway. She would have us refuse "an anti-science metaphysics, a demonology of technology" (Haraway 1991: 181).

Perhaps Haraway's most controversial statement of her position is the following one: "Though both are bound in the spiral dance, I would rather be a cyborg than a goddess" (1991: 181). That is to say, though both are fictions, ideological constructions that have a certain material and imaginative power to structure our experience in particular ways, Haraway chooses the cyborg rather than the goddess fiction. In a subsequent interview, Haraway claims that she would "rather go to bed with a cyborg than a sensitive man" (Penley and Ross 1991a: 18). The need to keep disrupting new fictions or positions before they have time to become fully entrenched orthodoxies is clearly important to Haraway's project.

From Haraway's work, then, an identity politics founded on "leaky distinctions" between organism and machine, the human and the non-human, can be seen to emerge. If cyborgs represent one version of this leak, a certain strain within the ecology movement focused on animal rights and wilderness preservation might be said to represent another. What happens when the critique of anthropocentrism takes the form of asserting, as "biocentric" ecologists do, that no form of organic life has any greater "intrinsic value" than any other form of life? Humans, in short, have no legitimate priority over lemmings, wolves, grizzly bears, dogs, cats, cattle, or any other animal. What right then have humans to take animal life, to kill animals for food, fur, or purposes of medical and other research, to eliminate habitats and exterminate whole species through human overpopulation and unchecked economic growth? The answer is, no right at all.

Animal People

In the US context especially, it should come as no surprise that the debate is often couched in terms of a discourse of legal rights, explicitly invoking the example of the Civil Rights and other social movements. An "Animal Bill of Rights," such as that proposed by the Animal Legal Defense Fund (ALDF), would assure "that animals, like all sentient beings," be "entitled to basic legal rights in our society. Deprived of legal protection, animals are defenseless against exploitation and abuse by humans." The petition to the US congress calls for:

> The right of animals to be free from exploitation, cruelty, neglect and abuse. The right of laboratory animals not to be used in cruel or unnecessary experiments. The right of farm animals to an environment that satisfies their basic physical and psychological needs. The right of companion animals to a healthy diet, protective shelter, and adequate medical care. The right of wildlife to a natural habitat, ecologically

sufficient to a normal existence and a self-sustaining species population. The right of animals to have their interests represented in court and safeguarded by the law of the land. (Tischler 1991: 5)

Within the US politico-legal context, ALDF executive director Joyce Tischler is sadly, but undoubtedly, correct when she states, in a letter accompanying the Animal Bill of Rights petition, "WITHOUT LEGAL PROTECTION, ANIMALS ARE DOOMED TO REMAIN HELPLESS VICTIMS OF ABUSE AND EXPLOITATION" (Tischler 1991: 1). The protection for which the ALDF is calling is surely only minimal once the anthropocentric point of view has been rejected sufficiently to recognize that animals should have rights, that humans do not have the right to exploit animals as in any sense inferior or less valuable or insentient beings.

The other side of such actions, as we have seen, is likely to be, regrettably, an extension of an already unwieldy legal apparatus in an increasingly litigious society. When the public airing of hearings and trials becomes an international media event, as in the recent hearings before the appointment of the controversial, though politically conservative, Clarence Thomas to the US Supreme Court, a great deal of space is opened up in which the legal apparatus does not so much guarantee civil rights as take the place of them. The staging of justice, or of a supposedly open and democratic legal process, as a spectacle becomes a substitute for the enactment and enforcement of the rights of relatively disenfranchised groups. And the spectacle of the law enacted via the mass media reinforces the notion of citizens' entitlement to compensation via the legal apparatus, so that liability cases and costs have increased exponentially over the past two decades.

From a radical ecological point of view, social and economic iniquities must be overthrown, not preserved under a gloss of liberal equality. The extension of civil rights to animal rights, while in some sense strategically useful in the current context, does not address more fundamental issues of how best to organize a more just and ecologically sound society, grounded in a social theory not limited to liberal notions of merely formal equality under the law.

Taking seriously Haraway's notion of "leaky distinctions" between such categories as cyborg and human, and human and animal, however, represents a first step towards rethinking our current assumptions in a radical way. If we are all cyborgs because of the deep deployment of technology within industrial and post-industrial societies increasingly globally connected in an international informational network, we are all also animal people. Haraway's book *Primate Visions* (1989) is the place to start for an historical understanding of how this plays out within twentieth-century science. Moreover, recognizing our exploitation of non-human as well as human beings as unjust *and* unecologically sound means recognizing the indisputable intrinsic value of life-forms other than human ones, regardless of their instrumental value to human society. In this sense, the critique of anthropocentrism both dethrones "man" and lets other sentient beings accede to the status of "animal people."

The Critique of Anthropocentrism

What are the political stakes of anti-anthropocentrism in the present moment? The debates among green consumers, vegetarians and animal rights activists, deep ecologists and wilderness preservationists, agricultural radicals and social ecologists, as well as eco-feminists and materialist feminists, constitute an imperatively new articulation that challenges the other social movements we have been examining. A Green cultural criticism informed by these debates represents what literary and cultural critics can contribute to reversing the tide of global ecological crisis: working for a Green revolution that would be anti-racist, anti-heterosexist, anti-imperialist, as well as anti-anthropocentric.

The question of animal rights opens up a split within the ecology movement, broadly conceived. So-called green consumers – according to Dobson, they should be called " 'green' " – who want to buy ecologically sound products, recycle as much as possible, and generally maintain their current standards of consumption in a less polluting and wasteful way, frequently take up vegetarianism as the diet of the future and the crucial node of controversy within a discourse of animal rights. Wilderness preservationists, on the other hand, who often espouse "deep ecology," the notion that human beings should subordinate themselves to ecological demands, frequently advocate a return to the social organization of gathering and hunting societies. Deep ecologist Dave Foreman, for example, one of the founders of the direct-action group Earth First!, has occasionally called for "a return to the Pleistocene" (see Chase 1991: 21) in the interests of helping "industrial civilization find its own dharma nature, and become an egalitarian, more tribal society" (Bookchin and Foreman 1991: 46; see also Foreman 1989). Hunting? What would a vegetarian say to that? What's the difference between not eating (other) animals, not eating other people, if you will, and eating only what you can find in the wild? What would a truly radical, Green relation to other animals, animal others, look like?

Foreman's primary concern is that we may lose "one-third of all species in the next 20 years because of multinational greed" (Bookchin and Foreman 1991: 40), but he wants to be very clear that his interest in preserving "biodiversity" does not mean preserving it instrumentally, for the sake of human use or pleasure:

> I believe a grizzly bear snuffling along Pelican Creek in Yellowstone National Park with her two cubs has just as much natural right to her life as any human has to his or hers. All living things have intrinsic value, inherent worth. Their value is not determined by what they will ring up on the cash register of the GNP [Gross National Product], nor by whether or not they are aesthetically pleasing to human beings. . . . They have traveled that same three-and-a-half-billion-year evolutionary course we have. They live for themselves, for their own sakes, regardless of any real or imagined value to human civilization. They should never be considered mere means to our ends for they are, like us, also ends in themselves. (Bookchin and Foreman 1991: 116)

From this point of view, not domesticating the planet but preserving as much wilderness as possible is the primary aim. Earth First!'s 1983 Wilderness Preserve System, for example, called not only for protecting all remaining roadless public lands over a few thousand acres, but for including large areas of privately owned and even already developed land which could be carefully restored to a wilder state (Chase 1991: 17–18). According to Christopher Manes, these preserves would permit:

> no human habitation (except, in some cases, indigenous peoples with traditional life-styles); no use of mechanized equipment or vehicles; no roads; no logging, mining, water diversion, industrial activity, agriculture, or grazing; no use of artificial chemical substances; no suppression of wildfires; no overflights by aircraft; and no priority given to the safety and convenience of human visitors over the functioning of the eco-system. (Manes 1990: 74; cited by Chase 1991: 17)

In the absence of agriculture and grazing, indigenous peoples would have to depend upon gathering and hunting, presumably without any livestock whatsoever. Whether this would prove acceptable to their "traditional life-styles" is unclear, since doing away with mechanization might well mean increased use of animals within these traditional lifestyles. What borderline space might the horse occupy in this economy, useful for the hunt within an indigenous tribal community, and not necessarily interchangeable with domestic livestock kept for food, clothing, and shelter?

Not surprisingly, the wilderness preservation movement is largely a US movement, though, as Williams notes, it has become a recent "cultural import" in the UK (Williams 1989: 236), with mixed results. Why is it that the preservation of wildlife, of endangered rare species, attracts such a disproportionate amount of attention from celebrities and elites? Williams takes his stand with the local cultivators of a hypothetical place, whose crops are trampled by a particular endangered species, and who are occasionally killed by it, against "the eminences of the world flying in and saying: 'you must save this beautiful wild creature.' . . . Such people are the friends of nobody, and to think that they are allies in the ecological movement is an extraordinary delusion" (1989: 220).

The Bookchin Story

The US social ecologist Murray Bookchin, while having much more to say than Williams about the crucial importance of wilderness and wildlife preservation for any radical ecology, concurs in the suspicion that certain aspects of the movement may be attractive to the political establishment because of its seeming disregard of issues of class, race, multinational corporate interests, and economic iniquities. According to Bookchin, deep ecology, despite its radical philosophical implications, "has actually become very trendy and chic these days. It has not only swept into its fold a large number of well-situated academics but also a lot of journalists and even royalty, like Prince Philip of England, and other movers and shakers in the elite 'ecology' establishment." Bookchin's question, which we think must be taken seriously, is whether these recent converts to deep ecology have "become radical social critics or is deep ecology congenial to their conventional, and sometimes even reactionary, social views?":

> Whatever its merits, the fact is that deep ecology, more than any other "radical" ecological perspective, blames "Humanity" as such for the ecological crisis – especially ordinary "consumers" and "breeders of children" – while largely ignoring the corporate interests that are really plundering the planet. This socially neutral aspect of deep ecol-

ogy appears to be very agreeable to the powers that be. I think this is the key reason that out of all the possible "radical" schools of ecological thought, deep ecology is being celebrated in popular magazines, in newspapers, on television, and in other media. (Bookchin and Foreman 1991: 123)

Bookchin reluctantly concludes, "Laudable as Earth First!'s reverence for wild areas and wildlife may be, the failure of deep ecology to provide a radical social orientation to its admirers often leaves them as mere acolytes of a wilderness cult" (Bookchin and Foreman 1991: 130; see also Bookchin 1989 and 1982).

Appeals to "our national heritage" take different forms in Britain and the United States, but their appearance in the media in both countries is on the upswing. In the guise of nature and environmental TV programs in the US, we are treated to eagles soaring over vast mountainous expanses at the same moment that the American eagle is employed as part of the imagery of jingoistic patriotism in the aftermath of the Gulf War – a war over corporate control of oil, and a war which for many months deflected both public attention and vast economic resources away from US domestic problems in the interests of an imperialist policing described as "peacekeeping." In the UK, corporations like British Petroleum and British Telecom boldly advertise themselves as "green," relaying images of beautifully depopulated pastoral landscapes, as if they were the chief guardians of the countryside – "our heritage" – against non-British invasions of (im)migrant, littering, and despoiling others.

Like Donna Haraway, Bookchin worries that the repudiation of technology, which goes along with a return to the Pleistocene or the Neolithic, means in effect a social irresponsibility regarding the technologies upon which we are currently so dependent, as well as an abandoning of a progressive social agenda – the demands of the new social movements. Bookchin's social ecology is in many ways parallel to Haraway's socialist feminism, though Bookchin is careful to align himself with anarchism rather than socialism when the question of the state comes up, since like Bahro he argues for decentralized, non-hierarchical, self-reliant "bioregional" communities. Both could well be described as materialist rather than socialist, in fact, because both acknowledge the crucial importance of race, gender, sexual identity, and ethnicity as well as class. The problem with materialism in this context, however, is that it seems a term so tainted by its popular usage – as synonymous with the commitment to conspicuous consumption in industrial societies – that Bookchin substitutes "naturalism":

> We should never lose sight of the fact that the project of human liberation has now become an ecological project, just as, conversely, the project of defending the Earth has also become a social project. Social ecology as a form of eco-anarchism weaves these two projects together, first by means of an organic way of thinking that I call *dialectical naturalism*; second, by means of a mutualistic social and ecological ethics that I call the *ethics of complementarity*; third, by means of a new technics that I call *eco-technology*; and last, by means of new forms of human association that I call *eco-communities*. (Bookchin and Foreman 1991: 131)

Thus Bookchin counters the potential inability of biocentrism to distinguish between bears and viruses, or between lemmings and humans as life-forms, by means of his "ethics of complementarity." This anti-anthropocentric ethics nevertheless acknowledges the disproportionate power humans exercise over the non-human world, and the extent to which this power is bound up with human sociality, so that humans are less subject to strictly biological imperatives than are, say, lemmings. "Human beings can play an appallingly destructive role for non-human life-forms, or by the same token, they can play a profoundly constructive role," Bookchin writes. "They can create an ecological society, or they can easily destroy their own tenure on the planet" (Bookchin and Foreman 1991: 126).

We might add that humans have already played such a constructive role in what we assume to be natural that the very notion of the biological per se must be treated with caution. Think of the many breeds within species of animals that have been created by humans for their use. One could almost argue that certain species have been so socialized by their domestication as to be nearly products of culture *rather than* of nature. And if we humans do succeed in destroying our own tenure on the planet, we will surely take most other species with us, species in no sense responsible for the ecological disaster to which they will have been subjected through our agency. If Bookchin is right, we should understand the roots of the ecological crisis to be social, even insofar as "the absence of an ecological sensibility" – which could, in a sense, be held largely responsible for the history of our deployment of resources in a corporate, state-capitalist, and militaristic fashion – might be said to have its roots in "social causes" and "human suffering" (Bookchin and Foreman 1991: 132).

A Green Paradox: Eco-Consumerism

These arguments between social ecologists and deep ecologists may seem rather far removed from the discourse of animal rights we find in activist organizations like the US group, People for the Ethical Treatment of Animals (PETA). The autumn 1991 issue of *PETA News*, for instance, features Paul and Linda McCartney (of Beatles and Wings fame) declaring their vegetarianism and commitment to what we might name lifestyle reform, a form of "green" consumerism. On the cover, which pictures the couple wearing T-shirts which read "GO Veggie" (Linda) and "STOP Eating Animals" (Paul), they are quoted as saying (singing?): "We don't *need* to eat flesh. We don't *need* to wear fur. We don't *need* to give dogs cancer to know not to smoke." The issue includes an article on "The Art of Vegetarianism" as conceived by them both, recipes by Linda for a festive holiday menu without meat, and an ad for the T-shirts displayed on the cover.

In general the message is consume, consume, without killing and eating animals, since slaughterhouses are sites of incredible brutality and pain. Because it is assumed that most of us wish to continue to have what we are accustomed to having, Linda's recipes are aimed at reproducing meat dishes – roasts, meatloaves, stews, and hashes – without meat, using "vegetarian ingredients like textured vegetable protein and commercial vegetarian burgers and sausages." In fact, we are told, Linda has "developed her own line of vegetarian burgers in England, now being sold in stores" (PETA 1991: 7).

This seems a good illustration of what Andrew Dobson calls "green" consumerism that cannot really be considered ecologically sound or sustainable in the long run. Most of Linda's recipes require an electric food processor. "Nature's Burger" and "Veggie Tofu" brand-name burgers are extremely upmarket, if not gourmet-supermarket purchases, out of the reach of many people, both logistically and financially. And simply saying "No" to the consumption of meat as a matter of personal choice does not get us very far towards a collective or regional, let alone a global, policy on agriculture, livestock, and animal rights, or on the deep ecologists' views on hunting. Whether there might be such a thing as just or humane livestock rearing and to what ends it might be considered necessary or acceptable, whether the occasional (ritual?) killing and eating of animals (cannibalism?) is ever permissible, whether there might be such a thing as ethically reformed agriculture, leading to humane conditions in slaughterhouses for both animals and the (other?) people who work there, the conditions in which animals historically produced for food and other human essentials (clothing, shelter) would be allowed to be produced, or to reproduce and continue living: these are just some of the questions that a principled individual choice not to cause animals pain by choosing vegetarianism, or its purer form, veganism, does not begin to address.

In the industrialized West, the extent to which contemporary urban, suburban, or even that much rarer thing, rural, vegetarianism depends upon global markets, industrial production of commodities and foodstuffs, and various forms of high-tech commercial appliances and agriculture, is the extent to which it fails, in Andrew Dobson's terms, to merit being called ecologically radical. What happens to even the principled, low-tech vegetarian or vegan when the only vegetables available are only the vegetables that can be grown not only organically but locally? Such a diet might remain possible in the Mediterranean, the Caribbean, subcontinental and southern Asian, and some African countries, but the northern hemisphere would not find it easy to support it. Southern California's growing areas, for example, are largely desert, dependent upon huge, ecologically unsound irrigation projects, namely, diverting the Colorado River and robbing other regions of their natural water supply. What price a seasonless assortment of fruits and vegetables?

Ironically, it seems that, other than recycling and purchasing "green," so-called environmentally safe, consumer products, vegetarianism and animal rights in the form of anti-fur and anti-animal experimentation are the kinds of ecological activism which have had the greatest impact on the younger generations of Western consumers. The convergence of vegetarianism with recent stands taken by rock and pop stars and other celebrities trying to be green is partly responsible for this phenomenon. For example, US fans of Morrissey, former lyricist and vocalist for the British band The Smiths, now performing very successfully on his own, often report that his pro-vegetarian stance has raised their consciousness about animal rights and green issues generally (Creekmur 1992). Another side of the story might well be that the modern focus on technologies of the body, as identified by Foucault, makes the question of controlling what we most literally consume particularly symbolically loaded in the present moment. Hence the prevalence of eating disorders (anorexia, bulimia, some forms of obesity) as well as food phobias and food fetishisms of various sorts.

Another Green Paradox: Hunting

What is needed from the radically ecological perspective is a more wide-sweeping, though locally determined, sense of whole sustainable economies of production and consumption in which animals and people, animal people, come to terms with their bioregional eco-systems in non-anthropocentric, though not necessarily vegetarian, ways. Surely carnivorous animals should be allowed to eat meat and not be subjected to industrially produced vegetarian dog and cat food, in order to satisfy some human principle of bloodless purity. Surely such controversial topics as human and animal blood sports, especially hunting in its various forms, should be investigated in open-minded, social, and ecological ways, not condemned out of hand as barbaric, if gatherer/hunters have been living in ecologically sustainable ways for centuries.

The issue of hunting in the modern world is extremely complex. Recognizing its complexity demands, on the one hand, broadening the usual industrialized terrain to include contemporary gathering and hunting peoples, whose modes of production may combine Paleolithic hunting practices with a cash economy. In locations on the modern capitalist periphery such as northern Canada, for instance, hunting for subsistence often conjoins hunting for food with hunting for fur, since fur can provide the cash necessary to support further hunting for food and so on. Thus to distinguish sharply between hunting for food and hunting for other purposes, as if only a strictly eat-or-die, utilitarian end justified hunting as a means, begs many questions, especially with regard to the social ecology of indigenous peoples (see Brody 1987; Kulchyski 1989; Emberley 1993). On the other hand, analyzing the complexities of modern hunting also requires attention to specific sites in which hunting occupies a very different relation to the ecosystem from hunting which is of crucial importance for gathering and hunting peoples.

Foxhunting in the UK and the US represents one such specific and particularly contested domain. In the UK the left is particularly prone to take an anti-hunting stance for reasons to do as much with its own traditional urbanity as with its sense of working-class solidarity – flying in the face of the foxhunting and grouse shooting toffs. This antagonism has a long history traceable to disputes over game laws and rights of access to common lands and resources, as analyzed by E. P. Thompson and others (see Thompson 1975). The struggle to preserve common rights, such as the right to gather wood and to kill game for food, has traditionally taken the form of a struggle against royal and upper-class game preservation for sport through the enactment of laws against poaching. This dispute exemplifies, in relation to a subsistence economy, one specific instance of the difference between residual gathering and proto-industrialized agriculture as modes of production and the historical slippage between the two, as well as the political question of access to means of subsistence.

But what about the place of foxhunting within specific regional and rural communities, in which the name of the game might well be preserving as much as possible the fox's existence in the wild while accommodating farmers' anxieties about the fox as a predator of sheep, poultry, and other livestock? Among hill farmers on Dartmoor, for instance, there is a conviction that a ban on foxhunting would probably bring about the disappearance of the fox from many "in country" areas surrounding southern England's last great wilderness and a drastic reduction in the number of foxes living on the moor itself.[1] In such communities, the class-fix of hunting, and its role in ecological preservation, can be quite different from the social and cultural space it occupies in other communities, such as the famous grasslands of the Midland shires, where it might be said to have become distinctly an upper-class preserve, dedicated to showing sport for the benefit of those who can afford to participate in a ritual that for many observers embodies conspicuous consumption.

So long as there is agriculture, rather than a complete "return" to gathering and hunting as a mode of production, and so long as there are wild animals like foxes that will prey upon domestic animals, foxes will be killed by humans. In what way should they be killed? What sort of hunting, shooting, trapping, or other form of population control would be justifiable? The pro-hunting lobby often argues that because foxhunting "has been for centuries an integral and important part of the life of rural Britain," it remains "the most humane and natural way to control foxes." The Masters of Foxhounds Association would have us believe that "the beneficial part [foxhunting] plays in conservation of the countryside and in the rural economy is beyond doubt."[2] What is the status of this claim that the fox would disappear almost entirely from its remaining natural habitats in rural and wilderness areas, as it already has from many places where intensive agriculture has driven it into towns and suburbs, if it were no longer preserved by foxhunting farmers?

To answer this question requires an investigation of the fox's place within the cultural formations of local communities. Foxhunting in areas like Dartmoor, at least, might be said to help preserve species habitats and local ecology through the performance of social rituals. It would seem that foxhunting farmers will tolerate foxes and other wildlife in greater numbers and even take pains to protect coverts and unprofitable or uncultivated land when the ritual of the chase is at stake. An exaggerated form of this logic carries over to foxhunting in the US, where the small red and grey fox populations are hunted but hardly ever killed, and attention is paid to preserving their habitats, stimulating a certain ecological awareness that would not otherwise exist. The ritual of the chase requires precisely that the fox live to give hounds and hunters a good run another day. In places like the Pine Barrens of New Jersey, where hounds follow a line through woods and cranberry bogs, and hunters follow by listening to hound voices, driving pickup trucks and keeping in touch with one another through CB radios, foxhunting constitutes the ground of a rural working-class identity through which the community's integrity is ritualized. The tension in this locale lies between occasional trappers and deer hunters who like to shoot foxes, and the foxhunters, who see themselves as dedicated preservationists. As Mary Hufford observes, this local subculture is a highly gendered one in which women play a marginal role, in contrast with their much greater visibility and importance in the upper-class "English-style" foxhunting of northern New Jersey (Hufford 1992: 96–103).

Within such a cultural formation, the fox takes on the status of a sacred animal with whom a ritual role-swapping takes place. Although this argument bears litttle relation to deep- or social-ecological arguments, and indeed must be seen as highly anthropo-centric, the controversies over hunting today invite some consider-ation of hunting's ritual dimension if we are to comprehend the social importance of hunting where it is still practiced, not on the capitalist periphery, but in the modern industrialized world. The historian Keith Thomas characterizes representations of foxhunting as "half battle, half morality-play" (Thomas 1983: 163). As Merrily Harpur has observed of foxhunting's mounted fields, "the hunters' highly evolved apparel is, in fact, the fox's livery: red coat, white bib and black extremities." Representations of the fox as sly Reynard, on the other hand, often depict him wearing hunting clothes, drinking wine, and eating chicken, surrounded by hunting prints "of riders upturned in hedges" (Harpur 1990: 40).

The social mix of hunters varies greatly from one location to the next. Harpur's description of an Irish field includes "the farmer, the vet, the bank manager, the nurse, the blacksmith, the soldier; the young and flash of every social standing; girls who would never wear gloves except to hunt; girls who knew that a woman never looks so well as on a horse, and an old woman just as well as a young one; country lads who fastened the white stock at their weatherbeaten throats with the baby's nappy pin" (1990: 40). From a social-ecological point of view, such questions of local social relations and the integrity of local communities and their cultural practices, especially when the border territory between the agriculturists' garden and the preservationists' wilderness is on the agenda, demand contextual, not universal solutions.

In the US, the question of hunting is usually posed rather differently, around the question of guns, bows and arrows, and their legal regulation, as well as around the question of "protecting" various species by selectively hunting them. The American right to bear arms is synonymous with the right to hunt game. The last great wild and natural frontier is often invoked when the issue of the ethics of hunting is on the agenda. The cult of American masculinity and the cult of the gun-bearing hunter, deep in the woods back-of-beyond, are mutually dependent, as the Vietnam film *The Deerhunter* amply demonstrated. The class-fix of hunting in the US is consequently much more populist, and even working-class, than it tends to be in the UK in popular debate. This difference brings the question of hunting back to the earliest moments of cultural difference between Britain as an imperial power and the colonies as sites of the genocide and expropriation of native people. One of the final ironies of Daniel Defoe's novel *Moll Flanders* (1722) is that in colonial Virginia hunting brings the English gentleman and the Indian male together in their disdain for extensive cultivation, which is left to women and less well-bred folks.

Thus, even when the issue might seem fairly clear-cut from an urban, left-leaning, green point of view, as in the case of hunting and blood sports, both deep ecology and social ecology frequently challenge such assumptions. Once we have agreed to reject any easy analogies between "women" and "nature," to problematize rather than make easy assumptions about the historical, social, and philosophical relations between dominating nature and oppressing women and racial and sexual minorities, and between hunting and the whole industrial infrastructure of producing animals for food without any attention to their subjectivity and natural rights, then even such a seemingly globally inconsequential matter as "a feminist position on hunting" becomes productively, and not reductively, problematical. A Green cultural criticism will seek to foreground the critical problems involved in such a project, while trying to think and practice long-term as well as short-term strategies in the interests of sustainable, radically ecological local and global cultures.

Notes

1 Interviews conducted during December 1991 and January 1992, and between May and August 1992, with some Graziers of the Dartmoor Commoners Association, not all of whom approve of foxhunting.
2 Masters of Foxhounds Association, *Code of Good Hunting Practice* (1992), p. 1.

Conclusion

Need materialism be only an alias for Marxism? We hope that by now the distinction between Marxist feminism and materialist feminism is clear. Marxist feminism holds class contradictions and class analysis to be central, and has tried various ways of working an analysis of gender oppression around this central contradiction. In addition to class contradictions and contradictions within gender ideology and gendered social practices, which have material bases and effects, we are arguing that materialist feminism should recognize as material other contradictions as well. These contradictions also have histories, operate in ideologies, and are grounded in material bases and effects. We think they should thus be granted material weight in social and literary analysis calling itself materialist. At the moment these categories would include, at least, the ideologies of race, sexuality, imperialism and colonialism, and anthropocentrism, with their accompanying radical critiques.

A materialist feminist criticism will, therefore, attend to such ideologically loaded categories whenever they are at work in a text, without confusing them. For these categories have their own histories. As Spivak cautions, the social movements within which critiques of these oppressive ideologies have been mounted – anti-racist, anti-imperialist, as well as Marxist and feminist – exist discontinuously and often contradict or interrupt one another. Sometimes oppressions may be seen to "interlock," as the Combahee River Collective has argued. Perhaps more often they are at odds with one another in peculiar congealings of complicity and resistance.

When, in the same year that the Earth Summit was held at Rio de Janeiro (1992), the World Bank can publish a report on world development concluding that the education of women is the most effective way to solve global poverty and environmental destruction, because women "control their fertility and the fertility of the soil," such an analysis is urgently called for (Erlichman 1992). Far from advocating fundamental changes in national and multinational policies that would check short-term profit and limitless economic growth in favor of long-term sustainability (see Shiva 1988 and Shiva et al. 1991), the World Bank targets women as those responsible for both overpopulation and inadequate food production. Their solution to impending ecological disaster: education as contraception, also leading to better crop and pest management. The report claims that, if a secondary education reduces from seven to three the number of children a woman has, herein lies the answer to this crisis of diminishing resources. In such an historical moment, being able to read between the lines and against the grain, as we have argued throughout this book, gives us at least some idea of what is at stake here. And that knowledge can provide a lever for more fundamental changes.

Works Cited

Adams, Parveen, and Elizabeth Cowie 1983. "Feminine Sexuality: Interview with Juliet Mitchell and Jacqueline Rose – 1982." *m/f* 8: 3–16.

Adams, Parveen, and Elizabeth Cowie 1986. "The Last Issue Between Us." *m/f* 11/12: 3.

Adams, Parveen, and Jeff Minson 1978. "The 'Subject' of Feminism." *m/f* 2: 43–61.

Aidoo, Ama Ata 1979. *Our Sister Killjoy or Reflections from a Black-Eyed Squint.* New York, London, Lagos: NOK Publishers International.

Althusser, Louis 1969. *For Marx.* Trans. Ben Brewster. Harmondsworth: Penguin; New York: Random House. Originally published in France as *Pour Marx.* Paris: Librairie François Maspero, 1965.

Althusser, Louis 1971. *Lenin and Philosophy and Other Essays.* Trans. Ben Brewster. New York and London: Monthly Review Press.

Amariglio, Jack, and Antonio Callari 1989. "Marxian Value Theory and the Problem of the Subject: The Role of Commodity Fetishism." *Rethinking Marxism* 2 (3): 31–60.

Amos, Valerie, and Pratibha Parmar 1984. "Challenging Imperial Feminism." *Feminist Review* 17: 3–19.

Anzaldúa, Gloria 1987. *Borderlands/La Frontera: The New Mestiza.* San Francisco: Spinsters/Aunt Lute.

Ardill, Susan, and Sue O'Sullivan 1986. "Upsetting an Applecart: Difference, Desire and Lesbian Sadomasochism." *Feminist Review* 23: 31–57.

Armstrong, Nancy 1987. *Desire and Domestic Fiction: A Political History of the Novel.* New York and Oxford: Oxford University Press.

Aveling, Edward, and Eleanor Marx Aveling 1886. *The Woman Question.* London: Swann Sonnenschein.

Bâ, Mariama 1981. *So Long a Letter.* Trans. Modupé Bodé-Thomas. African Writers Series 248. Oxford, Ibadan, Nairobi: Heinemann. First published Dakar: Les Nouvelles Editions Africaines, 1980.

Bahro, Rudolf 1984. *From Red to Green: Interviews with New Left Review.* Trans. Gus Fagan and Richard Hurst. London: Verso.

Baker, Houston A., Jr 1987. "In Dubious Battle." *New Literary History* 18 (2): 363–9.

Barker, Francis, Peter Hulme, Margaret Iversen, and Diana Loxley (eds) 1985. *Europe and Its Others*, Vol. 1: *Proceedings of the Essex Conference on the Sociology of Literature, July 1984*. Colchester: University of Essex.

Barrett, Michèle 1980. *Women's Oppression Today: Problems in Marxist Feminist Analysis*. London: Verso. Repr. with a new introduction and new subtitle, *The Marxist Feminist Encounter*, 1988.

Barrett, Michèle 1982. "Feminism and the Definition of Cultural Politics." In Brunt and Rowan (1982): 37–58.

Barrett, Michèle 1987. "Max Raphael and the Question of Aesthetics." *New Left Review* 161: 78–97. An earlier version appears as "The Place of Aesthetics in Marxist Criticism," in Nelson and Grossberg (1988): 697–713.

Barrett, Michèle 1988. "Introduction to the 1988 Edition." In *Women's Oppression Today: The Marxist Feminist Encounter*, pp. vii–xxxvi. London: Verso.

Barrett, Michèle 1991. *The Politics of Truth: From Marx to Foucault*. Cambridge: Polity Press.

Barrett, Michèle, and Mary McIntosh 1979. "Christine Delphy: Towards a Materialist Feminism?" *Feminist Review* 1: 95–106.

Barrett, Michèle, and Mary McIntosh 1985. "Ethnocentrism and Socialist-Feminist Theory." *Feminist Review* 20: 23–47.

Barrett, Michèle, and Mary McIntosh 1991. *The Anti-Social Family*. London and New York: Verso. 2nd edn with new postscript. Originally published 1982.

Beal, Frances M. 1986. "Black Women and the Science Fiction Genre: Interview with Octavia Butler." *Black Scholar* 17: 14–18.

Bebel, August 1971. *Woman under Socialism*. Trans. Daniel De Leon. New York: Schocken Books. Originally published 1904.

Belsey, Catherine 1980. *Critical Practice*. London and New York: Methuen.

Benhabib, Seyla, and Drucilla Cornell 1987. *Feminism as Critique: On the Politics of Gender*. Oxford: Basil Blackwell; Minneapolis: University of Minnesota Press.

Benstock, Shari (ed.) 1987. *Feminist Issues in Literary Scholarship*. Bloomington and Indianapolis: University of Indiana Press.

Bhabha, Homi K. 1985. "Signs Taken For Wonders: Questions of Ambivalence and Authority Under a Tree Outside Delhi, May 1817." In Barker et al. (1985): 89–106. First published in *Critical Inquiry* 12 (1) (1985): 144–65. Repr. in Gates (1986): 163–84.

Bono, Paola, and Sandra Kemp (eds) 1991. *Italian Feminist Thought: A Reader*. Oxford and New York: Basil Blackwell.

Bookchin, Murray 1982. *The Ecology of Freedom*. Palo Alto: Cheshire Books.

Bookchin, Murray 1989. *Remaking Society*. Montreal and New York: Black Rose Books.

Bookchin, Murray, and Dave Foreman 1991. *Defending the Earth: A Dialogue Between Murray Bookchin and Dave Foreman*. Boston: South End Press.

Brennan, Teresa (ed.) 1989. *Between Feminism and Psychoanalysis*. London and New York: Routledge.

Brody, Hugh 1987. *Living Arctic: Hunters of the Canadian North*. Toronto: Douglas & McIntyre.

Brunt, Rosalind, and Caroline Rowan (eds) 1982. *Feminism, Culture, and Politics*. London: Lawrence & Wishart.

Bunting, Madeleine 1992. "Derrida Debate Refuses to Die." *The Guardian*, May 18: 3.

Butler, Judith 1990. *Gender Trouble: Feminism and the Subversion of Identity*. New York and London: Routledge.

Butler, Octavia E. 1988. *Kindred*. Boston: Beacon Press. First published 1979.

Campbell, Colin 1986. "The Tyranny of the Yale Critics." *New York Times Magazine*, February 9: 20–48.

Carby, Hazel V. 1987. *Reconstructing Womanhood: The Emergence of the Afro-American Woman Novelist*. New York and Oxford: Oxford University Press.

Castle, Terry 1990. "Sylvia Townsend Warner and the Counterplot of Lesbian Fiction." *Textual Practice* 4 (2): 213–35.

Caudwell, Sarah 1982. *Thus Was Adonis Murdered*. New York, London, Harmondsworth: Penguin. First published New York: Charles Scribner's Sons, 1981.

Caudwell, Sarah 1986. *The Shortest Way to Hades*. New York, London, Harmondsworth: Penguin. First published London: Century Publishers, 1984.

Chase, Steve 1991. "Introduction: Whither the Radical Ecology Movement?" In Bookchin and Foreman (1991): 7–24.

Christian, Barbara 1985. *Black Feminist Criticism: Perspectives on Black Women Writers*. New York: Pergamon.

Christian, Barbara 1989. "The Race for Theory." In Kauffman (1989): 225–37. First published in *Cultural Critique* 6 (1987): 51–63.

Cixous, Hélène 1976. "The Laugh of the Medusa." Trans. Keith Cohen and Paula Cohen. *Signs* 1 (4): 875–93. Repr. in Marks and de Courtivron (1980): 245–64. First published as "Le Rire de la Méduse," *L'Arc* 61 (1975): 39–54.

Clements, Barbara Evans 1979. *Bolshevik Feminist: The Life of Aleksandra Kollontai*. Bloomington: Indiana University Press.

Combahee River Collective 1977. "A Black Feminist Statement." In Eisenstein (1979): 362–72. Repr. in Hull, Scott, and Smith (1982): 13–22; and in Moraga and Anzaldúa (1983): 210–18.

Connor, Steven 1989. *Postmodernist Culture: An Introduction to Theories of the Contemporary*. Oxford and Cambridge, MA: Basil Blackwell.

Coward, Rosalind 1980. " 'This Novel Changes Women's Lives': Are

Women's Novels Feminist Novels?" *Feminist Review* 5: 53–64. Repr. in Showalter (1985): 225–39.

Coward, Rosalind 1983. *Patriarchal Precedents: Sexuality and Social Relations*. London: Routledge.

Coward, Rosalind, and John Ellis 1977. *Language and Materialism: Developments in Semiology and the Theory of the Subject*. London: Routledge.

Creekmur, Corey 1992. Unpublished work in progress on fandom and popular music.

Dant, Tim 1991. *Knowledge, Ideology and Discourse: A Sociological Perspective*. London and New York: Routledge.

Davidson, Cathy N. 1986. *Revolution and the Word: The Rise of the Novel in America*. New York and Oxford: Oxford University Press.

Davis, Angela Y. 1981. *Women, Race & Class*. New York: Random House.

de Lauretis, Teresa (ed.) 1986. *Feminist Studies/Critical Studies*. Bloomington: Indiana University Press.

de Lauretis, Teresa 1989. "The Essence of the Triangle or, Taking the Risk of Essentialism Seriously: Feminist Theory in Italy, the U.S., and Britain." *differences: A Journal of Feminist Cultural Studies* 1 (2): 3–37. Revised as "Upping the Anti (sic) in Feminist Theory," in Hirsch and Fox Keller (1990): 255–70.

Delphy, Christine 1981. "For a Materialist Feminism." *Feminist Issues* 1 (2): 69–76. Originally published in France in *L'Arc* 61 (1975).

Derrida, Jacques 1974. "White Mythology: Metaphor in the Text of Philosophy." Trans. F. C. T. Moore. *New Literary History* 4 (1): 5–74. Originally published in France as "La Mythologie blanche," *Poétiques* 5 (1971).

Derrida, Jacques 1976. *Of Grammatology*. Trans. Gayatri Chakravorty Spivak. Baltimore and London: Johns Hopkins University Press. Originally published in France as *De la grammatologie*. Paris: Editions de Minuit, 1967.

Derrida, Jacques 1979. *Spurs: Nietzsche's Styles/Eperons: Les Styles de Nietzsche*. Trans. Barbara Harlow. Chicago and London: University of Chicago Press. Originally published in France as *Eperons*. Paris: Flammarion, 1978.

Derrida, Jacques 1980. "La Loi du Genre/The Law of Genre." Trans. Avital Ronell. *Glyph* 7 (1980): 176–232.

Derrida, Jacques 1982. *Positions*. Trans. Alan Bass. Chicago: University of Chicago Press. Originally published in France as *Positions*. Paris: Editions de Minuit, 1972.

Derrida, Jacques 1988a. *Limited Inc*. Trans. Samuel Weber and Jeffrey Mehlman. Evanston, Ill.: Northwestern University Press.

Derrida, Jacques 1988b. "Limited Inc a b c . . ." Trans. Samuel Weber. In Derrida (1988a): 29–110. First published in *Glyph* 2 (1977): 162–254.

Derrida, Jacques 1988c. "Signature Event Context." Trans. Samuel Weber and Jeffrey Mehlman. In Derrida (1988a): 1–24. First published in *Glyph* 1 (1977): 172–97.

Diamond, Irene, and Lee Quinby (eds) 1988. *Feminism & Foucault: Reflections on Resistance*. Boston: Northeastern University Press.

differences: A Journal of Feminist Cultural Studies 3 (2): 1991. "Queer Theory."

Dobson, Andrew 1990. *Green Political Thought: An Introduction*. London: Unwin Hyman.

Eisenstein, Zillah R. (ed.) 1979. *Capitalist Patriarchy and the Case for Socialist Feminism*. New York: Monthly Review Press.

Eisenstein, Zillah 1981. "Reform and/or Revolution: Towards a Unified Women's Movement." In Sargent (1981): 339–62.

Eisenstein, Zillah R. 1984. *Feminism and Sexual Equality: Crisis in Liberal America*. New York: Monthly Review Press.

Emberley, Julia V. 1990. "'A Gift for Languages': Native Women and the Textual Economy of the Colonial Archive." *Cultural Critique* 17: 21–50. To be reprinted in *Thresholds of Difference: Feminist Critique, Native Women's Writings and Post-Colonial Theory*. Toronto: University of Toronto Press, 1993.

Emberley, Julia 1993. "Simulated Politics: Animal Bodies, Fur-Bearing Women, and Indigenous Survival." Paper presented at the Society for the Humanities, Cornell University, February 10.

Erlichman, James 1992. "Women Hold Key to Saving Environment." *The Guardian*, May 18: 22.

Evans, Sara 1979. *Personal Politics: The Roots of Women's Liberation in the Civil Rights Movement and the New Left*. New York: Random House.

Farnsworth, Beatrice 1980. *Aleksandra Kollontai: Socialism, Feminism, and the Bolshevik Revolution*. Stanford: Stanford University Press.

Felperin, Howard 1987. "Making it 'Neo': The New Historicism and Renaissance Literature." *Textual Practice* 1 (3): 262–77.

Felski, Rita 1989. *Beyond Feminist Aesthetics: Feminist Literature and Social Change*. Cambridge, MA: Harvard University Press.

Feminist Review 34 1990. "Perverse Politics: Lesbian Issues."

Fields, Barbara Jeanne 1990. "Slavery, Race and Ideology in the United States of America." *New Left Review* 181: 95–118.

Foreman, Dave 1989. *Ecodefense: A Field Guide to Monkeywrenching*. Tucson: Ned Ludd Books.

Forrest, Katherine V. 1987. *Murder at the Nightwood Bar*. Tallahassee, FL: Naiad Press.

Foucault, Michel 1972. *The Archaeology of Knowledge*. Trans. A. M. Sheridan Smith. New York: Pantheon. Originally published in France as *L'Archéologie du savoir*. Paris: Editions Gallimard, 1969.

Foucault, Michel 1978. *The History of Sexuality*, Vol. I: *An Introduction*. Trans. Robert Hurley. New York: Pantheon. Originally published in France as *La Volonté de savoir*. Paris: Editions Gallimard, 1976.

Foucault, Michel 1980. *Power/Knowledge: Selected Interviews and Other Writings 1972–1977*. Ed. Colin Gordon. Brighton: Harvester; New York: Pantheon.

Fowler, Alastair 1982. *Kinds of Literature: An Introduction to the Theory of Genres and Modes*. Cambridge, MA: Harvard University Press.

Fraad, Harriet, Stephen Resnick, and Richard Wolff 1989. "For Every Knight in Shining Armor, There's a Castle Waiting To Be Cleaned: A Marxist-Feminist Analysis of the Household." *Rethinking Marxism* 2 (4): 9–69.

Fraad, Harriet, Stephen Resnick, and Richard Wolff 1990. "Class, Patriarchy, and Power: A Reply." *Rethinking Marxism* 3 (2): 124–44.

France, Marie 1984. "Sadomasochism and Feminism." *Feminist Review* 16: 35–42.

Fraser, Nancy 1989. *Unruly Practices: Power, Discourse and Gender in Contemporary Social Theory*. Cambridge: Polity Press.

Fraser, Nancy, and Linda Nicholson 1988. "Social Criticism without Philosophy: An Encounter between Feminism and Postmodernism." In Ross (1988): 83–104.

Fuss, Diana 1989. *Essentially Speaking: Feminism, Nature & Difference*. New York and London: Routledge.

Fuss, Diana (ed.) 1991. *inside/out: Lesbian Theories, Gay Theories*. New York and London: Routledge.

Gallop, Jane 1982. *The Daughter's Seduction: Feminism and Psychoanalysis*. Ithaca: Cornell University Press.

Gallop, Jane 1985. *Reading Lacan*. Ithaca and London: Cornell University Press.

Gallop, Jane 1992. *Around 1981: Academic Feminist Literary Theory*. New York and London: Routledge.

Gates, Henry Louis, Jr (ed.) 1986. *"Race," Writing, and Difference*. Chicago and London: University of Chicago Press.

Gates, Henry Louis, Jr 1987. "'What's Love Got to Do with It?': Critical Theory, Integrity, and the Black Idiom." *New Literary History* 18 (2): 345–62.

George, C. H. 1988. "Christopher Hill: A Profile." In *Reviving the English Revolution: Reflections on the Work of Christopher Hill*, pp. 15–29. Ed. Geoff Eley and William Hunt. London: Verso.

Gerstel, Judy 1991. "Foster Says Yale Helped Her Find Black Literature." *Detroit Free Press*, September 15: 7G.

Ghoussoub, Mai 1987. "Feminism – or the Eternal Masculine – in the Arab World." *New Left Review* 161: 3–18.

Gilbert, Sandra M., and Susan Gubar (eds) 1985. *The Norton Anthology of Literature by Women: The Tradition in English*. New York and London: W. W. Norton.

Grafton, Sue 1987. *"A" is for Alibi*. New York: Bantam. First published New York: Holt, Rinehart, & Winston, 1982.

Grafton, Sue 1988. *"D" is for Deadbeat*. New York: Bantam. First published New York: Henry Holt, 1987.

Grafton, Sue 1991. *"G" is for Gumshoe*. New York: Ballantine. First published New York: Holt, 1990.

Grossman, Rachel 1980. "Women's Place in the Integrated Circuit." *Radical America* 14 (1): 29–50.

Hamilton, Roberta, and Michèle Barrett (eds) 1986. *The Politics of Diversity: Feminism, Marxism and Nationalism.* London: Verso.

Haraway, Donna 1985. "A Manifesto for Cyborgs: Science, Technology, and Socialist Feminism in the 1980s." *Socialist Review* 80: 65–107. A revised version appears in Haraway (1991): 149–81.

Haraway, Donna 1988. "Situated Knowledges: The Science Question in Feminism and the Privilege of Partial Perspective." *Feminist Studies* 14 (3): 575–99. A revised version appears in Haraway (1991): 183–201.

Haraway, Donna 1989. *Primate Visions: Gender, Race, and Nature in the World of Modern Science.* New York and London: Routledge.

Haraway, Donna J. 1991. *Simians, Cyborgs, and Women: The Reinvention of Nature.* New York: Routledge.

Harlow, Barbara 1987. *Resistance Literature.* New York and London: Methuen.

Harpur, Merrily 1990. "Brush with Death." *The Listener* 20/27: 40–1.

Harris, Nigel 1987. *The End of the Third World: Newly Industrializing Countries and the Decline of an Ideology.* London and Harmondsworth: Penguin. First published London: I. B. Tauris, 1986.

Hartmann, Heidi 1981. "The Unhappy Marriage of Marxism and Feminism: Towards a More Progressive Union." In Sargent (1981): 1–41.

Hartsock, Nancy C. M. 1983. *Money, Sex, and Power: Toward a Feminist Historical Materialism.* New York: Longman. Repr. Boston: Northeastern University Press, 1985.

Harvey, David 1990. *The Condition of Postmodernity: An Enquiry into the Origins of Cultural Change.* Oxford and Cambridge, MA: Basil Blackwell.

Head, Bessie 1974. *A Question of Power.* African Writers Series 149. London, Nairobi, Ibadan: Heinemann.

Hekman, Susan J. 1990. *Gender and Knowledge: Elements of a Postmodern Feminism.* Cambridge: Polity Press.

Hennessy, Rosemary 1993. *Materialist Feminism and the Politics of Discourse.* New York and London: Routledge.

Hennessy, Rosemary, and Rajeswari Mohan 1989. "The Construction of Woman in Three Popular Texts of Empire: Towards a Critique of Materialist Feminism." *Textual Practice* 3 (3): 323–59.

Henwood, Doug 1990a. "Financial Collapse?" *Left Business Observer* 37: 1–3.

Henwood, Doug 1990b. "Miscellany: Frying Pans & Fires." *Left Business Observer* 38: 8.

Hill, Christopher 1972. *The World Turned Upside Down: Radical Ideas During the English Revolution.* New York: Viking.

Hirsch, Marianne and Evelyn Fox Keller (eds) 1990. *Conflicts in Feminism.* New York and London: Routledge.

Hobby, Elaine 1988. *Virtue of Necessity: English Women's Writing 1649–88.* London: Virago Press.

Hobby, Elaine 1991. "Katherine Philips: Seventeenth-Century Lesbian Poet." In Hobby and White (1991): 183–204.

Hobby, Elaine and Christine White (eds) 1991. *What Lesbians Do in Books*. London: The Women's Press.

Hollibaugh, Amber 1984. "Desire for the Future: Radical Hope in Passion and Pleasure." In Vance (1984): 401–10.

Hollibaugh, Amber, and Cherríe Moraga 1981. "What We're Rollin Around in Bed With: Sexual Silences in Feminism." *Heresies* 12. Repr. in Snitow, Stansell, and Thompson (1983): 394–405.

Hollinghurst, Alan 1988. *The Swimming-Pool Library*. New York: Random House. Originally published London: Chatto & Windus.

Holub, Robert C. 1984. *Reception Theory: A Critical Introduction*. London: Methuen.

hooks, bell [Gloria Watkins] 1981. *Ain't I A Woman: Black Women and Feminism*. Boston: South End Press.

hooks, bell 1990. *Yearning: Race, Gender, and Cultural Politics*. Boston: South End Press.

Hufford, Mary T. 1992. *Chaseworld: Foxhunting and Storytelling in New Jersey's Pine Barrens*. Philadelphia: University of Pennsylvania Press.

Hull, Gloria T., Patricia Bell Scott, and Barbara Smith (eds) 1982. *All the Women Are White, All the Blacks Are Men, But Some of Us Are Brave: Black Women's Studies*. Old Westbury, NY: The Feminist Press.

Hutcheon, Linda 1989. *The Politics of Postmodernism*. London and New York: Routledge.

Irigaray, Luce 1985. *This Sex Which Is Not One*. Trans. Catherine Porter with Carolyn Burke. Ithaca: Cornell University Press. Originally published in France as *Ce Sexe qui n'en est pas un*. Paris: Editions de Minuit, 1977.

Jacobus, Mary 1984. "The Law of/and Gender: Genre Theory and *The Prelude*." *Diacritics* 14 (4) (Winter): 47–57.

Jaggar, Alison M. 1983. *Feminist Politics and Human Nature*. Brighton: Harvester. Repr. Totowa, NJ: Rowman & Littlefield, 1988.

James, P. D. 1972. *An Unsuitable Job for a Woman*. New York: Fawcett Popular Library. First published New York: Charles Scribner's Sons.

James, P. D. 1987. *A Taste for Death*. New York: Warner Books. First published New York: Alfred A. Knopf, 1986.

Jameson, Fredric 1984. "Postmodernism, or The Cultural Logic of Late Capitalism." *New Left Review* 146: 53–92.

Jardine, Alice A. 1985. *Gynesis: Configurations of Woman and Modernity*. Ithaca and London: Cornell University Press.

Jardine, Alice 1989. "Notes for an Analysis." In Brennan (1989): 73–85.

Jones, Ann Rosalind 1981. "Writing the Body: Toward an Understanding of *l'écriture féminine*." *Feminist Studies* 7 (2): 247–63. Repr. in Newton and Rosenfelt (1985): 86–101.

Jones, Ann Rosalind 1984. "Julia Kristeva on Femininity: The Limits of a Semiotic Politics." *Feminist Review* 18: 56–73.

Joyce, Joyce A. 1987a. "The Black Canon: Reconstructing Black American Literary Criticism." *New Literary History* 18 (2): 335–44.

Joyce, Joyce A. 1987b. "'Who the Cap Fit': Unconsciousness and Unconscionableness in the Criticism of Houston A. Baker, Jr, and Henry Louis Gates, Jr." *New Literary History* 18 (2): 371–84.

Kaplan, Cora 1986. *Sea Changes: Culture and Feminism*. London: Verso.

Kauffman, Linda S. 1986. *Discourses of Desire: Gender, Genre, and Epistolary Fictions*. Ithaca and London: Cornell University Press.

Kauffman, Linda (ed.) 1989. *Gender & Theory: Dialogues on Feminist Criticism*. Oxford and New York: Basil Blackwell.

Kauffman, Linda (ed.) 1993. *American Feminist Thought: 1982–92*. Oxford and New York: Blackwell Publishers.

Kermode, Frank 1992. "Jacques or Master?" *The Guardian*, May 14: 19.

Khatibi, Abdelkebir 1983. *Maghreb pluriel*. Paris: Denoel.

King, Katie 1986. "The Situation of Lesbianism as Feminism's Magical Sign: Contests for Meaning and the U.S. Women's Movement, 1968–1972." *Communication* 9: 65–91.

King, Katie 1987. "Canons without Innocence: Academic Practices and Feminist Practices Making the Poem in the Work of Emily Dickinson and Audre Lorde." Dissertation, History of Consciousness, University of California, Santa Cruz.

King, Katie 1988. "Audre Lorde's Lacquered Layerings: The Lesbian Bar as a Site of Literary Production." *Cultural Studies* 2 (3): 321–42.

King, Katie 1990. "Producing Sex, Theory, and Culture: Gay/Straight Remappings in Contemporary Feminism." In Hirsch and Fox Keller (1990): 82–101.

King, Katie 1992. "Local and Global: AIDS Activism and Feminist Theory." *camera obscura: A Journal of Feminism and Film Theory* 28: 79–98.

Kollontai, Alexandra 1984. *Selected Articles and Speeches*. Trans. Cynthia Carlile. New York: International Publishers.

Kristeva, Julia 1986. "Stabat Mater." Trans. Léon S. Roudiez. In *The Kristeva Reader*, pp. 160–86. Ed. Toril Moi. Oxford: Basil Blackwell. Originally published in France as "Hérethique de l'amour," *Tel Quel* 74 (1977): 30–49.

Kuhn, Annette, and AnnMarie Wolpe (eds) 1978. *Feminism and Materialism: Women and Modes of Production*. London: Routledge.

Kulchyski, Peter 1989. "The Postmodern and the Paleolithic: Notes on Technology and Native Community in the Far North." *Canadian Journal of Political and Social Theory* 13 (3): 49–62.

Kureishi, Hanif 1988. *Sammy and Rosie Get Laid: The Screenplay and The Screenwriter's Diary*. Harmondsworth: Penguin.

Kureishi, Hanif 1990. *The Buddha of Suburbia*. London and Harmondsworth: Penguin; New York: Viking.

Lacan, Jacques 1977. *Ecrits: A Selection*. Trans. Alan Sheridan. New York and London: W. W. Norton. Originally published in France as *Ecrits*. Paris: Editions du Seuil, 1966.

LaCapra, Dominick 1985. *History and Criticism*. Ithaca and London: Cornell University Press.

Laclau, Ernesto, and Chantal Mouffe 1985. *Hegemony and Socialist Strategy: Towards a Radical Democratic Politics*. Trans. Winston Moore and Paul Cammack. London: Verso.

Landry, Donna, and Gerald MacLean 1992. "Rereading Laclau and Mouffe." *Rethinking Marxism* 4 (4): 41–60.

Lasch, Christopher 1977. *Haven in a Heartless World: The Family Besieged*. New York: W. W. Norton.

Laski, Marghanita 1985. "Heroic Scale." Review of Isabel Allende, *The House of Spirits*. *Country Life* 178 (4592), August 22: 528.

Linden, Robin Ruth, Darlene R. Pagano, Diana E. H. Russell, and Susan Leigh Star (eds), 1982. *Against Sadomasochism: A Radical Feminist Analysis*. San Francisco: Frog In The Well.

Lodge, David 1989. *Nice Work*. London and Harmondsworth: Penguin. First published London: Secker & Warburg, 1988.

Lonsdale, Sarah 1992a. "Cambridge Win for 'Subversive' Philosopher." *The Observer*, May 17: 2.

Lonsdale, Sarah 1992b. "What's it all about, Jacques?" *The Observer*, May 17: 19.

Lovell, Terry 1987. *Consuming Fiction*. London: Verso.

Lovell, Terry 1990. *British Feminist Thought: A Reader*. Oxford and New York: Basil Blackwell.

Lovibond, Sabina 1989. "Feminism and Postmodernism." *New Left Review* 178: 5–28.

Luxemburg, Rosa 1986. *The Mass Strike*. London, Chicago, and Melborne: Bookmarks.

Lyotard, Jean-François 1984. *The Postmodern Condition: A Report on Knowledge*. Trans. Geoff Bennington and Brian Massumi. Minneapolis: University of Minnesota Press. First published in France as *La Condition postmoderne: rapport sur le savoir*. Paris: Editions de Minuit, 1979.

McDonald, Christie V. 1982. "Choreographies." *Diacritics* 12 (2): 66–76.

McGann, Jerome J. 1985. "Introduction: A Point of Reference." *Historical Studies and Literary Criticism*, pp. 3–21. Ed. Jerome J. McGann. Madison: University of Wisconsin Press.

MacKinnon, Catharine A. 1982. "Feminism, Marxism, Method, and the State: An Agenda for Theory." *Signs* 7 (3): 515–44. Repr. in *Feminist Theory: A Critique of Ideology*, pp. 1–30. Ed. Nannerl O. Keohane, Michelle Z. Rosaldo, and Barbara C. Gelpi. Chicago: University of Chicago Press, 1982.

Manes, Christopher 1990. *Green Rage: Radical Environmentalism and the Unmaking of Civilization*. Boston: Little, Brown & Company.

Marks, Elaine, and Isabelle de Courtivron (eds) 1980. *New French Feminisms: An Anthology*. Amherst: University of Massachusetts Press. Repr. New York: Schocken Books, 1981.

Martin, Biddy 1988. "Feminism, Criticism, and Foucault." Revised version in Diamond and Quinby (1988): 3–19. First published in *New German Critique* 27 (1982): 3–30.

Martin, Biddy 1991. *Woman and Modernity: The (Life) Styles of Lou Andreas-Salomé.* Ithaca and London: Cornell University Press.

Martin, Biddy, and Chandra Talpade Mohanty 1986. "Feminist Politics: What's Home Got To Do With It?" In de Lauretis (1986): 191–212.

Marx, Karl 1970. *A Contribution to the Critique of Political Economy.* Trans. S. W. Ryazanskaya. Ed. Maurice Dobb. Moscow: Progress Publishers.

Marx, Karl 1973. *Grundrisse: Foundations of the Critique of Political Economy.* Trans. Martin Nicholas. Harmondsworth: Penguin.

Marx, Karl 1977. *Capital: A Critique of Political Economy*, Vol. 1. Trans. Ben Fowkes. New York: Vintage.

Miller, Nancy K. 1982. "The Text's Heroine: A Feminist Critic and Her Fictions." *Diacritics* 12 (2): 48–53. Repr. in Hirsch and Fox Keller (1990): 112–20.

Mitchell, Juliet 1966. "Women: The Longest Revolution." *New Left Review* 40: 11–37.

Mitchell, Juliet 1971. *Woman's Estate.* New York: Random House.

Mitchell, Juliet 1974. *Psychoanalysis and Feminism.* Harmondsworth: Penguin; New York: Pantheon.

Mitchell, Juliet 1984. *Women: The Longest Revolution.* London: Virago.

Mitchell, Juliet, and Jacqueline Rose (eds) 1982. *Feminine Sexuality: Jacques Lacan and the "école freudienne".* New York and London: W. W. Norton.

Modleski, Tania 1986. "Feminism and the Power of Interpretation: Some Critical Readings." In de Lauretis (1986): 121–38.

Modleski, Tania 1991. *Feminism Without Women: Culture and Criticism in a "Postfeminist" Age.* New York and London: Routledge.

Mohanty, Chandra Talpade 1984. "Under Western Eyes: Feminist Scholarship and Colonial Discourses." *Boundary 2* 12 (3)/13 (1) (1984): 333–58. Repr. in *Feminist Review* 30 (1988): 61–88. Revised version in Mohanty, Russo, and Torres (1991): 51–80.

Mohanty, Chandra Talpade, Ann Russo, and Lourdes Torres (eds) 1991. *Third World Women and the Politics of Feminism.* Bloomington and Indianapolis: Indiana University Press.

Moi, Toril 1985. *Sexual/Textual Politics: Feminist Literary Theory.* London and New York: Methuen.

Moi, Toril (ed.) 1987. *French Feminist Thought: A Reader.* Oxford and New York: Basil Blackwell.

Moraga, Cherríe 1983a. *Loving in the War Years: Lo que Nunca Pasó por Sus Labios.* Boston: South End Press. Five poems reprinted in Vance (1984): 417–24.

Moraga, Cherríe 1983b. "Preface." In Moraga and Anzaldúa (1983): xiii–xix.

Moraga, Cherríe and Gloria Anzaldúa (eds) 1983. *This Bridge Called My*

Back: Writings by Radical Women of Color. 2nd edn with new forewords. New York: Kitchen Table: Women of Color Press. First published Watertown, MA: Persephone Press, 1981.

Morrison, Toni 1973. *Sula*. New York: Alfred A. Knopf. Repr. New York: Bantam, 1975.

Moynihan, Daniel P. 1965. *The Negro Family: The Case for National Action*. Washington, DC: US Department of Labor.

Nancy, Jean-Luc, and Philippe Lacoue-Labarthe 1973. *Le Titre de la lettre*. Paris: Galilée.

Nash, June, and María Patricia Fernández-Kelly (eds) 1983. *Women, Men and the International Division of Labor*. Albany: State University of New York Press.

Naylor, Gloria 1989. *Mama Day*. New York: Vintage Books. First published New York: Ticknor & Fields, 1988.

Neale, R. S. 1985. *Writing Marxist History: British Society, Economy & Culture since 1700*. Oxford and New York: Basil Blackwell.

Nelson, Cary and Lawrence Grossberg (eds) 1988. *Marxism and the Interpretation of Culture*. Urbana and Chicago: University of Illinois Press.

Nestle, Joan 1981. "My Mother Liked to Fuck." *Womanews* 3 (1). Repr. in Snitow, Stansell, and Thompson (1983): 468–70; and in Nestle (1987): 120–2.

Nestle, Joan 1984. "The Fem Question." In Vance (1984): 232–41.

Nestle, Joan 1987. *A Restricted Country*. Ithaca, NY: Firebrand Books.

Newton, Judith and Deborah Rosenfelt (eds) 1985. *Feminist Criticism and Social Change: Sex, Class and Race in Literature and Culture*. London and New York: Methuen.

Nicholson, Linda 1987. "Feminism and Marx: Integrating Kinship with the Economic." In Benhabib and Cornell (1987): 16–30.

O'Brien, Meg 1990a. *The Daphne Decisions*. New York: Bantam of Bantam Doubleday Dell.

O'Brien, Meg 1990b. *Salmon in the Soup*. New York: Bantam of Bantam Doubleday Dell.

Paretsky, Sara 1988. *Bitter Medicine*. New York: Ballantine Books. First published New York: William Morrow, 1987.

Paretsky, Sara 1989. *Blood Shot*. New York: Dell of Bantam Doubleday Dell. First published New York: Delacorte, 1988. Published in the UK as *Toxic Shock*. London: Penguin, 1988.

Paretsky, Sara 1991. *Burn Marks*. New York: Dell of Bantam Doubleday Dell. First published New York: Delacorte, 1990.

Parry, Benita 1987. "Problems in Current Theories of Colonial Discourse." *Oxford Literary Review* 9 (1–2): 27–58.

Penley, Constance, and Andrew Ross 1991a. "Cyborgs at Large: Interview with Donna Haraway." In Penley and Ross (1991b): 1–20.

Penley, Constance, and Andrew Ross (eds) 1991b. *Technoculture*. Minneapolis and Oxford: University of Minnesota Press.

People for the Ethical Treatment of Animals (PETA) 1991. "The Art of Vegetarianism: Paul and Linda McCartney." *PETA News* 6 (4): 6–7.

Philipson, Ilene, for the *Socialist Review* Collective 1985. "The Impasse of Socialist-Feminism: A Conversation with Deirdre English, Barbara Epstein, Barbara Haber, and Judy MacLean." *Socialist Review* 79: 93–110.

Phillips, Anne (ed.) 1987. *Feminism and Equality*. New York: New York University Press.

Poovey, Mary 1984. *The Proper Lady and the Woman Writer: Ideology as Style in the Works of Mary Wollstonecraft, Mary Shelley, and Jane Austen.* Chicago and London: University of Chicago Press.

Poovey, Mary 1988. *Uneven Developments: The Ideological Work of Gender in Mid-Victorian England.* Chicago and London: University of Chicago Press.

Pryse, Marjorie, and Hortense J. Spillers (eds) 1985. *Conjuring: Black Women, Fiction, and Literary Tradition.* Bloomington: Indiana University Press.

Radhakrishnan, R. 1987. "Ethnic Identity and Post-Structuralist Differance." *Cultural Critique* 6: 199–220.

Reiter, Rayna R. (ed.) 1975. *Toward an Anthropology of Women*. New York: Monthly Review Press.

Rich, Adrienne 1980. "Compulsory Heterosexuality and Lesbian Existence." *Signs* 5 (4): 631–60. Repr. in Snitow, Stansell, and Thompson (1983): 177–205. Repr. with additions in *Blood, Bread, and Poetry: Selected Prose 1979–1985*, pp. 23–75. New York and London: W. W. Norton, 1986.

Rich, B. Ruby 1986. "Feminism and Sexuality in the 1980s." *Feminist Studies* 12: 525–61.

Riley, Denise 1988. *"Am I That Name?" Feminism and the Category of "Women" in History.* Minneapolis: University of Minnesota Press.

Rose, Jacqueline 1986. *Sexuality in the Field of Vision*. London: Verso.

Ross, Andrew (ed.) 1988. *Universal Abandon? The Politics of Postmodernism.* Minneapolis: University of Minnesota Press.

Rowbotham, Sheila 1973. *Woman's Consciousness, Man's World*. Harmondsworth: Penguin.

Rowbotham, Sheila 1977. *A New World for Women: Stella Browne – Socialist Feminist.* London: Pluto Press.

Rowbotham, Sheila, Lynne Segal, and Hilary Wainwright 1979. *Beyond the Fragments: Feminism and the Making of Socialism.* London: Merlin Press.

Rubin, Gayle 1975. "The Traffic in Women: Notes on the 'Political Economy' of Sex." In Reiter (1975): 157–210.

Rubin, Gayle 1984. "Thinking Sex: Notes for a Radical Theory of the Politics of Sexuality." In Vance (1984): 267–319.

Rubin, Gayle, with Deirdre English and Amber Hollibaugh 1982. "Talking Sex: A Conversation on Sexuality and Feminism." *Feminist Review* 11: 40–52. First printed in *Socialist Review* 58 (1981).

Rustin, Michael 1989. "The Politics of Post-Fordism: or, The Trouble with 'New Times.'" *New Left Review* 175: 54–77.

Ryan, Michael 1982. *Marxism and Deconstruction: A Critical Articulation*. Baltimore and London: Johns Hopkins University Press.

Said, Edward W. 1979. *Orientalism*. New York: Vintage. First published New York: Pantheon, 1978.

Salleh, Ariel 1991. Review of Vandana Shiva, *Staying Alive, Hypatia: A Journal of Feminist Philosophy* 6 (1) (Spring): 206–14.

SAMOIS, 1981. *Coming to Power: Writings and Graphics on Lesbian S/M*. Boston: Alyson Publications. Repr. 1982 and 1987.

Sandoval, Chela 1991. "U.S. Third World Feminism: The Theory and Method of Oppositional Consciousness in the Postmodern World." *Genders* 10: 1–24.

Sargent, Lydia (ed.) 1981. *Women and Revolution: A Discussion of the Unhappy Marriage of Marxism and Feminism*. Boston: South End Press.

Saussure, Ferdinand de 1972. *Course in General Linguistics*. Trans. Wade Baskin. Extract in *The Structuralists from Marx to Lévi-Strauss*, pp. 58–79. Ed. Richard and Fernande DeGeorge. New York: Doubleday.

Schulman, Sarah 1984. *The Sophie Horowitz Story*. Tallahassee, FL: Naiad Press.

Scott, Joan Wallach 1988. *Gender and the Politics of History*. New York: Columbia University Press.

Sedgwick, Eve Kosofsky 1985. *Between Men: English Literature and Male Homosocial Desire*. New York: Columbia University Press.

Sedgwick, Eve Kosofsky 1990. *Epistemology of the Closet*. Berkeley: University of California Press.

Shiva, Vandana 1988. *Staying Alive: Women, Ecology and Development*. London: Zed Books.

Shiva, Vandana, Patrick Anderson, Heffa Schücking, Andrew Gray, Larry Lohmann, and David Cooper 1991. *Biodiversity: Social & Ecological Perspectives*. London and New Jersey: Zed Books.

Showalter, Elaine (ed.) 1985. *The New Feminist Criticism: Essays on Women, Literature, and Theory*. New York: Pantheon.

Signs: Journal of Women in Culture and Society 9 (4) 1984. "The Lesbian Issue."

Smith, Barbara 1977. "Toward a Black Feminist Criticism." *Conditions Two* 1 (2): 25–44. Repr. in Hull, Scott, and Smith (1982): 157–75; in Newton and Rosenfelt (1985): 3–18; and in Showalter (1985): 168–85.

Smith, Valerie 1989. "Black Feminist Theory and the Representation of the 'Other.'" In Wall (1989): 38–57.

Smith, Valerie 1990. "Split Affinities: The Case of Interracial Rape." In Hirsch and Fox Keller (1990): 271–87.

Snitow, Ann, Christine Stansell, and Sharon Thompson (eds) 1983. *Powers of Desire: The Politics of Sexuality*. New York: Monthly Review Press.

Solomon-Godeau, Abigail 1988. "Living with Contradictions: Critical Practices in the Age of Supply-Side Aesthetics." In Ross (1988): 191–213.

Spencer, Jane 1986. *The Rise of the Woman Novelist: From Aphra Behn to Jane Austen*. Oxford and New York: Basil Blackwell.

Spender, Dale 1980. *Man Made Language*. London and Boston, MA: Routledge & Kegan Paul.

Spillers, Hortense J. 1985. "Afterword: Cross-Currents, Discontinuities: Black Women's Fiction." In Pryse and Spillers (1985): 249–61.

Spillers, Hortense J. 1987a. "A Hateful Passion, a Lost Love." Repr. in Benstock (1987): 181–207. First published in *Feminist Studies* 9 (2) (1983): 293–323.

Spillers, Hortense J. 1987b. "Mama's Baby, Papa's Maybe: An American Grammar Book." *Diacritics* 17 (2): 65–81.

Spivak, Gayatri Chakravorty 1985. "The Rani of Sirmur." In Barker et al. (1985): 128–51.

Spivak, Gayatri Chakravorty 1987. *In Other Worlds: Essays in Cultural Politics*. New York and London: Methuen.

Spivak, Gayatri Chakravorty 1988. "Can the Subaltern Speak?" In Nelson and Grossberg (1988): 271–313.

Spivak, Gayatri Chakravorty 1989a. "Feminism and Deconstruction, Again: Negotiating with Unacknowledged Masculinism." In Brennan (1989): 206–23.

Spivak, Gayatri Chakravorty 1989b. "In Praise of *Sammy and Rosie Get Laid*." *Critical Quarterly* 31 (2): 80–8.

Spivak, Gayatri Chakravorty 1989c. Plenary lecture delivered at the "Marxism Now: Traditions and Difference" conference, University of Massachusetts, Amherst, December 1, 1989.

Spivak, Gayatri Chakravorty 1990. *The Post-Colonial Critic: Interviews, Strategies, Dialogues*. Ed. Sarah Harasym. New York and London: Routledge.

Spy: The New York Monthly (November) 1990: 1. Advertisement for *Forbes Magazine*.

Stimpson, Catharine R. 1988. "Nancy Reagan Wears a Hat: Feminism and its Cultural Consensus." *Critical Inquiry* 14 (2): 223–43.

Swindells, Julia, and Lisa Jardine 1990. *What's Left? Women in Culture and the Labour Movement*. London and New York: Routledge.

Taylor, Barbara 1983. *Eve and the New Jerusalem: Socialism and Feminism in the Nineteenth Century*. London: Virago; New York: Pantheon.

Textual Practice 4 (2): 1990. "Lesbian and Gay Cultures: Theories and Texts." Ed. Joe Bristow.

Thomas, Keith 1983. *Man and the Natural World: A History of the Modern Sensibility*. New York: Pantheon.

Thompson, E. P. 1975. *Whigs and Hunters: The Origin of the Black Act*. New York: Pantheon. Originally published London: Penguin.

Tischler, Joyce 1991. Letter from the Executive Director of the Animal Legal Defense Fund, 1363 Lincoln Avenue, San Rafael, California 94901, with an Animal Bill of Rights, a petition to the 102nd United States Congress.

Todd, Janet 1989. *The Sign of Angellica: Women, Writing, and Fiction, 1660–1800*. London: Virago.

Tompkins, Jane P. 1985. *Sensational Designs: The Cultural Work of American Fiction*. New York: Oxford University Press.

Tucker, Robert C. 1978. *The Marx–Engels Reader*. 2nd edn. New York and London: W. W. Norton. First published 1972.

Vance, Carole S. (ed.) 1984. *Pleasure and Danger: Exploring Female Sexuality*. Boston: Routledge & Kegan Paul.

Vlasopolos, Anca 1990. *Missing Members*. Detroit: Corridors Press.

Vogel, Lise 1983. *Marxism and the Oppression of Women: Toward a Unitary Theory*. New Brunswick, NJ: Rutgers University Press; London: Pluto Press.

Vološinov, V. N. 1973. *Marxism and the Philosophy of Language*. Trans. Ladislav Matejka and I. R. Tutinik. Cambridge, MA: Harvard University Press. Repr. 1986.

Wall, Cheryl A. (ed.) 1989. *Changing Our Own Words: Essays on Criticism, Theory, and Writing by Black Women*. New Brunswick and London: Rutgers University Press.

Ware, Cellestine 1970. *Woman Power: The Movement for Women's Liberation*. New York: Tower Publications.

Watt, Ian 1957. *The Rise of the Novel*. London: Chatto & Windus; Berkeley: University of California Press.

Wayne, Valerie (ed.) 1991. *The Matter of Difference: Materialist Feminist Criticism of Shakespeare*. Ithaca, NY: Cornell University Press.

Weeks, Jeffrey 1981. *Sex, Politics and Society: The Regulation of Sexuality Since 1800*. London and New York: Longman. 2nd edn 1989.

White, Christine 1990. "'Poets and lovers evermore': Interpreting Female Love in the Poetry and Journals of Michael Field." *Textual Practice* 4 (2): 197–212.

Williams, Raymond 1961. *The Long Revolution*. London: Chatto & Windus. Repr. with new foreword, Harmondsworth: Penguin, 1965.

Williams, Raymond 1977. *Marxism and Literature*. Oxford: Oxford University Press.

Williams, Raymond 1980. *Problems in Materialism and Culture*. London: Verso.

Williams, Raymond 1983. *Keywords: A Vocabulary of Culture and Society*.

Revised edn. London: Fontana; New York: Oxford University Press. Originally published 1976.

Williams, Raymond 1989. *Resources of Hope: Culture, Democracy, Socialism.* Ed. Robin Gale. London and New York: Verso.

Winterson, Jeanette 1987. *Oranges Are Not the Only Fruit.* New York: Atlantic Monthly Press. First published London and New York: Pandora Press, 1985.

Winterson, Jeanette 1988. *The Passion.* New York: Atlantic Monthly Press. First published London: Bloomsbury Publishing, 1987.

Winterson, Jeanette 1990. *Sexing the Cherry.* London: Vintage. First published London: Bloomsbury Publishing, 1989.

Wittig, Monique 1980. "The Straight Mind." *Feminist Issues.* 1 (1): 103–11.

Woodhull, Winifred 1991. "Unveiling Algeria." *Genders* 10: 112–31.

Woolf, Virginia 1957. *A Room of One's Own.* New York and London: Harcourt Brace Jovanovich. First published 1929.

Index of Names

Index of Subjects

Index compiled by Frank Pert